"The Count looked at the ... ... Owen ... own height, and behind it the hunched scaly back and thick hind legs. The vestigal wings were folded flat, fanning open and shut slightly as Sherez breathed. *What a creature is dragon,* the poets sang, *though for his wisdom he resigned the air to crawl* . . ."

John M. Lord, *As Above, So Below*

"He trod the air with regal impunity. His glinting jade talons, five to each foot, opened and closed on the invading night wind like those of a hawk in full expectation of its prey."

Michael Bishop, *One Winter in Eden*

". . . the dragon finally molted, patchworking into a red. The nails on its foreclaws, which had been as brittle as jingle shells, were now as hard as golden oak and the same color. Its hind claws were dull and strong as steel. Its eyes were two black shrouds and it had not roared yet, but Jakkin knew that roar would come, loud and full and fierce . . ."

Jane Yolen, *Cockfight*

" 'Two things are true about every dragon in the world: they like to brag, and they're jealous as can be over their territory. If a ship sails into their waters, they burn it. And often as not, they'll save one man, fly him back to land, and leave him to tell the story. But they don't always leave him whole . . .' "

Dave Smeds, *Dragon Touched*

"The ice dragon was a crystalline white, the shade of white that is so hard and cold that it is almost blue. It was covered with hoarfrost, so when it moved its skin broke and crackled as the crust on the snow crackles beneath a man's boots, and flakes of rime fell off.

"Its eyes were clear and deep and icy.

"Its wings were vast and batlike, colored all a faint translucent blue. Adara could see the clouds through them, and oftentimes the moon and stars, when the beast wheeled in frozen circles through the skies."

George R.R. Martin, *The Ice Dragon*

DRAGONS OF LIGHT

DEDICATION

For all the talented,
dedicated, imaginative
writers and artists,
as yet undiscovered:
this book.

DRAGONS OF LIGHT

ORSON SCOTT CARD

BART

NEW YORK

ISBN: 1-55785-037-2

First Bart Books edition: 1988

Bart Books
155 E. 34th Street
New York, New York 10016

Manufactured in the United States of America

TABLE OF CONTENTS

INTRODUCTION

BY ORSON SCOTT CARD

It's not that Michael Goodwin and I are in love with dragons. What we're in love with is good writing and good illustration -- fantasy conceived and visualized with lively imagination and consummate skill. Dragons were merely a theme to bind together the works of some of our favorite writers and illustrators. How were we to know that old masters and fine new talents would create such marvelous serpents that we couldn't even fit them all into one book? Dragons of Light is only the first of two volumes. The second, Dragons of Darkness, will be published in the fall of 1981.

These books are unique in several respects. First, to our knowledge no publisher in recent years has tried to create such a close bonding of story and art, with each illustrator selected because his style of work is particularly well-suited to the story he is visualizing. Second, because the book is so unusual, publishers were naturally a bit wary about committing themselves to it before the stories had actually been put together. This meant that we had to ask authors for stories before we had a contract with a publisher; and because all things in the world of publishing take time, many authors and artists waited, with varying degrees of patience, for a good long time before getting paid. In a world where mortgages fall due far more regularly than freelance writers' and artists' checks arrive, such forebearance is rare. Yet without that cooperative spirit from all whose work appears here and in the next volume, this book would have been impossible.

The worms that wait for you within these pages are strange, chameleonic creatures. One lurks within the heart of a southern schoolteacher; another dwells in a nest in an incredibly tall tree in the ancient American Northwest. The variety goes on: a dragon that gambles its life for its master's freedom; a dragon that sets up in business with an erstwhile enemy; a serpent made of ice; and one who faces his showdown in a grocery store gone mad.

I was delighted as these stories, one by one, were sent to me as I prepared the book; I was delighted again as, one by one, the artists brought the tales to life with paint, pastels, or pen. Perhaps it is audacious of me to predict, but I think you will be delighted, too.

"It was true that Adara was always a child apart."

THE ICE DRAGON

GEORGE R.R. MARTIN

ILLUSTRATIONS BY
ALICIA AUSTIN

Adara liked the winter best of all, for when the world grew cold the ice dragon came.

She was never quite sure whether it was the cold that brought the ice dragon or the ice dragon that brought the cold. That was the sort of question that often troubled her brother Geoff, who was two years older than her and insatiably curious, but Adara did not care about such things. So long as the cold and the snow and the ice dragon all arrived on schedule, she was happy.

She always knew when they were due because of her birthday. Adara was a winter child, born during the worst freeze that anyone could remember, even Old Laura, who lived on the next farm and remembered things that had happened before anyone else was born. People still talked about that freeze. Adara often heard them.

They talked about other things as well. They said it was the chill of that terrible freeze that had killed her mother, stealing in during her long night of labor past the great fire that Adara's father had built, and creeping under the layers of blankets that covered the birthing bed. And they said that the cold had entered Adara in the womb, that her skin had been pale blue and icy to the touch when she came forth, and that she had never warmed in all the years since. The winter had touched her, left its mark upon her, and made her its own.

It was true that Adara was always a child apart. She was a very serious little girl who seldom cared to play with the others. She was beautiful, people said, but in a strange, distant sort of way, with her pale skin and blond hair and wide clear blue eyes. She smiled, but not often. No one had ever seen her cry. Once when she was five she had stepped upon a nail imbedded in a board that lay concealed beneath a snowbank, and it had gone clear through her foot, but Adara had not wept or screamed even then. She had pulled her foot loose and walked back to the house, leaving a trail of blood in the snow, and when she had gotten there she had said only, "Father, I hurt myself." The sulks and tempers and tears of ordinary childhood were not for her.

Even her family knew that Adara was different. Her father was a huge, gruff bear of a man who had little use for people in general, but a smile always broke across his face when Geoff pestered him with questions, and he was full of hugs and laughter for Teri, Adara's older sister, who was golden and freckled, and flirted shamelessly with all the local boys. Every so often he would hug Adara as well, especially when he was drunk, which was frequent during the long winters. But there would be no smiles then. He would only wrap his arms around her, and pull her small body tight against him with all his massive strength, sob deep in his chest, and fat wet tears would run down his ruddy cheeks. He never hugged her at all during the summers. During the summers he was too busy.

Everyone was busy during the summers except for Adara. Geoff would work with his father in the fields and ask endless questions about this and that, learning everything a farmer had to know. When he was not working he would run with his friends to the river, and have adventures. Teri ran the house and did the cooking, and worked a bit at the inn by the crossroads during the busy season. The innkeeper's daughter was her friend, and his youngest son was more than a friend, and she would always come back giggly and full of gossip and news from travellers and soldiers and king's messengers. For Teri and Geoff the summers were the best time, and both of them were too busy for Adara.

Their father was the busiest of all. A thousand things needed to be done each day, and he did them, and found a thousand more. He worked from dawn to dusk. His muscles grew hard and lean in summer, and he stank from sweat each night when he came in from the fields, but he always came in smiling. After supper he would sit with Geoff and tell him stories and answer his questions, or teach Teri things she did not know about cooking, or stroll down to the inn. He was a summer man, truly.

He never drank in summer, except for a cup of wine now and again to celebrate his brother's visits.

That was another reason why Teri and Geoff loved the summers, when the world was green and hot and bursting with life. It was only in summer that Uncle Hal, their father's younger brother, came to call. Hal was a dragonrider in service to the king, a tall slender man with a face like a noble. Dragons cannot stand the cold, so when winter fell Hal and his wing would fly south. But each summer he returned, brilliant in the king's green-and-gold uniform, en route to the battlegrounds to the north and west of them. The war had been going on for all of Adara's life.

Whenever Hal came north, he would bring presents; toys from the king's city, crystal and gold jewelry, candies, and always a bottle of some expensive wine that he and his brother could share. He would grin at Teri and make her blush with his compliments, and entertain Geoff with tales of war and castles and dragons. As for Adara, he often tried to coax a smile out of her, with gifts and jests and hugs. He seldom succeeded.

For all his good nature, Adara did not like Hal; when Hal was there, it meant that winter was far away.

Besides, there had been a night when she was only four, and they thought her long asleep, that she overheard them talking over wine. "A solemn little thing," Hal said. "You ought to be kinder to her, John. You cannot blame *her* for what happened."

"Can't I?" her father replied, his voice thick with wine. "No, I suppose not. But it is hard. She looks like Beth, but she has none of Beth's warmth. The winter is in her, you know. Whenever I touch her I feel the chill, and I remember that it was for her that Beth had to die."

"You are cold to her. You do not love her as you do the others."

Adara remembered the way her father laughed then. "Love her? Ah, Hal. I loved her best of all, my little winter child. But she has never loved back. There is nothing in her for me, or you, any of us. She is such a cold little girl." And then he began to weep, even though it was summer and Hal was with him. In her bed, Adara listened and wished that Hal would fly away. She did not quite understand all that she had heard, not then, but she remembered it, and the understanding came later.

She did not cry; not at four, when she heard, or six, when she finally understood. Hal left a few days later, and Geoff and Teri waved to him excitedly when his wing passed overhead, thirty great dragons in proud formation against the summer sky. Adara watched with her small hands by her sides.

There were other visits in other summers, but Hal never made her smile, no matter what he brought her.

Adara's smiles were a secret store, and she spent of them only in winter. She could hardly wait for her birthday to come, and with it the cold. For in winter she was a special child.

She had known it since she was very little, playing with the others in the snow. The cold had never bothered her the way it did Geoff and Teri and their friends. Often Adara stayed outside alone for hours after the others had fled in search of warmth, or run off to Old Laura's to eat the hot vegetable soup she liked to make for the children. Adara would find a secret place in the far corner of the fields, a different place each winter, and there she would build a tall white castle, patting the snow in place with small bare hands, shaping it into towers and battlements like those Hal often talked about on the king's castle in the city. She would snap icicles off from the lower branches of trees, and use them for spires and spikes and guardposts, ranging them all about her castle. And often in the dead of winter would come a brief thaw and a sudden freeze, and overnight her snow castle would turn to ice, as hard and strong as she imagined real castles to be. All through the winters she would built on her castle, and no one ever knew. But always the spring would come, and a thaw not followed by a freeze; then all the ramparts and walls would melt away, and Adara would begin to count the days until her birthday came again.

Her winter castles were seldom empty. At the first frost each year, the ice lizards would come wriggling out of their burrows, and the fields would be overrun with the tiny blue creatures, darting this way and that, hardly seeming to touch the snow as they skimmed across it. All the children played with the ice lizards. But the others were clumsy and cruel, and they would snap the fragile little animals in two, breaking them between their fingers as they might break an icicle hanging from a roof. Even Geoff, who was too kind ever to do something like that, sometimes grew curious, and held the lizards too long in his efforts to examine them, and the heat of his hands would make them melt and burn and finally die.

Adara's hands were cool and gentle, and she could hold the lizards as long as she liked without harming them, which always made Geoff pout and ask angry questions. Sometimes she would lie in the cold, damp snow and let the lizards crawl all over her, delighting in the light touch of their feet as they skittered across her face. Sometimes she would wear ice lizards hidden in her hair as she went about her chores, though she took care never to take them inside where the heat of the fires would kill them. Always she would gather up scraps after the family ate, and bring them to the secret place where her castle was a-building, and there she would scatter them. So the castles she erected were full of kings and courtiers every winter; small furry creatures that snuck out from the woods, winter birds with pale white plumage, and hundreds and hundreds of squirming, struggling ice lizards, cold and quick and fat. Adara liked the ice lizards better than any of the pets the family had kept over the years.

But it was the ice dragon that she loved.

She did not know when she had first seen it. It seemed to her that it had always been a part of her life, a vision glimpsed during the deep of winter, sweeping across the frigid sky on wings serene and blue. Ice dragons were rare, even in those days, and whenever it was seen the children would all point and wonder, while the old folks muttered and shook their heads. It was a sign of a long and bitter winter when ice dragons were abroad in the land. An ice dragon had been seen flying across the face of the moon on the night Adara had been born, people said, and each winter since it had been seen again, and those winters had been very bad indeed, the spring coming later each year. So the people would set fires and pray and hope to keep the ice dragon away, and Adara would fill with fear.

But it never worked. Every year the ice dragon returned. Adara knew it came for her.

The ice dragon was large, half again the size of the scaled green war dragons that Hal and his fellows flew. Adara had heard legends of wild dragons larger than mountains, but she had never seen any. Hal's dragon was big enough, to be sure, five times the size of a horse, but it was small compared to the ice dragon, and ugly besides.

The ice dragon was a crystalline white, that shade of white that is so hard and cold that it is almost blue. It was covered with hoarfrost, so when it moved its skin broke and crackled as the crust on the snow crackles beneath a man's boots, and flakes of rime fell off.

Its eyes were clear and deep and icy.

Its wings were vast and batlike, colored all a faint translucent blue. Adara could see the clouds through them, and oftentimes the moon and stars, when the beast wheeled in frozen circles through the skies.

Its teeth were icicles, a triple row of them, jagged spears of unequal length, white against its deep blue maw.

When the ice dragon beat its wings, the cold winds blew and the snow swirled and scurried and the world seemed to shrink and shiver. Sometimes when a door flew open in the cold of winter, driven by a sudden gust of wind, the householder would run to bolt it and say, "An ice dragon flies nearby."

And when the ice dragon opened its great mouth, and exhaled, it was not fire that came streaming out, the burning sulfurous stink of lesser dragons.

The ice dragon breathed *cold*.

Ice formed when it breathed. Warmth fled. Fires guttered and went out, shriven by the chill. Trees froze through to their slow secret souls, and their limbs turned brittle and cracked from their own weight. Animals turned blue and whimpered and died, their eyes bulging and their skin covered over with frost.

The ice dragon breathed death into the world; death and quiet and *cold*. But Adara was not afraid. She was a winter child, and the ice dragon was her secret.

She had seen it in the sky a thousand times. When she was four, she saw it on the ground.

She was out building on her snow castle, and it came and landed close to her, in the emptiness of the snow-covered fields. All the ice lizards ran away. Adara simply stood. The ice dragon looked at her for ten long heartbeats, before it took to the air again. The wind shrieked around her and through her as it beat its wings to rise, but Adara felt strangely exalted.

Later that winter it returned, and Adara touched it. Its skin was very cold. She took off her glove nonetheless. It would not be right otherwise. She was half afraid it would burn and melt at her touch, but it did not. It was much more sensitive to heat than even the ice lizards, Adara knew somehow. But she was special, the winter child, cool. She stroked it, and finally gave its wing a kiss that hurt her lips. That was the winter of her fourth birthday, the year she touched the ice dragon.

The winter of her fifth birthday was the year she rode upon it for the first time.

It found her again, working on a different castle at a different place in the fields, alone as ever. She watched it come, and ran to it when it landed, and pressed herself against it. That had been the summer when she had heard her father talking to Hal.

They stood together for long minutes until finally Adara, remembering Hal, reached out and tugged at the dragon's wing with a small hand. And the dragon beat its great wings once, and then extended them flat against the snow, and Adara scrambled up to wrap her arms about its cold white neck.

Together, for the first time, they flew.

She had no harness or whip, as the king's dragonriders use. At times the beating of the wings threatened to shake her loose from where she clung, and the coldness of the dragon's flesh crept through her clothing and bit and numbed her child's flesh. But Adara was not afraid.

They flew over her father's farm, and she saw Geoff looking very small below, startled and afraid, and knew he could not see her. It made her laugh an icy, tinkling laugh, a laugh as bright and crisp as the winter air.

They flew over the crossroads inn, where crowds of people came out to watch them pass.

They flew above the forest, all white and green and silent.

They flew high into the sky, so high that Adara could not even see the ground below, and she thought she glimpsed another ice dragon, way off in the distance, but it was not half so grand as *hers*.

They flew for most of the day, and finally the dragon swept around in a great circle, and spiraled down, gliding on its stiff and glittering wings. It let her off in the field where it had found her, just after dusk.

Her father found her there, and wept to see her, and hugged her savagely. Adara did not understand that, nor why he beat her after he had gotten her back to the house. But when she and Geoff had been put to sleep, she heard him slide out of his own bed and come padding over to hers. "You missed it all," he said. "There was an ice dragon, and it scared everybody. Father was afraid it had eaten you."

Adara smiled to herself in the darkness, but said nothing.

She flew on the ice dragon four more times that winter, and every winter after that. Each year she flew farther and more often than the year before, and the ice dragon was seen more frequently in the skies above their farm.

Each winter was longer and colder than the one before.

Each year the thaw came later.

And sometimes there were patches of land, where the ice dragon had lain to rest, that never seemed to thaw properly at all.

There was much talk in the village during her sixth year, and a message was sent to the king. No answer ever came.

"A bad business, ice dragons," Hal said that summer when he visited the farm. "They're not like real dragons, you know. You can't break them or train them. We have tales of those that tried, found frozen with their whip and harness in hand. I've heard about people that have lost hands or fingers just by touching one of them. Frostbite. Yes, a bad business."

"Then why doesn't the king do something?" her father demanded. "We sent a message. Unless we can kill the beast or drive it away, in a year or two we won't have any planting season at all."

Hal smiled grimly. "The king has other concerns. The war is going badly, you know. They advance every summer, and they have twice as many dragonriders as we do. I tell you, John, it's hell up there. Some year I'm not going to come back. The king can hardly spare men to go chasing an ice dragon." He laughed. "Besides, I don't think anybody's ever killed one of the things. Maybe we should just let the enemy take this whole province. Then it'd be *his* ice dragon."

But it wouldn't be, Adara thought as she listened. No matter what king ruled the land, it would always be *her* ice dragon.

Hal departed and summer waxed and waned. Adara counted the days until her birthday. Hal passed through again before the first chill, taking his ugly dragon south for the winter. His wing seemed smaller when it came flying over the forest that fall, though, and his visit was briefer than usual, and ended with a loud quarrel between him and her father.

"They won't move during the winter," Hal said. "The winter terrain is too treacherous, and they won't risk an advance without dragonriders to cover them from above. But come spring, we aren't going to be able to hold them. The king may not even try. Sell the farm now, while you can still get a good price. You can buy another piece of land in the south.

"*This* is my land," her father said. "I was born here. You too, though you seem to have forgotten it. Our parents are buried here. And Beth too. I want to lie beside her when I go."

"You'll go a lot sooner than you'd like if you don't listen to me," Hal said angrily. "Don't be stupid, John. I know what the land means to you, but it isn't worth your life." He went on and on, but her father would not be moved. They ended the evening swearing at each other, and Hal left in the dead of night, slamming the door behind him as he went.

Adara, listening, had made a decision. It did not matter what her father did or did not do. She would stay. If she moved, the ice dragon would not know where to find her when winter came, and if she went too far south it would never be able to come to her at all.

It did come to her, though, just after her seventh birthday. That winter was the coldest one of all. She flew so often and so far that she scarcely had time to work on her ice castle.

Hal came again in the spring. There were only a dozen dragons in his wing, and he brought no presents that year. He and her father argued once again. Hal raged and pleaded and threatened, but her father was stone. Finally Hal left, off to the battlefields.

That was the year the king's line broke, up north near some town with a long name that Adara could not pronounce.

Teri heard about it first. She returned from the inn one night flushed and excited. "A messenger came through, on his way to the king," she told them. "The enemy won some big battle, and he's to ask for reinforcements. He said our army is retreating."

Their father frowned, and worry lines creased his brow. "Did he say anything of the king's dragonriders?" Arguments or no, Hal was family.

"I asked," Teri said. "He said the dragonriders are the rear guard. They're supposed to raid and burn, delay the enemy while our army pulls back safely. Oh, I hope Uncle Hal is safe!"

"Hal will show them," Geoff said. "Him and Brimstone will burn 'em all up."

Their father smiled. "Hal could always take care of himself. At any rate, there is nothing we can do. Teri, if any more messengers come through, ask them how it goes."

She nodded, her concern not quite covering her excitement. It was all quite thrilling.

In the weeks that followed, the thrill wore off, as the people of the area began to comprehend the magnitude of the disaster. The king's highway grew busier and busier, and all the traffic flowed from north to south, and all the travellers wore green-and-gold. At first the soldiers marched in disciplined columns, led by officers wearing plumed golden helmets, but even then they were less than stirring. The columns marched wearily, and the uniforms were filthy and torn, and the swords and pikes and axes the soldiers carried were nicked and oftimes stained. Some men had lost their weapons; they limped along blindly, empty-handed. And the trains of wounded that followed the columns were often longer than the columns themselves. Adara stood in the grass by the side of the road and watched them pass. She saw a man with no eyes supporting a man with only one leg, as the two of them walked together. She saw men with no legs, or no arms, or both. She saw a man with his head split open by an axe, and many men covered with caked blood and filth, men who moaned low in their throats as they walked. She *smelled* men with bodies that were horribly greenish and puffed-up. One of them died and was left abandoned by the side of the road. Adara told her father and he and some of the men from the village came out and buried him.

Most of all, Adara saw the burned men. There were dozens of them in every column that passed, men whose skin was black and seared and falling off, who had lost an arm or a leg or half of a face to the hot breath of a dragon. Teri told them what the officers said, when they stopped at the inn to drink or rest; the enemy had many, many dragons.

For almost a month the columns flowed past, more every day. Even Old Laura admitted that she had never seen so much traffic on the road. From time to time a lone messenger on horseback rode against the tide, galloping towards the north, but always alone. After a time everyone knew there would be no reinforcements.

An officer in one of the last columns advised the people

of the area to pack up whatever they could carry, and move south. "They are coming," he warned. A few listened to him, and indeed for a week the road was full of refugees from towns farther north. Some of them told frightful stories. When they left, more of the local people went with them.

But most stayed. They were people like her father, and the land was in their blood.

The last organized force to come down the road was a ragged troop of cavalry, men as gaunt as skeletons riding horses with skin pulled tight around their ribs. They thundered past in the night, their mounts heaving and foaming, and the only one to pause was a pale young officer, who reigned his mount up briefly and shouted, "Go, go. They are burning everything!" Then he was off after his men.

The few soldiers who came after were alone or in small groups. They did not always use the road, and they did not pay for the things they took. One swordsman killed a farmer on the other side of town, raped his wife, stole his money, and ran. His rags were green-and-gold.

Then no one came at all. The road was deserted.

The innkeeper claimed he could smell ashes when the wind blew from the north. He packed up his family and went south. Teri was distraught. Geoff was wide-eyed and anxious and only a bit frightened. He asked a thousand questions about the enemy, and practiced at being a warrior. Their father went about his labors, busy as ever. War or no war, he had crops in the field. He smiled less than usual, however, and he began to drink, and Adara often saw him glancing up at the sky while he worked.

Adara wandered the fields alone, played by herself in the damp summer heat, and tried to think of where she would hide if her father tried to take them away.

Last of all, the king's dragonriders came, and with them Hal.

There were only four of them. Adara saw the first one, and went and told her father, and he put his hand on her shoulder and together they watched it pass, a solitary green dragon with a vaguely tattered look. It did not pause for them.

Two days later, three dragons flying together came into view, and one of them detached itself from the others and circled down to their farm while the other two headed south.

Uncle Hal was thin and grim and sallow-looking. His dragon looked sick. Its eyes ran, and one of its wings had been partially burned, so it flew in an awkward, heavy manner, with much difficulty. "Now will you go?" Hal said to his brother, in front of all the children.

"No. Nothing has changed."

Hal swore. "They will be here within three days," he said. "Their dragonriders may be here even sooner."

"Father, I'm scared," Teri said.

He looked at her, saw her fear, hesitated, and finally turned back to his brother. "I am staying. But if you would, I would have you take the children."

Now it was Hal's turn to pause. He thought for a moment, and finally shook his head. "I can't, John. I would, willingly, joyfully, if it were possible. But it isn't. Brimstone is wounded. He can barely carry me. If I took on any extra weight, we might never make it."

Teri began to weep.

"I'm sorry, love," Hal said to her. "Truly I am." His fists clenched helplessly.

"Teri is almost full-grown," their father said. "If her weight is too much, then take one of the others."

Brother looked at brother, with despair in their eyes. Hal trembled. "Adara," he said finally. "She's small and light." He forced a laugh. "She hardly weighs anything at all. I'll take Adara. The rest of you take horses, or a wagon, or go on foot. But go, damn you, *go*."

"We will see," their father said non-committally. "You take Adara, and keep her safe for us."

"Yes," Hal agreed. He turned and smiled at her. "Come, child. Uncle Hal is going to take you for a ride on Brimstone."

Adara looked at him very seriously. "No," she said. She turned and slipped through the door and began to run.

They came after her, of course, Hal and her father and even Geoff. But her father wasted time standing in the door, shouting at her to come back, and when he began to run he was ponderous and clumsy, while Adara was indeed small and light and fleet of foot. Hal and Geoff stayed with her longer, but Hal was weak, and Geoff soon winded himself, though he sprinted hard at her heels for a few moments. By the time Adara reached the nearest wheat field, the three of them were well behind her. She quickly lost herself amid the grain, and they searched for hours in vain while she made her way carefully towards the woods.

When dusk fell, they brought out lanterns and torches and continued their search. From time to time she heard her father swearing, or Hal calling out her name. She stayed high in the branches of the oak she had climbed, and smiled down at their lights as they combed back and forth through the fields. Finally she drifted off to sleep, dreaming about the coming of winter and wondering how she would live until her birthday. It was still a long time away.

Dawn woke her; dawn and a noise in the sky.

Adara yawned and blinked, and heard it again. She shinnied to the uppermost limb of the tree, as high as it would bear her, and pushed aside the leaves.

There were dragons in the sky.

She had never seen beasts quite like these. Their scales were dark and sooty, not green like the dragon Hal rode. One was a rust color and one was the shade of dried blood and one was black as coal. All of them had eyes like glowing embers, and steam rose from their nostrils, and their tails flicked back and forth as their dark, leathery wings beat the air. The rust-colored one opened its mouth and roared, and the forest shook to its challenge, and even the branch that held Adara trembled just a little. The black one made a noise too, and when it opened its maw a spear of flame lanced out, all orange and blue, and touched the trees below. Leaves withered and blackened, and smoke began to rise from where the dragon's breath had fallen. The one the color of blood flew close overhead, its wings creaking and straining, its mouth half-open. Between its yellowed teeth Adara saw soot and cinders, and the wind stirred by its passage was fire and sandpaper, raw and chafing against her skin. She cringed.

On the backs of the dragons rode men with whip and lance, in uniforms of black-and-orange, their faces hidden behind dark helmets. The one on the rust dragon gestured with his lance, pointing at the farm buildings across the fields. Adara looked.

Hal came up to meet them.

His green dragon was as large as their own, but somehow it seemed small to Adara as she watched it climb upwards from the farm. With its wings fully extended, it was plain to see how badly injured it was; the right wing tip was charred, and it leaned heavily to one side as it flew. On its back, Hal looked like one of the tiny toy soldiers he had brought them as a present years before.

The enemy dragonriders split up and came at him from three sides. Hal saw what they were doing. He tried to turn, to throw himself at the black dragon head-on, and flee the other two. His whip flailed angrily, desperately. His green dragon opened its mouth, and roared a weak challenge, but its flame was pale and short and did not reach the oncoming enemy.

The others held their fire. Then, on a signal, their dragons all breathed as one. Hal was wreathed in flames.

His dragon made a high wailing noise, and Adara saw that it was burning, *he* was burning, they were all burning, beast and master both. They fell heavily to the ground, and lay smoking amidst her father's wheat.

The air was full of ashes.

Adara craned her head around in the other direction, and saw a column of smoke rising from beyond the forest and the river. That was the farm where Old Laura lived with her grandchildren and *their* children.

When she looked back, the three dark dragons were circling lower and lower above her own farm. One by one they landed. She watched the first of the riders dismount and saunter towards their door.

She was frightened and confused and only seven, after all. And the heavy air of summer was a weight upon her, and it filled her with a helplessness and thickened all her fears. So Adara did the only thing she knew, without thinking, a thing that came naturally to her. She climbed down from her tree and ran. She ran across the fields and through the woods, away from the farm and her family and the dragons, away from all of it. She ran until her legs throbbed with pain, down in the direction of the river. She ran to the coldest place she knew, to the deep caves underneath the river bluffs, to chill shelter and darkness and safety.

And there in the cold she hid. Adara was a winter child, and cold did not bother her. But still, as she hid, she trembled.

Day turned into night. Adara did not leave her cave.

She tried to sleep, but her dreams were full of burning dragons.

She made herself very small as she lay in the darkness, and tried to count how many days remained until her birthday. The caves were nicely cool; Adara could almost imagine that it was not summer after all, that it was winter, or near to winter. Soon her ice dragon would come for her, and she would ride on its back to the land of always-winter, where great ice castles and cathedrals of snow stood eternally in endless fields of white, and the stillness and silence were all.

It almost felt like winter as she lay there. The cave grew colder and colder, it seemed. It made her feel safe. She napped briefly. When she woke, it was colder still. A white coating of frost covered the cave walls, and she was sitting on a bed of ice. Adara jumped to her feet and looked up towards the mouth of the cave, filled with a wan dawn light. A cold wind caressed her. But it was coming from outside, from the world of summer, not from the depths of the cave at all.

She gave a small shout of joy, and climbed and scrambled up the ice-covered rocks.

Outside, the ice dragon was waiting for her.

It had breathed upon the water, and now the river was frozen, or at least a part of it was, although she could see that the ice was fast melting as the summer sun rose. It had breathed upon the green grass that grew along the banks, grass as high as Adara, and now the tall blades were white and brittle, and when the ice dragon moved its wings the grass cracked in half and tumbled, sheared as clean as if it had been cut down with a scythe.

The dragon's icy eyes met Adara's, and she ran to it and up its wing, and threw her arms about it. She knew she had to hurry. The ice dragon looked smaller than she had ever seen it, and she understood what the heat of summer was doing to it.

"Hurry, dragon," she whispered. "Take me away, take me to the land of always-winter. We'll never come back here, never. I'll build you the best castle of all, and take care of you, and ride you every day. Just take me away, dragon, take me home with you."

The ice dragon heard and understood. Its wide translucent wings unfolded and beat the air, and bitter arctic winds howled through the fields of summer. They rose. Away from the cave. Away from the river. Above the forest. Up and up. The ice dragon swung around to the north. Adara caught a glimpse of her father's farm, but it was very small and growing smaller. They turned their back to it, and soared.

Then a sound came to Adara's ears. An impossible sound, a sound that was too small and too far away for her to ever have heard it, especially above the beating of the ice dragon's wings. But she heard it nonetheless. She heard her father scream.

Hot tears ran down her cheeks, and where they fell upon the ice dragon's back they burned small pockmarks in the frost. Suddenly the cold beneath her hands was biting, and when she pulled one hand away Adara saw the mark that it had made upon the dragon's neck. She was scared, but still she clung. "Turn back," she whispered. "Oh, *please*, dragon. Take me back."

She could not see the ice dragon's eyes, but she knew what they would look like. Its mouth opened and a blue-white plume issued, a long cold streamer that hung in the air. It made no noise; ice dragons are silent. But in her mind Adara heard the wild keening of its grief.

"Please," she whispered once again. "Help me." Her voice was thin and small.

The ice dragon turned.

The three dark dragons were outside of the barn when Adara returned, feasting on the burned and blackened carcasses of her father's stock. One of the dragonriders was standing near them, leaning on his lance and prodding his dragon from time to time.

He looked up when the cold gust of wind came shrieking across the fields, and shouted something, and sprinted for the black dragon. The beast tore a last hunk of meat from her father's horse, swallowed, and rose reluctantly into the air. The rider flailed his whip.

Adara saw the door of the farmhouse burst open. The other two riders rushed out, and ran for their dragons. One of them was struggling into his pants as he ran. He was barechested.

The black dragon roared, and its fire came blazing up at them. Adara felt the searing blast of heat, and a shudder went through the ice dragon as the flame played along its belly. Then it craned its long neck around, and fixed its baleful empty eyes upon the enemy, and opened its frost-rimed jaws. Out from among its icy teeth its breath came streaming, and that breath was pale and cold.

It touched the left wing of the coal-black dragon beneath them, and the dark beast gave a shrill cry of pain, and when it beat its wings again, the frost-covered wing broke in two. Dragon and dragonrider began to fall.

The ice dragon breathed again.

They were frozen and dead before they hit the ground.

The rust-colored dragon was flying at them, and the dragon the color of blood with its barechested rider. Adara's ears were filled with their angry roaring, and she could feel their hot breath around her, and see the air shimmering with heat, and smell the stink of sulfur.

Two long swords of fire crossed in midair, but neither

touched the ice dragon, though it shriveled in the heat, and water flew from it like rain whenever it beat its wings.

The blood-colored dragon flew too close, and the breath of the ice dragon blasted the rider. His bare chest turned blue before Adara's eyes, and moisture condensed on him in an instant, covering him with frost. He screamed, and died, and fell from his mount, though his harness hand remained behind, frozen to the neck of his dragon. The ice dragon closed on it, wings screaming the secret song of winter, and a blast of flame met a blast of cold. The ice dragon shuddered once again, and twisted away, dripping. The other dragon died.

But the last dragonrider was behind them now, the enemy in full armor on the dragon whose scales were the brown of rust. Adara screamed, and even as she did the fire enveloped the ice dragon's wing. It was gone in less than an instant, but the wing was gone with it, melted, destroyed.

The ice dragon's remaining wing beat wildly to slow its plunge, but it came to earth with an awful crash. Its legs shattered beneath it, and its wing snapped in two places, and the impact of the landing threw Adara from its back. She tumbled to the soft earth of the field, and rolled, and struggled up, bruised but whole.

The ice dragon seemed very small now, and very broken. Its long neck sank wearily to the ground, and its head rested amid the wheat.

The enemy dragonrider came swooping in, roaring with triumph. The dragon's eyes burned. The man flourished his lance and shouted.

The ice dragon painfully raised its head once more, and made the only sound that Adara ever heard it make: a terrible thin cry full of melancholy, like the sound the north wind makes when it moves around the towers and battlements of the white castles that stand empty in the land of always-winter.

When the cry had faded, the ice dragon sent cold into the world one final time: a long smoking blue-white stream of cold that was full of snow and stillness and the end of all living things. The dragonrider flew right into it, still brandishing whip and lance. Adara watched him crash.

Then she was running, away from the fields, back to the house and her family within, running as fast as she could, running and panting and crying all the while like a seven year old.

Her father had been nailed to the bedroom wall. They had wanted him to watch while they took their turns with Teri. Adara did not know what to do, but she untied Teri, whose tears had dried by then, and they freed Geoff, and then they got their father down. Teri nursed him and cleaned out his wounds. When his eyes opened and he saw Adara, he smiled. She hugged him very hard, and cried for him.

By night he said he was fit enough to travel. They crept away under cover of darkness, and took the king's road south.

Her family asked no questions then, in those hours of darkness and fear. But later, when they were safe in the south, there were questions endlessly. Adara gave them the best answers she could. But none of them ever believed her, except for Geoff, and he grew out of it when he got older. She was only seven, after all, and she did not understand that ice dragons are never seen in summer, and cannot be tamed nor ridden.

Besides, when they left the house that night, there was no ice dragon to be seen. Only the huge dark corpses of three war dragons, and the smaller bodies of three dragon-riders in black-and-orange. And a pond that had never been there before, a small quiet pool where the water was very cold. They had walked around it carefully, headed towards the road.

Their father worked for another farmer for three years in the south. His hands were never as strong as they had been, before the nails had been pounded through them, but he made up for that with the strength of his back and his arms, and his determination. He saved whatever he could, and he seemed happy. "Hal is gone, and my land," he would tell Adara, "and I am sad for that. But it is all right. I have my daughter back." For the winter was gone from her now, and she smiled and laughed and even wept like other little girls.

Three years after they had fled, the king's army routed the enemy in a great battle, and the king's dragons burned the foreign capital. In the peace that followed, the northern provinces changed hands once more. Teri had recaptured her spirit and married a young trader, and she remained in the south. Geoff and Adara returned with their father to the farm.

When the first frost came, all the ice lizards came out, just as they had always done. Adara watched them with a smile on her face, remembering the way it had been. But she did not try to touch them. They were cold and fragile little things, and the warmth of her hands would hurt them.

THE GEORGE BUSINESS

ROGER ZELAZNY

ILLUSTRATIONS BY
GEOFREY DARROW

Deep in his lair, Dart twisted his green and golden length about his small hoard, his sleep troubled by dreams of a series of identical armored assailants. Since dragons' dreams are always prophetic, he woke with a shudder, cleared his throat to the point of sufficient illumination to check on the state of his treasure, stretched, yawned and set forth up the tunnel to consider the strength of the opposition. If it was too great, he would simply flee, he decided. The hell with the hoard, it wouldn't be the first time.

As he peered from the cavemouth, he beheld a single knight in mismatched armor atop a tired-looking gray horse, just rounding the bend. His lance was not even couched, but still pointing skyward.

Assuring himself that the man was unaccompanied, he roared and slithered forth.

"Halt," he bellowed, "you who are about to fry!"

The knight obliged.

"You're the one I came to see," the man said. "I have—"

"Why," Dart asked, "do you wish to start this business

up again? Do you realize how long it has been since a knight and dragon have done battle?"

"Yes, I do. Quite awhile. But I—"

"It is almost invariably fatal to one of the parties concerned. Usually your side."

"Don't I know it. Look, you've got me wrong—"

"I dreamt a dragon-dream of a young man named George with whom I must do battle. You bear him an extremely close resemblance."

"I can explain. It's not as bad as it looks. You see—"

"*Is* your name George?"

"Well, yes. But don't let that bother you—"

"It *does* bother me. You want my pitiful hoard? It wouldn't keep you in beer money for the season. Hardly worth the risk."

"I'm not after your hoard—"

"I haven't grabbed off a virgin in centuries. They're usually old and tough, anyhow, not to mention hard to find."

"No one's accusing—"

"As for cattle, I always go a great distance. I've gone out of my way, you might say, to avoid getting a bad name in my own territory."

"I know you're no real threat here. I've researched it quite carefully—"

"And do you think that armor will really protect you when I exhale my deepest, hottest flames?"

"Hell, no! So don't do it, huh? If you'd please—"

"And that lance . . . You're not even holding it properly."

George lowered the lance.

"On that you are correct," he said, "but it happens to be tipped with one of the deadliest poisons known to Herman the Apothecary."

"I say! That's hardly sporting!"

"I know. But even if you incinerate me, I'll bet I can scratch you before I go."

"Now that would be rather silly—both of us dying like that—wouldn't it?" Dart observed, edging away. "It would serve no useful purpose that I can see."

"I feel precisely the same way about it."

"Then why are we getting ready to fight?"

"I have no desire whatsoever to fight with you!"

"I'm afraid I don't understand. You said your name is George, and I had this dream—"

"I can explain it."

"But the poisoned lance—"

"Self-protection, to hold you off long enough to put a proposition to you."

Dart's eyelids lowered slightly.

"What sort of proposition?"

"I want to hire you."

"Hire me? Whatever for? And what are you paying?"

"Mind if I rest this lance a minute? No tricks?"

"Go ahead. If you're talking gold your life is safe."

George rested his lance and undid a pouch at his belt. He dipped his hand into it and withdrew a fistful of shining coins. He tossed them gently, so that they clinked and shone in the morning light.

"You have my full attention. That's a good piece of change there."

"My life's savings. All yours—in return for a bit of business."

"What's the deal?"

George replaced the coins in his pouch and gestured.

"See that castle in the distance—two hills away?"

"I've flown over it many times."

"In the tower to the west are the chambers of Rosalind,

daughter of the Baron Maurice. She is very dear to his heart, and I wish to wed her."

"There's a problem?"

"Yes. She's attracted to big, brawny barbarian types, into which category I, alas, do not fall. In short, she doesn't like me."

"That *is* a problem."

"So, if I could pay you to crash in there and abduct her, to bear her off to some convenient and isolated place and wait for me, I'll come along, we'll fake a battle, I'll vanquish you, you fly away and I'll take her home. I am certain I will then appear sufficiently heroic in her eyes to rise from sixth to first position on her list of suitors. How does that sound to you?"

Dart sighed a long column of smoke.

"Human, I bear your kind no special fondness—particularly the armored variety with lances—so I don't know why I'm telling you this . . . Well, I do know, actually . . . But never mind. I could manage it, all right. But, if you win the hand of that maid, do you know what's going to happen? The novelty of your deed will wear off after a time—and you know that there will be no encore. Give her a year, I'd say, and you'll catch her fooling around with one of those brawny barbarians she finds so attractive. Then you must either fight him and be slaughtered or wear horns, as they say."

George laughed.

"It's nothing to me how she spends her spare time. I've a girlfriend in town myself."

Dart's eyes widened.

"I'm afraid I don't understand . . ."

"She's the old baron's only offspring, and he's on his last legs. Why else do you think an uncomely wench like that would have six suitors? Why else would I gamble my life's savings to win her?"

"I see," said Dart. "Yes, I can understand greed."

"I call it a desire for security."

"Quite. In that case, forget my simple-minded advice. All right, give me the gold and I'll do it." Dart gestured with one gleaming vane. "The first valley in those western mountains seems far enough from my home for our confrontation."

"I'll pay you half now and half on delivery."

"Agreed. Be sure to have the balance with you, though, and drop it during the scuffle. I'll return for it after you two have departed. Cheat me and I'll repeat the performance, with a different ending."

"The thought had already occurred to me. —Now, we'd better practice a bit, to make it look realistic. I'll rush at you with the lance, and whatever side she's standing on I'll aim for it to pass you on the other. You raise that wing, grab the lance and scream like hell. Blow a few flames around, too."

"I'm going to see you scour the tip of that lance before we rehearse this."

"Right. —I'll release the lance while you're holding it next to you and rolling around. Then I'll dismount and rush toward you with my blade. I'll whack you with the flat of it—again, on the far side—a few times. Then you bellow again and fly away."

"Just how sharp is that thing, anyway?"

"Damned dull. It was my grandfather's. Hasn't been honed since he was a boy."

"And you drop the money during the fight?"

"Certainly. —How does that sound?"

"Not bad. I can have a few clusters of red berries under my wing, too. I'll squash them once the action gets going."

"Nice touch. Yes, do that. Let's give it a quick rehearsal now and then get on with the real thing."

"And don't whack too hard . . ."

"A red substance dribbled from beneath the thundering creature's left wing."

That afternoon, Rosalind of Maurice Manor was abducted by a green and gold dragon who crashed through the wall of her chamber and bore her off in the direction of the western mountains.

"Never fear!" shouted her sixth-ranked suitor—who just happened to be riding by—to her aged father who stood wringing his hands on a nearby balcony. "I'll rescue her!" and he rode off to the west.

Coming into the valley where Rosalind stood backed into a rocky cleft, guarded by the fuming beast of gold and green, George couched his lance.

"Release that maiden and face your doom!" he cried.

Dart bellowed, George rushed. The lance fell from his hands and the dragon rolled upon the ground, spewing gouts of fire into the air. A red substance dribbled from beneath the thundering creature's left wing. Before Rosalind's wide eyes, George advanced and swung his blade several times.

". . . and that!" he cried, as the monster stumbled to its feet and sprang into the air, dripping more red.

It circled once and beat its way off toward the top of the mountain, then over it and away.

"Oh George!" Rosalind cried, and she was in his arms. "Oh, George . . ."

He pressed her to him for a moment.

"I'll take you home now," he said.

That evening as he was counting his gold, Dart heard the sound of two horses approaching his cave. He rushed up the tunnel and peered out.

George, now mounted on a proud white stallion and leading the gray, wore a matched suit of bright armor. He was not smiling, however.

"Good evening," he said.

"Good evening. What brings you back so soon?"

"Things didn't turn out exactly as I'd anticipated."

"You seem far better accoutered. I'd say your fortunes had taken a turn."

"Oh, I recovered my expenses and came out a bit ahead. But that's all. I'm on my way out of town. Thought I'd stop by and tell you the end of the story. —Good show you put on, by the way. It probably would have done the trick—"

"But—?"

"She was married to one of the brawny barbarians this morning, in their family chapel. They were just getting ready for a wedding trip when you happened by."

"I'm awfully sorry."

"Well, it's the breaks. To add insult, though, her father dropped dead of a heart attack during your performance. My former competitor is now the new baron. He rewarded me with a new horse and armor, a gratuity and a scroll from the local scribe lauding me as a dragon-slayer. Then he hinted rather strongly that the horse and my new reputation could take me far. Didn't like the way Rosalind was looking at me now I'm a hero."

"That *is* a shame. Well, we tried."

"Yes. So I just stopped by to thank you and let you know how it all turned out. It would have been a good idea—if it had worked."

"You could hardly have foreseen such abrupt nuptials. —You know, I've spent the entire day thinking about the affair. We *did* manage it awfully well."

"Oh, no doubt about that. It went beautifully."

"I was thinking . . . How'd you like a chance to get your money back?"

"What have you got in mind?"

"Uh— When I was advising you earlier that you might

not be happy with the lady, I was trying to think about the situation in human terms. Your desire was entirely understandable to me otherwise. In fact, you think quite a bit like a dragon."

"Really?"

"Yes. It's rather amazing, actually. Now—realizing that it only failed because of a fluke, your idea still has considerable merit."

"I'm afraid I don't follow you."

"There is—ah—a lovely lady of my own species whom I have been singularly unsuccessful in impressing for a long while now. Actually, there are an unusual number of parallels in our situations."

"She has a large hoard, huh?"

"Extremely so."

"Older woman?"

"Among dragons, a few centuries this way or that are not so important. But she, too, has other admirers and seems attracted by the more brash variety."

"Uh-huh. I begin to get the drift. You gave me some advice once. I'll return the favor. Some things are more important than hoards."

"Name one."

"My life. If I were to threaten her she might do me in all by herself, before you could come to her rescue."

"No, she's a demure little thing. Anyway, it's all a matter of timing. I'll perch on a hilltop nearby—I'll show you where—and signal you when to begin your approach. Now, this time I have to win, of course. Here's how we'll work it . . ."

George sat on the white charger and divided his attention between the distant cavemouth and the crest of a high hill off to his left. After a time, a shining winged form

"As the creature advanced, he felt himself seized by the shoulders."

flashed through the air and settled upon the hill. Moments later, it raised one bright wing.

He lowered his visor, couched his lance and started forward. When he came within hailing distance of the cave he cried out:

"I know you're in there, Megtag! I've come to destroy you and make off with your hoard! You godless beast! Eater of children! This is your last day on earth!"

An enormous burnished head with cold green eyes emerged from the cave. Twenty feet of flame shot from its huge mouth and scorched the rock before it. George halted hastily. The beast looked twice the size of Dart and did not seem in the least retiring. Its scales rattled like metal as it began to move forward.

"Perhaps I exaggerated . . ." George began, and he heard the frantic flapping of giant vanes overhead.

As the creature advanced, he felt himself seized by the shoulders. He was borne aloft so rapidly that the scene below dwindled to toy-size in a matter of moments. He saw his new steed bolt and flee rapidly back along the route they had followed.

"What the hell happened?" he cried.

"I hadn't been around for awhile," Dart replied. "Didn't know one of the others had moved in with her. You're lucky I'm fast. That's Pelladon. He's a mean one."

"Great. Don't you think you should have checked first?"

"Sorry. I thought she'd take decades to make up her mind—without prompting. Oh, what a hoard! You should have seen it!"

"Follow that horse. I want him back."

They sat before Dart's cave, drinking.

"Where'd you ever get a whole barrel of wine?"

"Lifted it from a barge, up the river. I do that every now and then. I keep a pretty good cellar, if I do say so."

"Indeed. Well, we're none the poorer, really. We can drink to that."

"True, but I've been thinking again. You know, you're a very good actor."

"Thanks. You're not so bad yourself."

"Now supposing—just supposing—you were to travel about. Good distances from here each time. Scout out villages, on the continent and in the isles. Find out which ones are well off and lacking in local heroes . . ."

"Yes?"

". . . And let them see that dragon-slaying certificate of yours. Brag a bit. Then come back with a list of towns. Maps, too."

"Go ahead."

"Find the best spots for a little harmless predation and choose a good battle site—"

"Refill?"

"Please."

"Here."

"Thanks. Then you show up, and for a fee—"

"Sixty-forty."

"That's what I was thinking, but I'll bet you've got the figures transposed."

"Maybe fifty-five and forty-five then."

"Down the middle, and let's drink on it."

"Fair enough. Why haggle?"

"Now I know why I dreamed of fighting a great number of knights, all of them looking like you. You're going to make a name for yourself, George."

ONE WINTER IN EDEN

MICHAEL BISHOP

ILLUSTRATIONS BY
VAL and JOHN LAKEY

One way or another, there were dragons in Eden.

(Carl Sagan)

i

"Read this one, Mr. Lang."

The child's high-pitched Steamboat Willie voice made no impression on Lang. Two weeks and a day after assuming his teaching duties in Barclay, a trackside Georgia town twenty miles from the Alabama border, he was holding his classroom door open so that the rear guard of his third-graders filing back along the breezeway from the cafeteria could pass inside. It was January, and very cold. Blackbirds in the pecan trees near the school fluttered like ribbons of mortuary crepe. The stray dogs cavorting in the marshy quadrangle seemed to be doing so only to keep warm.

"Mr. Lang," the same piping voice insisted, "I want you to read this one."

The voice belonged to Skipper Thornley, a stocky eight-year-old with an unappeasable air of blue-eyed expectation. The large, flat picture book he had thrust at

Lang was blocking traffic, and Skipper, Lang had learned, was capable of waiting centuries for what he wanted.

"Come on, Skipper, let's let everyone get inside. You don't want me to read the blasted thing out here, do you?"

"Mrs. Banks always read to us after lunch," the boy replied.

"*Get inside!*" Lang exclaimed. He could make his voice boom in a sonorous, no-nonsense way altogether outside the capabilities of his fellow teachers at the Barclay Public Primary School, all but one of whom were female. Skipper and the others reacted by skipping mock-fearfully indoors.

Owing to a precedent established by Mrs. Banks, who had just departed for Colorado with her husband, the period after lunch was devoted either to Story Time or to the children's own excruciatingly painful sessions of—ah, yes—Friendship Sharing. Friendship Sharing required everyone, not excepting the teacher, to listen to some chosen child's interminable monologue about pets, or parents, or favorite TV programs. And the principal beneficiary of this activity, Lang understood, was whichever self-inebriated kid happened to be holding center stage at the moment. Few of his third-graders had much narrative savvy, and the "stories" they told fishtailed, backed up on themselves, and usually disintegrated into incoherent repetition. That was why, four days after Lang's arrival, Friendship Sharing had fallen victim to the less nerve-wracking institution of Story Time, which, by ritual precedent, the teacher conducted. Since most of the kids liked to be read to, especially if there were pictures you could show around, Lang was content to indulge them. Rather incredibly, Story Time had begun to make Lang feel that maybe he belonged in Barclay. Maybe he had found a home.

"All right, Skipper, what you got for us today?" Lang

stood at the front of the room, his foot on a metal folding chair and his right hand nonchalantly cupping his chin as he surveyed the class.

From a desk in the back Skipper Thornley passed his library book forward, and Lang could see its glossy plastic cover picking up finger prints as it flopped from hand to hand. Skipper's parents had probably checked the book out from the regional library in Ladysmith, eighteen miles up the road, since the primary school's books were mostly ancient volumes that had been taped and rebound many times over. Finally, Vanessa Copeland, a black girl in a front-row desk, received the book and read its title aloud.

"Everyone . . . Knows . . . What . . . a . . . Dragon . . . Looks . . . Like," Vanessa enunciated carefully. Then she handed the book to Lang, who, without actually recoiling, accepted it, lowered his foot to the floor, and stumbled backward a step or two. In his hesitation the children apparently perceived a hint of their teacher's reluctance, if nothing at all of his surprise and dismay, for they immediately began chanting, "*Read* it, *read* it, *read* it, *read* it. . . ." Their pitiless trochees meant nothing to Lang. He was unshaken by the hubbub of their incantation; he was, in fact, vaguely in sympathy with the desire for diversion that drove it. But the *book* unsettled him, and the beauty of its almost iridescent cover illustration—a dragon floating above an Oriental landscape—had no power to defuse the threat implicit in the title.

Everyone Knows What a Dragon Looks Like.

The hell you say! thought Lang irrationally, hatefully. The stinking *hell* you say! He began tearing pages out of the book and dropping them to the floor. The chants of "*Read* it, *read* it" died in his third-graders' mouths and Skipper Thornley stood up in the back of the room wearing a look of reproachful astonishment. Lang saw the

boy's expression smear suddenly into one of inconsolable
heartbreak and heard all around him a silence as bleak as
January.

Stricken, he stopped tearing pages out of Skipper's
book. Half torn from the binding, an exquisitely detailed
illustration of routed barbarian horsemen tick-tocked back
and forth in Lang's fingers, hypnotizing him with memory
and regret.

Lang forced his head up to meet the uncomprehending
gazes of his students. They seemed to be waiting for him to
explain, as if intuitively convinced that he had destroyed
the book with some premeditated lesson in mind. He
hadn't. He had acted out of fear and rage.

"I'll give you the money for the book," Lang told Skipper. "Don't worry about that. I'll give you the money."

ii.

Lang's arrival in Barclay had gone virtually unre-
marked. To date, the only people with whom he had had
any significant commerce were the children in his class, his
fellow teachers, and Mr. E. H. Norton, the principal.

Mr. Norton, a small man with pinched but patrician
features, presided over a divided kingdom. The primary
school (kindergarten through third grade) had once been a
black educational plant. It was located on the western
outskirts of Barclay, near a tumbledown Negro church and
a semicircular drive of small, one-story, government-
funded apartments. The school's playground abutted a
field canopied by lush kudzu in the summer but at this time
of year wired and crosswired with leafless vines. Vandals
repeatedly stripped the playground's slides and teeter-
totters of the bolts, clasps, and fittings that held them
together. No one knew exactly why.

The elementary school, Mr. Norton's other bastion, lay

almost two miles away—near the post office, the First
Methodist Church, the medical clinic, and the highway
going north to Ladysmith. It housed grades four through
seven, as well as Mr. Norton's office, and because this
facility had once served only whites, it boasted a detached
gymnasium of barnlike proportions and indoor corridors
rather than open breezeways.

(Children in higher grades were bused to schools in
Wickrath, twelve miles away, the county seat.)

A few minutes before seven on a chilly Wednesday
morning, Lang found himself standing in a corridor outside his superior's office. He was there because the previous evening, during a curt but hardly cryptic telephone
call, Mr. Norton had requested his presence. Now the
temperature outside was several degrees below freezing,
and, rising from bed in the dark, Lang had scarcely been
able to get his blood coursing and his brain even margin-
ally alert. He had not realized that it could be so cold in
Georgia.

Precisely at seven Mr. Norton appeared in the corridor.
He was wearing a rich-looking leather coat with fur-lined
lapels, doeskin gloves, and a knitted muffler. He led Lang
through his secretary's office to the carpeted and paneled
sanctorum where, a little over three weeks ago, he had
conducted Lang's employment interview. Nodding Lang
into an armchair opposite his huge oaken desk (whose
surface reminded Lang of the deck of an aircraft carrier),
Mr. Norton shed his coat, gloves, and muffler and opened
his Venetian blinds on the bleak, narrow vista of the
teachers' parking lot. He viewed this grey auroral landscape with distaste.

Mr. Norton had a reputation as a disciplinarian, of his
staff as well as of his students. Many thought him severe
and humorless, although this judgment may not have

reflected the trying circumstances of his tenure. Eight and a
half years before, Mr. Norton had agreed to remain as
principal for the onset of court-ordered integration. Since
then, it was said, he had weathered changes and disrup-
tions before which less gritty administrators would have
trembled and retreated. A great many white parents had
yanked their children from the public schools in favor of
private "academies" in Ladysmith and other surrounding
towns. This loss of students, in addition to limiting the state
and federal funds at Mr. Norton's disposal, had necessi-
tated a painful reconstitution and intermural shuffling of
his faculty. Two kingdoms were more difficult to rule than
one. Mr. Norton had succeeded in establishing his authority over both. He took great pride in his attention to the
cleanliness and order of his otherwise obsolescent buildings, and no one in the county disputed that Mr. E. H.
Norton ran a pair of tight ships. His attitude toward blacks,
however, was alternately suspicious and autocratic, try as
he might to disguise his true feelings and to administer
fairly—for without once in his youth suspecting that such a
thing could happen, Mr. Norton had become a human
bridge between two distinctive eras of race relations in
Barclay. More than a few townspeople—not all of them
blacks or disaffected former teachers—believed that he
had outserved his usefulness and deserved to be replaced.

Lang had picked up on this enduring scuttlebutt from a
variety of sources, mostly other teachers, but he really had
no opinion in the matter. A single disquieting thing was on
his mind this morning, and his heart was a lump of ice in his
chest.

"Skipper Thornley's daddy called me last night. He said
you tore up a library book the boy took to school yesterday." Mr. Norton continued to stare through the parted
slats of his blinds into the outer greyness. "Said you did it
right in front of the class. Is that right?"

"Maybe he had found a home."

"Yes, sir."

Mr. Norton grimaced and finally looked at Lang. "You hadn't been drinking, had you?"

"No, sir."

"Then why'n hell would you do an asinine thing like that?"

"I didn't like the book."

"Skipper's daddy said it was about dragons. You don't approve of books about dragons? You tear 'em up and throw the pages on the floor. That's instructive, I guess. That teaches respect for property. Because afterwards you apologize and pay for the damages."

"I didn't apologize," Lang said. "I paid, though."

Mr. Norton clamped his lips and shook his head. "I don't appreciate such shenanigans, Lang," he finally said. "They don't make any sense. Was it a dirty book? Did it contain unsavory pictures or language?"

"By Barclay's standards?"

"Who else's standards make a snit of difference?"

"No, then—it wasn't unsavory in its text or illustrations. I just didn't care for the subject. The book's title was a lie."

Mr. Norton took a slip of paper from his shirt pocket and smoothed it out on the oaken landing strip of his desk. "Everyone Knows What a Dragon Looks Like," he read from the paper.

"Which is a lie," Lang insisted.

"It's a picture book for kids. You're not supposed to *believe* a title. It's just what you *call* something." Mr. Norton grimaced in exasperation, unable to explain what he felt was already self-evident. "A title's just what you call something," he repeated gently, as if for the benefit of a mental deficient who was also blood kin.

Lang remained silent.

"I recommended you for Mrs. Banks's job over three

other applicants, Lang. One of the people I interviewed was a nice young black woman. She was lacking several credits toward her degree. She was a nice person, but she wasn't qualified. I didn't want her teaching my kids." Mr. Norton paused, then resumed animatedly: "There's folks around here who'd rather have her than you, though, even if you do sport a sheepskin from Columbia. They wonder what you're doing here. No lie. He can't be such hot stuff if he had to come to Barclay, they tell each other. Ol' E. H. is playing Jim Crow with us again, they say.

"Listen, I'm walking a tightrope every time I recommend we hire a white in a spot vacated by a black. The only person of color on the county board of education is Darius Copeland, right here from our town, and his little girl Vanessa's in your class. I understand Mr. Copeland registered a nay when the superintendent took your application before the board, Lang. He said the complexion of the faculty here in Barclay was getting a little too pale. You pinched your job by a three-to-one vote. If you hadn't applied at midyear—when applicants are scarce and generally a trifle puny in their credentials—you wouldn't't've got on with us at all. I don't know what your chances for coming back next year are. I mentioned that in our interview, didn't I? Well, if you keep tearing up kids' library books in front of every last wet-eyed yearling in your room, you ain't, pardon me, going to make it till *February*. That's a promise. I'll get you out of here before Darius Copeland does."

Lang remained silent, but his blood was moving.

"Now will you tell me—settin' aside that business about its title being a lie—why'n hell you tore up Skipper Thornley's book?"

Lang took a deep, bitter breath. "I'm a dragon myself," he said.

Mr. Norton snorted and shook his head humorlessly. "So am I. But I'm not half the dragon folks say I am. I keep it in check. That's what I'd advise you to do, too, Lang. Otherwise, you'll go coastin' out of here on a sled with greased runners."

"Yes, sir."

Braving the cold, Lang walked downtown and then out along the Alabama Station Highway to the primary school. When he arrived, several of his third-graders were huddled in the breezeway outside his room waiting for him to unlock the door and let them in.

iii.

Lang got through February by "keeping a low profile." Then, early in March, when the possibility seemed especially remote, an epidemic of pediculosis swept the county school system.

Head lice.

Mr. Norton drove over one morning from the elementary school, gathered his primary teachers in the cafeteria, and informed them that they would have to subject every single one of their students to a scalp examination. The county health department had too few employees to handle the task. Mr. Norton put a magnifying glass on the lunchroom table at which they were all sitting, then had Lang pass out packages of tongue depressors to the teachers. As the principal perfunctorily explained the basics of scalp examination (the tongue depressors were instruments of search), Lang noticed the looks of bewilderment or muted outrage on the faces of his five female colleagues.

Finally, Miss Pauline Winter could take no more. A young black woman who along with Mrs. Kaye taught first-graders in an open-classroom situation, she pushed her package of tongue depressors away from her and very deliberately stood up. "I didn't sign on to give scalp inspections," she said. "I'm not a doctor and I don't see how this has got *anything* to do with education." Her indignation had overcome her mixed feelings of respect and fearful contempt for Mr. Norton, and, like any mutineer confronting authority, she trembled with both determination and nervousness. She was wearing a lemon-colored pant suit and a pale shade of lip ice that, together, were either too elegant or too foxy for the cinderblock cafeteria. At the same time, though, the vividness of her clothes and makeup made her seem a formidable opponent for Mr. Norton, and Lang could tell she had clearly and forthrightly voiced the reservations of all the other teachers.

"Do you want to resign?" Mr. Norton asked Miss Winter.

Mrs. Kaye, a woman in her mid to late forties with a greyish-blonde beehive hairdo, said, "I would hope we didn't have to resign to keep from doing this. I don't care for the idea myself, Mr. Norton. One time, I'll do it. Ask me again, though, and I'll quit for sure."

Mr. Norton, reining in his dragon, explained that they would not be able to eradicate the head lice unless they inspected daily for at least ten or twelve days. The lice attachd eggs, or *nits*, to the base of an individual shaft of hair; and if not effectively treated, these nits, borne outward from the scalp by the growing hairs, would in ten days' time hatch a new and active population of tiny parasites. The Wickrath County schools were under siege. Unless inspections were thorough and frequent during the next several days, the head lice might well shut down the schools. Did everyone understand that? Is that what they all wanted? No one teacher, Mr. Norton stressed, was going to have more than thirty children a day to inspect,

and that was certainly a burden they could all live with if
they cared for either the children or their jobs.

Miss Winter, Mrs. Kaye, Mrs. Conley, Miss Geter, Mrs.
Belflower, and the physical education instructor Russell
Fountain heard their principal out with a palpable skepti-
cism. Only Fountain appeared resigned to the task
ahead—but he had already carried out an inspection of
fifth-graders at the elementary school and the success of a
number of these searches had both disturbed and af-
fronted him. Lang saw revulsion as well as reluctance in
the faces of his associates.

"I'll inspect for the others," he heard himself say, "if
they'll take turns watching my class while I'm busy with
theirs."

"So long as it gets done, I don't give a bassoonist's toot
how you all handle it," Mr. Norton said. And when he
squeezed Lang's shoulder before leaving the cafeteria,
Lang knew there would be no administrative reprisal for
his charity toward the other teachers.

iv.

Lang was fearless in his scalp inspections. He met the
children in the mornings as they walked onto the school
grounds or disembarked the brontosaurian yellow buses
in the parking lot. Before they entered their own class-
rooms, he led as many as he could to the administrative
office and lined them up along the corridor outside its
door. Inside, standing with his back to an electric heater
whose incandescent coils reminded him of the element of
an enormous pop-up toaster, Lang juggled a tongue depressor, a magnifying glass, and a utility flashlight in his
perusals of the children's heads. The sheep were separated from the goats.

On the first day, out of a student population of approximately two hundred, Lang found only sixteen kids with pediculosis. As the inspection program proceeded, however, this number dropped until on Tuesday of the second week Lang could find no one at all who qualified as a bonafide louse- or nit-carrier. All those who had been infested were either still confined to their homes or back in school with notes from doctors attesting to their cure and absolution. Others had returned with labels from such proprietary medications as Kwell. These notes and labels were passports to renewed respectability within the kingdom of Barclay's educational system. The siege appeared to be over. For safety's sake, Lang continued the inspections through Friday of the second week. For the duration of the program he put in a minimum of three hours a day, and by the time he broke for lunch he lacked either the appetite or the necessary energy to eat.

Miss Winter visited Lang on Friday as he was finishing his nit-picking head count of Mrs. Belflower's third-graders. She brought with her Antonio Johnson, a solemn six-year-old with a face as dark and unforthcoming as an eggplant. He had come to school late and so had missed having his scalp examined with Miss Winter's other first-graders.

"How you doin'?" the woman asked Lang.

"Lousy."

Miss Winter vouchsafed him a wan smile. "I brought this child by in order to be in full compliance with Mr. Norton's say-so about the lice problem. That isn't Antonio's problem, but I brought him anyway, just to be in compliance. He's got other troubles. Black children just don't fetch in that many head lice, do they, Mr. Lang?"

Despite a few irate phone calls from redneck parents attributing their children's head lice to contact with "niggers," Lang's experience as Chief Scalp & Nape Inspector pretty much bore out Miss Winter's claim. For each black kid with a minor case of pediculosis, there were eight or nine white children with a veritable population explosion of lice, the consequence in many instances being a secondary bacterial infection such as impetigo—so that the backs of their necks were spotted brown like a giraffe's. Miss Winter, Lang observed, took an odd pride in the relative immunity of the black children, even as she commiserated at a distance with the afflicted whites.

At last Mrs. Belflower's charges were gone, and Lang dropped the tongue depressor he had been using into a waste basket. Although he had found no lice, he felt crawly and dirty. Lousy. Still, the job was done, and an unobtrusive vein of exultation underlay his weariness, just waiting to be tapped. Bellicose memories of mightier victories and more potent deeds invaded him from some primitive portion of his brain, but, in contrast to what he had just accomplished, these antiquated tableaux struck him as grandiose and petty. He wanted nothing more to do with them. They were a corruption he had been trying for centuries to dislodge.

"Mr. Lang," Miss Winter was saying. "You listenin' to me?"

He came back to the moment. Miss Winter had brought Antonio Johnson not simply to have his scalp inspected but to get Lang's opinion about an unrelated medical matter. Look at Anotnio's eyes, Miss Winter urged. Didn't Lang think there might be an infection in the boy's eyes? Lang washed his hands at a discolored basin in the office's restroom, then returned to comply with Miss Winter's request. He wasn't a doctor, but Miss Winter obviously valued his opinion and Lang was flattered to oblige her. He hunkered in front of Antonio Johnson and found the whites of the boy's eyes aflame with a reticulate redness.

Lang said, "You haven't been drinking, have you?"

Antonio Johnson stared tunnels through him. Lang had rarely encountered such a bleak, cheerless stare in a small child. Blessedly, he supposed, he could no longer pick out precedents from the veiled past. In the here and now, though, Antonio Johnson stank. His flesh and clothes gave off the fetor of neglect, the sourness of mildewed laundry and week-old sweat.

"I think it's pink eye," Miss Winter said. "I think it's a bad case. Antonio's missed three days of school this week. Who knows how long he's had it?"

"Is that contagious? Pink eye?"

Miss Winter regarded Lang with surprise. "You bet it is, if it's pink eye. And I think it is. I was wondering what you thought. He don't need to come back to class any more'n those children with head lice, if it is. What he needs is to see a doctor."

After learning that Antonio's mama had no phone, and that his house was across the Alabama Station Highway in a pine copse about three blocks from the comfortable middle-class neighborhood in which Lang had an apartment, Lang volunteered to use his lunch period to walk the boy home. He would search for whoever was around to talk with and urge that person to take little Antonio to the doctor.

"I don't know Antonio's mama," Miss Winter said. Then her voice dropped as if to disguise from Antonio what she next had to say: "I been by that house, Mr. Lang. It's a sorry place. I don't know how anyone can live in such a house." Suddenly Miss Winter was angry. "It's a crime!" she declared, and Lang intercepted the force of her declaration as if she were indicting *him* for the crime. Clearly, he had not yet oriented himself to the complexity of industrial-era relationships. America was impervious to the

auguries of serpent skins and bamboo straws. "A disgrace
and a crime!" said Miss Winter emphatically.

v.

Lang got his coat and walked Antonio Johnson across
the Alabama Station Highway and down the weed-grown
asphalt road toward the boy's house. The jacket the child
wore was a ratty windbreaker missing its zipper clasp. Its
sleeves and tail danced in the wind like Monday-morning
washing. Three or four of the houses on the west side of
the road were shanties faced with discarded roofing tiles or
irregular sheets of plywood. Their open doors were windows on another way of life. As if to contradict the squalor
and oppression that these ramshackle houses seemed to
embody, another pair of nearby dwellings were well-kept
bungalows with painted shutters and neatly spaced
shrubs. Antonio's sprawling house was at the end of the
street. Even before they reached its muddy front yard and
climbed the collapsing steps, Lang knew that no one was
home. Through the open door you could see a kitchen
chair with a soiled blanket draped across its back and the
end of a wooden bed piled high with varicolored quilts.
Everything else was darkness and weathered wood.

"Where's your mama, Antonio?"

Antonio shrugged indifferently, then faced away. From
the sagging front porch Lang watched a pair of scrawny
chickens parade across the yard. He decided to take the
boy to the doctor himself.

The clinic was in downtown Barclay, about ten or fifteen
minutes by foot, and Lang told himself that he could no
more abandon Antonio at this empty house than he could
return him untreated to school. He said as much aloud.
Patron and escort, he set off for town. Antonio followed
him docilely up the asphalt street. A dog barked at them.

On Railroad Street—Barclay's main drag, contiguous for three miles with the highway passing north to Ladysmith and south to Columbus—Lang noticed that Antonio had halted near the gas pumps at McKillian's Corner Grocery. The boy was rubbing his eyes with his jacket sleeve and grimacing as if in pain. Lang returned to him, withdrew a handkerchief, and wiped Antonio's runny nose. "Don't rub 'em," he advised. "You'll probably just make it worse." Antonio's stare, fathomless and uninterpretable, seared Lang from emotional recesses he hadn't yet plumbed. When a train hauling wood chips came rumbling into Barclay from the north and sounding its deep but ear-splitting warning horn, all over town dogs began howling in piteous response. "Damn," said Lang, straightening. The clinic lay on the other side of the tracks, as did the elementary school, and they would have to wait until the train had passed to complete their journey.

The door to McKillian's Corner Grocery opened, and a short, well-built black man came out, gingerly tearing the top off a new package of cigarettes. He wore well-pressed maroon trousers, a shirt of pale grey, a white tie, and a leather car coat. When he saw Antonio, he smiled glancingly, then approached the boy without really acknowledging Lang's presence. This oblique approach tactic, Lang understood, was a function of the man's complicated sense of decorum rather than an intentional slight; in fact, it seemed to derive from a residual shyness which he was even today attempting to exorcise.

"Hey, Tony," he said. "Don't you belong in school?"

"Hey," Antonio Johnson replied, almost inaudibly. The first word out of his mouth that morning.

"I'm taking him to the clinic to see about his eyes," Lang said.

The black man finally permitted himself a gander at

Lang. "Who are you?" he asked, shoving his hands into the pockets of his coat and squinting sidelong at the huge, swaying cars of the passing train.

Lang introduced himself.

"Vanessa's new teacher?" the man inquired skeptically. "Mrs. Banks's replacement?" He retrieved his right hand from his pocket and extended it toward Lang. "I'm Darius Copeland," he said. "I'm on the school board, and you're my baby's new teacher, I presume."

Lang shook hands with Copeland, who avoided his direct gaze as if he were a basilisk. Did each perceive a threat in the other? The cold March breeze, along with the rumbling iron wheels and the creaking iron hitches of the wood-chip cars, harassed and estranged the two men. Even though they had never met before, they were naked to each other in the chill, uncertain noon. This lasted an eyeblink.

"You couldn't find Mrs. Johnson?" Copeland asked.

"I tried. She wasn't home."

"She's been lookin' for a job. Six kids in school, no papa at home, and her with arthritis bad. School's the only time she got to get out and look." The train's caboose trundled by. "I'll take Tony to the doctor. Seems to me Vanessa and her fellow students need a teacher, right?"

"They're at lunch. Mrs. Belflower's with them."

Darius Copeland laughed and looked self-consciously to heaven. "Then I was talking straight," he said, dropping his eyes. "They really do need a teacher." Disconcertingly, he seemed embarrassed to have said such a thing aloud. He fetched a Cricket from his pants, bent his head, and lit a cigarette. The smoke trailed away like milkweed ticking.

"If you really don't mind," Lang said, "I will let you take Antonio to the doctor. I probably should get back and I don't have a car."

"Hey, then, I'll carry you both."

Copeland's automobile, a Corvair with a badly rusted lower body, was parked cattywampus in front of the Barclay Barbecue House next door to the grocery. Everyone climbed in, and Copeland, crossing the tracks running parallel to Railroad Street, drove to the clinic. He took Antonio inside to register with the nurse at the front desk, then emerged from the little brick building and trotted back to his Corvair. A moment later he was hauling Lang out the Alabama Station Highway toward the primary school. The two men kept an uneasy silence, listening to the car's engine make loud *ker-chunking* sounds each time its spark plugs misfired.

At the school Copeland parked in the loading/ unloading zone for buses. He patted the pockets of his coat. "Vanessa doin' okay?"

"She's a good reader," Lang said. "She's doing fine."

"I work two jobs. She's usually in bed when I get home." At last Copeland found what he was searching for, a handful of yellow tickets with detachable stubs. "The Barclay Elementary P.T.O.'s sellin' these," he explained. "Dollar a throw. Teachers are automatic members. You like to make a contribution toward winnin' a nineteen-inch G.E. television set? This is one of the ways our Parent-Teacher Organization raises money. It's a raffle, but we don't call it that. Each dollar's a contribution, not a chance. Set's gonna be give away at the next meetin', and I been too busy to sell very many of the tickets I was allotted."

Lang bought five tickets. Copeland painstakingly filled out the stubs with a ballpoint pen, separated the stubs from the tickets, and stuffed them in a car-coat pocket. Lang escaped Copeland's Corvair with a feeling of relief akin to that he had sometimes experienced getting out of taxi cabs in New York City. And yet, he knew, Copeland would not have taken it amiss if he had bought only one ticket or maybe even begged off altogether. Copeland had simply been doing his best to make conversation.

vi.

Like any other bachelor schoolteacher of moderate good sense, Lang lived quietly and frugally. After spending his first night in Barclay in an expensive motel, he had rented the upstairs apartment in a two-story duplex on a residential street lined with elms and dogwoods. All the surrounding houses were either tall Victorian affairs or modest clapboard dwellings with screened-in porches and low brick walls along their unpaved connecting sidewalks. For that reason, perhaps, Lang's apartment building—of scaly green stucco—was set well back from the street, with a magnolia tree in the center of the yard to intercept or deflect the gazes of casual passers-by.

Late Sunday evening Lang telephoned Mr. Norton to tell him that he wished to take a day of sick leave. Mr. Norton was more understanding than Lang had anticipated, probably because of his yeoman efforts during the head-lice epidemic and the fact that he had given Mr. Norton an entire evening in which to find a substitute for him. Winter, season of antihistamines and sallow-making viruses, frequently took teachers out with scarcely any warning at all, and Mr. Norton was apparently grateful for small favors. After hanging up the telephone, Lang padded in his stocking feet to the bathroom, where he looked at himself in the medicine-cabinet mirror and felt his heart go as hard in his chest as a petrified serpent's egg.

He had contacted Antonio Johnson's pink eye.

For two weeks he had probed and prodded the scalps of nearly two hundred children a day, without himself falling prey to head lice. Antonio Johnson, on the other hand, he

"Like any other bachelor school teacher of moderate good sense, Lang lived quietly and frugally."

had merely led downtown to McKillian's Corner Grocery, and the result was a case of acute conjunctivitis. The eyes staring back at him in the mirror looked as if they belonged to a ghoul in a Technicolor horror film. Worse, the redness accentuated the fact that in each eye a vaguely pointed growth was encroaching on the iris; these growths looked like tiny volcanic cones floating on the enflamed whites, and their prominence was such that Lang could not shut his eyes without feeling them scrape against his lids. Ah, Antonio, he thought. It was a revelation to learn of his susceptibility. He turned off the bathroom light and went to bed.

The downstairs apartment belonged to the Rowells, a young couple with two small children. The wife was small and blonde. Lang saw her only in the afternoons when she came outside to backpack her baby and to cruise her Eskimo-faced toddler up and down the street in a creaky stroller. More than once, those kids had awakened Lang out of a dreamless sleep with their crying. At such times Lang believed himself as human as any other. He lay listening in the dark, content to share with the Rowells the inconvenience of a feverish or colic-stricken child. He gloried in his physical closeness to these people whom he really didn't know.

If his downstairs neighbors or his colleagues at work perceived anything odd about him, Lang was certain that they attributed it to his being from out of town. Aside from the book-ripping incident, and perhaps his eagerness in volunteering for the post of Chief Scalp & Nape Inspector, he had given no one any cause to wonder about his origins or to doubt his sanity. Nevertheless, his status in Barclay was still probationary, and people were curious about him. Although the Rowells were too busy with work and child-rearing to bother him (except at night, inadvertently), his fellow teachers had taken advantage of recesses and the daily lunch break to ask him questions.

Early on they had asked him where he had gone to school, what kind of job he had had in New York, and how he had come to accept a teaching position in, of all places, itty-bitty Barclay, Georgia.

Listening to young Mrs. Rowell singing a lullaby to one of her children, Lang told himself that the lies he had passed off during these polite, dog-sniffing information exchanges were better proofs of his humanity than his desire to renounce the past. You lied in order to fit in. You lied in order not to give offense. The sounds of Mrs. Rowell's crying infant, considering all he had done and all he knew, were as soothing as any Mozart string quintet, even if they did overwhelm the poor young woman's lullaby. Even before the suffering child had quieted, Lang was drifting off to sleep. The crying, together with the lullaby, gave him occasion to dream.

His dreams dredged up the serpentine past. It was a novelty to dream. Prior to sleep, immediately prior to his drifting off, Lang was always in a blue wood in the Southern Appalachians, waiting for spring. Afterwards, other centuries and other climes recalled to him the innumerable glories and barbarisms of human and mythic history. Lang knew the places at which the two intersected. Today there was a price on his head, a bounty, and the fact of that bounty was the sole remaining point of intersection. Lang had opted to evade this development by plunging wholeheartedly into the more perilous of the two historical streams.

In dreams, though, reptilian landscapes and longings rose up in hideous panoply to tempt him with their old, sad promises of power. Flight and fire. Heroism and terror. How could anyone—especially someone who had already been corrupted—resist?

vii.

Early the following morning Lang bundled up and walked to the clinic. It was still unseasonably cold for March, even though the dogwood and redbud trees had begun to bloom. Barclay's clinic was run by a married couple whom townspeople referred to affectionately as Dr. Sam and Dr. Elsa; their last name was Kensington. Dr. Sam and Dr. Elsa alternated days in the Barclay medical center since they were also physicians to the Wickrath community and operated a similar service in that town. Although Lang had never met either of them, he had heard their names many times and so felt only slightly ill at ease about reporting to one of them for medical attention.

Monday was Dr. Elsa's day, and Lang arrived early enough to be ushered to an examination room without having to endure a long stay in the waiting area out front. He alienated Dr. Elsa's young nurse, however, by insisting that he had come only to get a prescription for his pink eye and by refusing to let her take his blood pressure.

"We always take our patients' blood pressure," the nurse said. "It's standard operating procedure and a necessary precaution."

Lang rebuttoned his coat so that she could not possibly take a reading, whereupon the nurse departed with a twitch of the butt symbolically consigning him to her own private mental set of troublemakers and insupportable eccentrics. A few minutes later, Dr. Elsa came in.

She was a tall, curly-haired woman of fifty-five or so whose face exuded the fatigued good humor of a performer on a March of Dimes telethon. Her smile was not so much forced as self-effacing. Why am I here at this hour, and what good can I really do? As if she were neither a doctor nor an unfamiliar woman, she shook hands with Lang heartily, and he was pleased that she didn't mention his refusal to submit to the blood-pressure test. He liked Dr. Elsa's smile. He admired her long, expressive hands, which nevertheless betrayed a poignant dishwater redness. She smelled of soap and lemons, as did the very brand of kitchen detergent to which Lang himself had converted after moving to Barclay.

Leaning forward and peering into his eyes, Dr. Elsa said, "It's conjunctivitis. Just like little Antonio's. A tube of Cortisporin ought to take care of it. I'll write you a prescription, honey."

"What's that? Cortisporin?"

"Goose grease," Dr. Elsa said, scribbling on her prescription pad.

"What?"

Dr. Elsa chuckled. "It's an ointment with cortisone and three killer-diller antibiotics. Apply it four times a day. It's liable to be Thursday, though, before the case you've got begins to clear up." She handed him the prescription.

Lang was sitting on the examination table, his feet dangling down to some sort of chromium footrest. Why hadn't she mentioned the bumps in his eyes? Surely they were conspicuous enough to warrant comment. He was afraid to bring the matter up, but even more afraid to leave without having asked. Hospitalization. Surgery. These were prospects that would destroy his impersonation and reduce to ruins the hopes of his inchoate, pre-human dreams. He would never be a very good or a very convincing blind man.

"It's not just pink eye," he said. "It's . . . it's—"

"Those pimples on your sclera aren't anything to worry about, honey. It's a little unusual you should have 'em, but they're not going to drift over into your baby blues draggin' blood vessels and blindness. Just clear up that infection and you'll be fine." Dr. Elsa smiled. "Trust me."

"But what are they?" Lang persisted.

"Oh, my goodness. It's been a long time, honey. I think they're called *pinguecula,* if you want the medical term. They're just pieces of degenerate tissue that collect on the surface of the whites. Utterly harmless. You see 'em in older people all the time. I think I've got the beginnings of one in my right eye myself. Perfectly natural."

"Oh," said Lang.

"How old are you, by the way?"

"Twenty-eight." The response was automatic. Lang had been twenty-eight for the past five years.

"Well, folks twenty-eight don't usually have enough degenerate tissue to make a pinguecula. That's the only extraordinary thing in your case. How long have you been twenty-eight?"

Lang looked into Dr. Elsa's face with sudden alarm.

"That's a joke, honey. You'd pass for a teenager in some circles. Mine, for instance." She opened the examination-room door. "Now go on over to the druggist's and do what I told you and you'll be as good as new in three or four days. It's nice to have you in town."

"Should I go back to work tomorrow? Will I contaminate the kids?"

"I don't know about their minds, honey, but if you keep your hands away from your face and just exercise reasonable caution you won't give 'em all the pink eye. Sure. I'd say to go on back to work. I truly would." Dr. Elsa chuckled, backed out of the room, and pulled the door to as if Lang were yet in line for a battery of excruciating ophthalmological tests.

He waited a minute or two to see if anyone intended to look in on him again, then got up and strolled through the narrow corridor to the front desk. Dr. Elsa's nurse-cum-receptionist, whose blood pressure he had raised by denying her an opportunity to measure his, told him the bill was eight dollars. Lang wrote out a check and gave it to her.

viii.

At nine-thirty that evening Lang was sitting in the dark listening to Mrs. Rowell crooning a lullaby to one of her children when someone suddenly began pounding on his door. Lang was surprised to discover Darius Copeland standing on his porch in blue jeans and a denim coat, with a sailor's cap rolled down over his ears as a makeshift rain bonnet. The rain also surprised Lang. The clarity and timbre of Mrs. Rowell's lullaby had held all his attention; the apathetic patter of the rain had made no impression at all. Copeland was holding something that could have been a suitcase or a birdcage or maybe even a breadbox. It was draped with a yellow mackintosh.

"Evenin', Mr. Lang. Sorry to come botherin' you." Copeland's expression was uncertain and sheepish. "Heard you wasn't feelin' well, but thought I'd come over with the news—the *good* news—and just sort of try to see how you was gettin' along."

"What good news?" Lang gestured Copeland inside. The ointment in his eyes blurred and faceted the rainy night, imparting to it a mythic strangeness for which he was oddly homesick. He was loath to close the door.

"You won the TV," Copeland informed him, and Lang, shaking off his fugue, hurried to turn on a light. "We had the drawin' at the P.T.O. meetin' tonight, and you won the set. I brought it over." Copeland hefted the burden in his right hand, then pulled the mackintosh aside like a matador performing a hasty veronica. *Voilà*, a G.E. portable with rabbit ears and an astonishingly ample screen. "You got an outlet anywhere? I'll plug it in for you."

In two minutes the set was resting on an end table beside

Lang's split and stuffing-depleted sofa. Restless mono-
chrome images bristled back and forth across the face of
the set like an animated pointillist nightmare. Mercifully,
Copeland had not turned up the volume.

"How you feelin', anyway?"

"All right," Lang responded. "But I've got 'goose
grease' in my eyes and everything's really a blur to me
right now . . . What about Antonio Johnson? You ever
get any word on how he's doing?"

"Miss Winter said he wasn't in school again today, that's
all I know. I 'magine his mama's takin' care of him,
though." Copeland crooked a thumb at the TV. "How
you like the set? We raised nigh on to four hunner' dollars
sellin' tickets. That's about three hunnerd profit. Ain't it
something how you won?" Copeland turned the set off by
bending and unplugging it. "When you're over that pink
eye, you'll be glad to have it. Place like this gets lonely for
an unmarried fella who don't know too many folks yet
. . . Well, you take care."

Lang let Copeland out and watched him trot down the
wet exterior steps as if viewing him through a kaleido-
scope. Bejeweled by rain, faceted by the latter-day magic
of Cortisporin, the elms and dogwoods glittered like trees
in a fairy tale.

ix.

At school the next day Lang found that the ointment in
his eyes was less of an obstacle to his classroom performance than he had feared. Its fluid glaze passed up and
down each eyeball like a nictitating membrane. This was a
sensation to which he easily adjusted, as if through some
ancient familiarity hinting at his origins and mocking his
present self.

Antonio Johnson was back in school on Wednesday.

He was wearing frayed but well-scrubbed clothes. His mother had apparently acquired the proper medication and held him out of school until he was well again. Lang, watching the boy enter Miss Winter's first-grade classroom, had a chilling, empathic picture of what it must be like to take a bath in the house where Antonio and his family lived. He reflected, too, that Cortisporin was more than six dollars a tube. Each tube contained an eighth of an ounce of ointment. Even the druggist had joked that imported French perfume and a bottle of aged-in-the-cask Tennessee bourbon were cheaper. Where had Antonio's mama got the money? Welfare? Credit? Someone's private charity? Lang would probably never know, and, in truth, the question was not one he really wished to pursue . . .

A strange tension pervaded the relationships of the primary school's staff that week. Lang had already noticed that at the midmorning recess when the teachers congregated in the shelter of Mrs. Belflower's building to keep watch on the children gamboling on the playground across the drive, Miss Winter always stood a little apart from her white colleagues. Or they stood apart from her. The others, Miss Winter included, had at first spoken politely to Lang when he perforce joined these playground-watching sessions in January—but he had proved a dull and tight-lipped conversationalist, and they had eventually left him alone at recess and restricted their interrogations of him to lunch periods and library breaks.

Now Lang went out on the playground with the kids. He pushed them on the swings, sent them flying on the merry-go-round, and tried to judge their impossible free-for-all relay races. It pained and perplexed Lang to look back at the school building and see his fellow teachers arrayed against the wall as if they had been sorted by color, like beads or buttons. And this week they seemed to have separated and subdivided by some arcane criterion in addition to that of race. Mrs. Kaye and Miss Winter, without standing together, stood apart from the others, while Miss Geter of the second grade was excluded from a huddle consisting of Mrs. Conley and Mrs. Belflower, neither of whom had very much to say to the other.

To complicate matters for Lang, Barclay's mysterious playground vandal had struck again. The bolts supporting the steps on the slide had been removed, the metal clasps on the teeter-totter were nowhere to be found, and several of the struts on the monkey bars had been dangerously unsocketed. The children had to entertain themselves without benefit of this equipment, with the result that Lang had to supervise their activities more closely than usual. He issued frequent commands to stay off the unbolted equipment and broke up the inevitable disputes arising from a great many clever varieties of improvised roughhouse. The only consolation he derived from this self-appointed duty was that it kept him from standing in the lee of Mrs. Belflower's classroom with his sour and uncommunicative cohorts.

Their reasons for remaining silent, Lang told himself, had to be even more sinister than his own. He wanted to shout redemptive curses at them, rub their noses in their childish and vindictive behavior. Once, he had a brief but terrifying vision of a soldier with a flamethrower raking the five of them with cruel, brilliant bursts of destruction. The soldier was Lang himself. The entire vision was an unsettling reminder of the old corruption he had vowed to renounce forever.

Ashamed and chastened, Lang awaited the bell that would end the recess. He ignored the kids crying for him to start yet another of their scrambling, undisciplined dashes across the playground.

By Friday afternoon Lang was emotionally exhausted, but his pink eye had been cured. That evening he prepared a supper of hot dogs, ate it slowly, and then turned on his television set for the first time since Darius Copeland had delivered it to him. Lang rationalized that this evening marked his first chance to watch the set without the impediment of artificial nictitating membranes. His sight was clear.

Between nine and ten o'clock, then, Lang found himself engrossed in a program whose protagonist, owing to some unlikely radiation-induced alteration of his metabolism and blood chemistry, turned into a muscle-bound brute whenever he was angered or physically abused. This metamorphosis occurred three times during the program, and on each occasion it enabled the protagonist either to escape or to evert a difficult situation.

Transfixed, Lang pulled himself up in his armchair.

Despite the power at the protagonist's disposal when he was changed from man to roaring brute, the poor fellow was seeking a cure. He wanted to be free of the monster resident in his blood and brain. He wanted to be a human being like those from whom his hideous, underlying self so pitiably estranged him. Lang sympathized. He identified. The parallel with his own masquerade was too explicit and exacting to permit him the luxury of a cynical objectivity. How could he fail to be moved by the plight of his television counterpart? He could not.

After the third and final manifestation of the monster, however, Lang became aware of several dismaying facts. First, the program he had just watched was merely one episode of a weekly series devoted to the deeds and tribulations of the protagonist's divided self. Next Friday the man would be back, shredding expensive shirts as his pectorals irresistibly expanded and tossing bad guys

around as if they were basketballs. Second, the continuing
nature of the program suggested that its entire *raison
d'être* lay less in an elaboration of the protagonist's sickness and cure than in a gaudy exploitation of the monster's
inhuman prowess. Finally, because no one who exists in a
social context can hope to avoid absolutely the major and
minor provocations of daily life, the protagonist was altogether helpless to contain his beast. At this point, Lang
realized, the astonishing parallel was suddenly wrenched
askew. Unlike the television character, Lang was not helpless to contain *his* beast. Nor was he any longer a prisoner
of the serpentine impulses that had once informed his
motion and his mind. Not by any means.

Lang unplugged the TV and went to bed. From
downstairs he could hear Mrs. Rowell singing limpid, un-
placeable lullabies to her husband or her babies. The
bittersweet clarity of her voice had nothing to do with the
noise that had emanated from the television set. Nothing
whatever.

x.

On Monday at recess Skipper Thornley wandered into
the kudzu field next to the playground and found a metal
fitting from one of the partially dismantled slides. Lang
tried to summon the boy out of the field, but Skipper held
the fitting above his head and shouted that he could see "a
whole mess" of such fasteners, along with a few slide
steps, scattered about among the leafless kudzu vines. This
intelligence precipitated a scavenger hunt that began like
an Oklahoma Territory land rush. Kids charged into the
kudzu field, tripped one another, plunged headlong into
the vines, scrambled up, elbowed for position, rooted
about like banties or porkers, and, with surprising fre-
quency, actually found a bolt or a metal clasp or a slide

step for their pains. Lang could not reasonably hope to discourage them in their search. Finally, he simply shouted that when the bell rang, they must come out of the field at once and lay the items they had found on the sidewalk near Mrs. Belflower's building. Then he joined the adults on the other side of the drive.

Aloud, goaded to speech by the silence of his fellow teachers, Lang observed that he had previously supposed the playground vandal had been dismantling the equipment for the parts, perhaps because he was a mechanic of some sort or knew a shady hardware entrepreneur to whom he could pawn his midnight booty. But why, Lang wondered, would anyone take apart a slide or teeter-totter merely to hurl the metal fasteners into a nearby field? The vandal's purpose could only be to satisfy a reckless compulsion or to indulge a thirsty mean streak. His principal victims, after all, were the children and the public school system in Barclay. Unless approached from these relatively well-defined perspectives, Lang said, the vandalism made no sense.

The silence that met these observations was charged with a static hostility whose field Lang could neither encompass nor neutralize. For two or three minutes no one said anything. The teachers were still paired or isolated singly against one another, and Lang's attempt to unite them in a discussion about the vandal appeared to be suffocating in the thin but electric air of their indifference or ill feeling.

Then Miss Winter said, "What do *you* think of that, Mrs. Belflower? What's *your* opinion on the subject? You certainly had a lot to say last Monday when Mr. Fountain told us the equipment had been unbolted again."

Mrs. Belflower turned to face her adversary. She was a thin-faced woman with short brown hair, which she had

hidden today beneath a colorful silk kerchief. Her eyes
were pale blue, and her figure had only recently—very
gently—begun to spread. Her manner with the children,
Lang had noted, was patient and methodical, if not overtly
affectionate, and he had always been disposed to think
well of her. Now, though, her nostrils dilated and her
feathery brown eyebrows met above her nose in a Tar-
tarish V. Lang could scarcely believe that this was the same
Mrs. Belflower who had once plied him with inconsequen-
tial questions at lunch—as if purposely trying *not* to rattle
the skeletons, if any, in his closet.

"I didn't have a *lot* to say about it, Miss Winter. I wasn't
even talking to you, if I remember correctly."

"But you wanted me to overhear, didn't you?"

"I didn't even know you were in the lunchroom. And all
I said, Miss Winter, was that some poor black man was
probably taking the parts and selling them. It wasn't intended as a racial slur, for Pete's sake."

"Then why didn't you just say it was some poor *man*
stealin' the parts and leave it at that? What was the point of
specifyin' the thief was black if you weren't tryin' to imply
something narrow and low?"

Mrs. Belflower's eyes flared, but her voice remained
incongruously calm. "Oh, my. It's as if I'm being grilled by
a policeman, it's as if—"

"And now it turns out the parts wasn't stolen at all,"
interrupted Miss Winter. "It turns out the 'thief' was only
trashin' the equipment to keep the kids from playin' on it.
That's not any poor black man at work, Mrs. Belflower.
That's someone that can't handle the notion of black and
white playin' together in the same front yard. That's the
sort of sick old bigotry that badmouths our schools and
plunks its kids in fat-cat private ones to keep 'em from
seein' too soon how the world really operates! You

wouldn't know fair, Mrs. Belflower, if it bit you on the big toe!" Miss Winter clasped her arms across her midriff, looked out toward the kudzu field, and bitterly shook her head.

Mrs. Belflower recoiled from this attack as if she had been anticipating it for weeks. "My life away from school isn't any of your business," she said carefully. "Until you've made yourself dictator of the United States, Miss Winter, don't you try to tell me how to run my life. Don't you try to tell me how to raise my family or where to work. Not until you have declared Freedom of Choice un-American and made yourself dictator, Miss Winter." She walked away several steps and opened the door to her classroom. "Alice," she said, addressing Mrs. Conley, "would you see to it my kids come in when the bell rings? I've got to sit down a minute." The red door closed behind her.

"You tell me is it fair," Miss Winter suddenly appealed to Lang. "She sends her kids to that fat-cat 'cademy in Ladysmith and gets paid to teach in the public schools. That shows her contempt for public education, doesn't it? It's an insult to all of us, what she's doin'. You tell me it isn't an insult."

Mrs. Kaye stepped up to Miss Winter and put an arm around her shoulder. "One of her children has a special problem, Pauline."

"My ass," said Miss Winter. "My sweet ass."

xi.

In the cafeteria the next day Mrs. Kaye told Lang that Pauline Winter had been summoned out of class that morning and asked to report to the principal's office at the elementary school. She had been gone ever since. Two and a half hours. All the signs pointed to a chewing-out of

Churchillian eloquence and Castrovian duration. Poor Miss Winter was really getting her ears singed. She was being eviscerated by a master.

"Two and a half hours?" said Lang incredulously. Mr. Norton had taken only twenty minutes to chew him out for tearing up Skipper Thornley's book. Could Mr. Norton really get wound up two-and-a-half-hours' worth, even for a breach of etiquette stemming from a set-to with racial overtones? Maybe for that he could. Maybe that was precisely the sort of faux pas to unwind Mr. Norton's yo-yo. "Do you think he fired her?" Lang asked.

"Not in the middle of the school day," Mrs. Kaye replied. "Mr. Norton wouldn't leave me with her kids and mine, too. Not for a whole day, anyway."

But they telephoned the elementary school to check. Mrs. Kaye got through to Mrs. Dorn, Mr. Norton's secretary, and Mrs. Dorn said that Miss Winter had left the elementary school well over an hour ago, with her superior's emphatic order to return to the classroom. Mr. Norton had given Miss Winter a reprimand and a warning—if she kept meddling in administrative matters and other folks' personal affairs, she'd find herself cleaning out her desk quicker than she could say Jack Robinson.

Holding the telephone receiver as if it were someone else's empty beer can, Mrs. Kaye hung up without telling Mrs. Dorn that her colleague still had not come back from the elementary school.

"What's the matter?" asked Lang.

"I don't know. It looks like Pauline is playing hooky."

Miss Winter played hooky Tuesday through Thursday. Late on Tuesday afternoon, however, Mr. Norton learned of her unexcused absence and tried throughout the evening to reach her by phone, only to get a busy signal and to conclude that she had taken her receiver off the hook. He tried again the following morning, with the same results. Angered and frustrated, Mr. Norton had then contacted the school board's official attorney in Wickrath; with the attorney's approval, late Wednesday afternoon he mailed Miss Winter a registered letter informing her that she had been relieved of her job. The grounds were "abandonment of position." Miss Winter received this letter early Thursday morning, and at eleven o'clock she showed up at the elementary school, accosted Mr. Norton in a corridor, and proclaimed that she had merely been taking the three days of personal leave to which every certified county teacher was entitled each year, and that her dismissal was not only an affront to her loyalty and talent but an out-and-out violation of the law. She demanded to be reinstated. Mr. Norton apoplectically demurred, threatening to call in the local police if she didn't remove herself instantly from his building. Miss Winter departed under scathing protest, counterthreatening a suit against Mr. Norton himself and another against the entire fascist educational mock-up for which he fagged. According to Mrs. Kaye, half the student body at the elementary school had overheard all or part of this vehement exchange, and things didn't look too good for Miss Winter.

"I think she's blown it," Mrs. Kaye told Lang at lunch on Friday. "She's a smart cookie, Pauline is, and she can really be sweet—but this time I do believe she's done herself in."

A woman from Wickrath was substituting for Miss Winter, and she seemed convinced that she would be on hand until the end of the school year.

Lang was walking home that same afternoon when Miss Winter's small, silver automobile—something foreign with racing stripes—headed in toward the curb and coasted along it beside him. The Alabama Station Highway glittered with dogwood blossoms and the flowers of a few early, flame-colored azeleas.

"Hop in," Miss Winter called. "I'll give you a ride."

Lang hopped in while her car was still moving. Slamming the door, he glanced at Miss Winter's profile to determine her mood. Never before had she offered to give him a ride.

"I just been cleanin' my stuff out of my desk at school," she said, her foot easing down gently on the accelerator. A flotilla of dogwood blossoms drifted across the windshield, then eddied violently away as the car picked up speed.

They drove without speaking to Lang's apartment building. Miss Winter, despite his protests that he could walk from the street, pulled up the long unpaved drive and stopped at the foot of the stairway to his second-story apartment. When he started to get out, she killed the motor and touched him on the arm with her outstretched fingers. "Just a minute," she said. "Give me just a minute of your time, Mr. Lang." He let go of the door handle and turned to face her. Her expression—her hand to her mouth as if to cover an imminent fit of coughing—conveyed her uncertainty about what she was going to say, and Lang was discomfited by her nervousness. Finally, though, she dropped her hand and resolutely lifted her chin.

"Was I ever snotty to you, Mr. Lang? Did I ever make you feel you didn't have any right to be teachin' in Barclay's schools, even if you wasn't a hometown boy? Please answer me as you feel it."

Lang declared that she had always behaved cordially toward him.

"Well, I tried to. I know what it is to have folks choosin' up sides against you. And you were a trial to me, too, because you come in for Rose—Mrs. Banks is how you'd

know her—and she was a special comfort to Pauline
Winter, someone to talk to and just be natural around.
Mrs. Kaye and I get along all right, I'm not sayin' we
don't—but it isn't the same as it was with Rose and me.
Lord, Mr. Lang, do you know how much I hurt to see you
come in for Rose when I'd been hopin' for . . . ?" She
waved her left hand.

"Another black person," Lang concluded for her.

"Right on, Mr. Lang. Preferably a woman. Boy friends I
got plenty of; too many, maybe. But at work you need a
friend and ally, someone you can just be natural
around—even if it's only at lunch time and plannin' sessions and so forth. I knew *you* weren't gonna be that
person soon's I laid eyes on you."

Lang said he was sorry for not having been that person.
It occurred to him that his present incarnation had
emerged from a ready-to-hand cultural template rather
than from his own careful formulation of his likely needs
and safeguards as a human being. Because the template
had seemed to provide for both, he had unquestioningly
surrendered to it.

Miss Winter smiled. "Well, I 'preciate your bein' sorry
for what you couldn't help. But that's not the reason I gave
you a ride home, Mr. Lang. You want to know the real
reason?"

Lang said he did.

"There's gonna be a school-board meetin' in Wickrath
next Tuesday night, and I'm gonna be presentin' my side
of this business at an informal hearing. I'm askin' them to
overturn my dismissal. It's an open meetin', Mr. Lang—all
the sessions of the board are—and I want you to come.
You don't have to bring a banner sayin' 'E. H. Norton
Unfair to Pauline Winter' or nothin' like that. I just want
you to come and sit in on the meetin' and be some of my

moral support. In your mind, I mean. You don't have to say a word. I just want you to be on my side in your mind. Rose would've come if this had happened while she was still here. Some of my friends are gonna be there, but probably not any teachers. Teachers shy away from school-board meetin's like they would a rabid dog. Mrs. Kaye might come, she's a friend, and Mr. Copeland he's got a seat on the board, but most of the folks there that evenin' are gonna think me bein' fired was only what I asked for."

"You stayed away from school," Lang reminded Miss Winter gently.

"Every teacher in this county gets three days of personal leave they don't have to explain the reason for!"

"But you have to apply for it. You have to give notice."

Miss Winter sighed and slumped across her steering wheel. "That's what this whole nasty business backs up to, doesn't it? 'Abandonment of position.' That man Norton had just put me through his grinder for sayin' the truth about Mrs. Belflower—she didn't get *her* hand slapped, did she now?—and I wasn't thinkin' straight. I couldn't talk to nobody, let alone ol' Mr. Norton His Highness. One mistake, Mr. Lang, and my six years of teachin' in this county are bein' pulled out from under me like a no-account rug. It isn't fair, Mr. Lang. You know it isn't."

"I know it isn't."

She lifted her head from the steering wheel and looked at him. "Will you come Tuesday evenin', then? Just to be on my side in your mind?"

xii.

Lang caught a ride to Wickrath with Darius Copeland. The trip took about fifteen minutes down a narrow two-lane highway bordered by shaggy pines. It was dark when they arrived in the parking lot outside the small prefabricated building in which Mr. Hendricks, the county superintendent of education, had his office. So many automobiles and pickup trucks crowded the lot that Copeland had to drive through it and park on a sidestreet.

As they walked toward the superintendent's prefab, Lang noticed that Copeland played anxiously with his tie and then plunged his hands deep into his pants pockets. People were congregated on the prefab's rickety front porch, shadowy under a single exterior lamp, and also along the gravel walk from the parking lot. Others milled about among their vehicles.

"Are all these people here because of Miss Winter?" Lang asked.

Copeland led Lang around the building, through the crowd, and up a set of stairs to a rear entrance. "Most of 'em," he conceded, opening the door. "But a few of 'em have come with a two-bit petition to get a bus driver thrown off his route. The others, well, they're here to see what the board is goin' to do about Miss Winter's request to be reinstated in Barclay."

"How are you voting?"

"It's no secret, man. I'm with Miss Winter down the line. You think I could go home tonight if I voted with that pale-face bloc through there?" Copeland nodded at a group down the hall.

Lang and Copeland were standing in a utility area given over to a soft-drink cooler and a broken-down copying machine. The inside of the building reminded Lang of the interior of a somewhat outsized mobile home, cramped and temporary-seeming. In the corridor beyond the utility room Lang could see Mr. Hendricks, a burly six-footer in his late forties, conversing good-humoredly with the other four board members, including a bespectacled woman in a

navy-blue skirt with a severely cut matching jacket. The
men were wearing either suits or slacks with sports
jackets—two fellows approaching sixty from decidedly different metabolic routes, one heavy in the gut, the other as
thin and gnarled as a piece of beef jerky; and a young man
a half a head taller than anyone else in the building.

In a reception area to the left of this corridor sat Miss
Winter and a florid-looking man whom Lang assumed to
be her attorney. With them was a skinny young fellow with
moustaches like a pair of wind-blown caterpillars; he was
scribbling in a stenographer's notebook, and Copeland
identified him as a reporter from the county newspaper.
The group in the reception area totally disregarded the
presence of the school officials in the corridor, who were
meticulous in repaying this favor. Meanwhile, the hubbub
of the people outside suggested to Lang the persistent
monotone of an army at siege.

"We haven't got room for that crowd in our conference
room," said the woman in navy-blue.

"Good," said the portly man in pinstripes. "I guess we'll
just have to keep 'em out there."

"Ah," said Mr. Hendricks. "There's always the courthouse."

And what they did almost immediately, perceiving now
that Darius Copeland had arrived, was initiate a removal
en masse from the superintendent's building to the trial
facilities in the Wickrath County Courthouse. Lang was
separated from Copeland. Almost before he could accommodate himself to what was happening, he was
marching up an asphalt drive with a horde of parents and
curiosity seekers. He noted that blacks and whites seemed
to be about equally well represented. They crowded together into the old-fashioned courthouse, and two or three
minutes later Lang found himself sitting on a hardwood

bench in the balcony overlooking the courtroom floor. He had the balcony to himself, and realized that he had climbed the hollow-sounding stairs not only to get a better view of the proceedings but to render his person as inconspicuous as possible during the evening's scheduled discussions. Miss Winter had seen him climbing the stairs, had acknowledged his presence with a daunted look and a curt nod of the head. Surely she would not regard his desire for a little anonymity here in Wickrath as cowardly. She knew that she valued his job at least as much as she valued hers, and she would certainly understand his reluctance to appear before the board as either a malcontent or a firebrand. He was there, wasn't he? He had kept his part of the bargain. He had shown up to be on her side in his mind

Copeland, along with Mr. Hendricks and the other four members of the school board, was seated now at a long folding table facing the spectators' section of the courtroom. The crowd filing in continued to be disorganized and restive, slow to settle into the benches behind the courtroom railing; and Lang reflected that Miss Winter's informal hearing was beginning, more and more, to approach the dimensions and the ceremonial solemnity of a full-blown murder trial. The courtroom creaked and echoed as onlookers and participants alike stumbled to their places. Lang, watching all this, became aware of the subtle drafts and crosswinds swirling through the balcony. His feet ached with the cold.

At last Mr. Hendricks gaveled the session to order. A secretary stood up and read the minutes of the previous meeting. Mr. Hendricks gave a detailed report of his activities in March.

A man in overalls and boots rose in the spectator section—Lang could see only his narrow back and his

bright pink bald spot—and waved a petition at the board
members. He charged that the bus driver on his son's
route was guilty of harassment and inconsistent discipli-
nary standards. "He kicked my boy off his bus for passin'
gas!" the man angrily declared. "That's jes' natural,
passin' gas! How was my Billy s'posed to help that, I
wonder." The superintendent countered that these unfortunate attacks of flatulence were usually preceded
by Billy's ribald warnings to the effect that everyone had
better grab a gas mask or throw open a window. Sometimes, Mr. Hendricks went on patiently, Billy even stood
up on his seat to make these announcements, chicken-
flapping his arms to draw his schoolmates' attention. The
boy obviously delighted in fouling not only his own nest
but everyone else's too. Laughter greeted the superintendent's countercharges, and after some nearly inaudible
discussion the board voted unanimously to reject the
complainant's request to sack the bus driver. This single
agenda item took almost twenty minutes, however, and
immediately after it had been decided, a commotion
erupted at the rear of the courtroom—out of Lang's
sight—as the disappointed petitioner and several of his
cohorts turned at the door to shout threats and profanities
at the school board. Others in the audience retaliated with
boos and cries of "Beat it, rednecks!" until Lang, relatively
safe in the balcony, began to fear a wholesale internecine
riot. The courtroom reverberated for a time with shouts,
stampings, and slammings, but eventually settled again
into a quiet riven only by the wind and an occasional
cough.

Miss Winter's case was called.

xiii.

Lang watched as a courtroom stenographer set up her

machine near the head table, and as the youngest male
board member pulled a folding chair into place to serve, in
the stead of the boxlike stall next to the courtroom's official
bench, as a witness stand.

Because Mr. Norton was not on hand, Carter Ewing, the
school board's attorney, summarized the events leading
up to Miss Winter's dismissal and stressed that she would
still be employed if she had formally requested leave to
cover the period of her intended absence from the classroom. Since she had done absolutely nothing to make
her plans clear, however, it was mortally impossible to
conclude that she had not simply abandoned her position.
As a consequence, she was legally subject to dismissal.
Ewing made no mention of the reprimand and warning
that had goaded Miss Winter to heedless flight—for, Lang
understood, that matter would have required further and
more perilous explanations.

Miss Winter's attorney, like a five-and-dime parody of
William Jennings Bryan, prowled along the front edge of
the school board's table asking his client questions about
her long service to the county and her own recollections of
the events of the previous week. As a consequence, Miss
Winter did a great deal of talking. She wore a pale beige
suit, with a single white azalea pinned on her coat, and
most of her remarks she addressed to Mr. Hendricks, who
was sitting immediately to her left. The superintendent's
expression remained neutral throughout her testimony,
but he never flinched from meeting her gaze and his
attentiveness and lack of any discernible hostility seemed
to Lang decidedly good omens. Then he recalled that the
superintendent never took part in the voting of the board.

After answering her attorney's initial questions, Miss
Winter backtracked and came at every one of them from a
different angle. She discussed her relationships with Mr.

Norton and her colleagues at the Barclay primary school,
then began an oblique animadversion on the hiring prac-
tices of the board. Her attorney cut her off before she could
really get going on this subject, but Miss Winter was clearly
beginning to feel comfortable in front of her audience,
even righteously heroic in her perceived martyrdom, with
the result that she veered at once into a catalogue of Mr.
Norton's manifold tyrannies. She told of his attempt to
make his teachers head-lice experts, and of his eagerness
in asking if she wished to resign when she pointed out that
neither she nor any of the others were medical doctors.
She rehearsed for the board the ill feelings that had followed upon Mrs. Belflower's speculations about the iden-
tity of the playground vandal, who was still at large. She
wondered aloud how a woman who sent her children to a
private academy could justifiably secure employment with
the county school system. Again Miss Winter's attorney cut
her off, but a moment later she was recreating the scene in
Mr. Norton's office that had stemmed directly from her
argument with Mrs. Belflower. She asked rhetorically if Mr.
Norton's decision to call only Pauline Winter on the carpet
didn't seem to reflect a telltale glare into the darkness of his
heart. Then she began enumerating abuses of power and
privilege dating back to her employment by the board in
the fall of—

    Lang noticed that Darius Copeland, head down, was
toying apprehensively with a pencil. Earlier, on the drive
from Barclay, Copeland had told Lang that one of the
board members had children in a private school in eastern
Alabama. Copeland knew that Miss Winter had come
before the board with three strikes against her and only a
scant chance of persuading its members to reverse Mr.
Norton's final, perhaps overhasty call. Now Miss Winter
was kicking up dirt around home plate, virtually begging

for an indefinite suspension from the game. That the dirt
had a gritty palpability quite apart from Miss Winter's
untidy refusal to let it lie wasn't going to win her any friends
in this place. And Lang, up in the balcony, began to realize
that the possibilities for either a simple or a complicated
compromise were being squeezed relentlessly out the
courtroom door. His feet ached with a searing cold, and his
blood turned icy in the alien labyrinth of his veins.

"Why don't we go ahead and vote?" said Darius Copeland, interrupting Miss Winter and glancing helplessly up
into the balcony.

Mrs. Shetland, the board's lone female member,
suggested that they retire to one of the jury rooms. She
was the group's official chair, and she seemed to wish to
take the vote itself out of the public arena of the courtroom. Perhaps that was a sensible rather than a craven
desire, especially if the board intended to debate the
matter—but Copeland lifted his pencil and voiced an ob-
jection.

"Everybody here knows what they're gonna do. Let's
just go ahead and do it, okay?"

" 'S all right with me," said the lean, elderly board
member. "I don't have a damn thing to hide."

The others agreed, whereupon the portly man in
pinstripes moved that the board sustain Mr. Norton's dismissal of Miss Pauline Winter. There was an immediate
second from the tall young man beside him. Mrs. Shelton
then called the roll of her colleagues. By a three-to-one
decision, the chair having no vote, the board sustained Mr.
Norton's dismissal of Miss Winter. The decision was official
if still not incontestable at a higher level.

Murmurs of mild indignation stirred through the spectators sitting beneath Lang. There was also a feeble smat-
tering of applause. Lang could feel inside himself a swell-

ing not of outrage but of empty futility. It was as if there were a balloon in his chest that someone with a bicycle pump was inflating steadily with great quantities of stale air. Miss Winter had not yet moved, but Lang, carrying this burden, stood up and gripped the balcony rail.

"She deserves another chance," he said loudly enough to be heard over the continuing susurrus of protest and approval. None of the icy terror uncoiling inside him was betrayed in his voice, nor any of his perplexity in the face of so many untenable options. "She's worked in Barclay six years without misstep or error, and she deserves another chance to go back to her job." Lang found that, like Miss Winter earlier, he was speaking exclusively to Mr. Hendricks, the superintendent. Precisely why he had no idea.

Mr. Hendricks pushed back his chair and rose to address Lang, whom he recognized as a new employee of the school system. "We've just completed our discussion of that particular agenda item, Mr. Lang, and the board has voted. Now we have other business to see to." He spoke without heat, or threat, or condescension, as a grandfather might speak to a small child. That Lang was implicitly challenging the authority, and the wisdom, of the board appeared to fluster Mr. Hendricks not at all.

"She deserves another chance," Lang reiterated, panicked by the pressures building in his chest and the thousands of conflicting electrical impulses shooting into his brain like BBs.

"Mr. Lang," said the superintendent, "I was inclined to think the same thing until Miss Winter began testifying on her own behalf. I think she lost control of herself up here, and I think that may very well tell us something significant about her character. In any case, my opinion doesn't—"

"Have you ever considered the degree of provocation," Lang said, still painstakingly civil in spite of his inner turmoil. "Have you ever really tried to see the matter from—"

"Mister," said the board member who didn't have a damn thing to hide, "it's past time for you to shut up and sit down."

Darius Copeland averted his gaze, looking toward the courtroom's tall empty windows, and Miss Winter sat staring at the ceiling with wet, naked eyes, heedless of the renewed activity around her.

"Please," said Mr. Hendricks, addressing Lang with gentle urgency, "if you persist in this, you may be placing your own job in jeopardy. The board has three or four more items to take care of this evening. So please, if you care anything for the forms of everyday courtesy, please sit down."

"Is that man one of ours?" asked Mrs. Shetland.

"I'm simply trying to point out that the straws had all been cast even before Miss Winter got here, not excluding Mr. Copeland's. I'm simply trying to say that powerlessness and frustration breed—"

"Costly government programs," said the portly man in pinstripes.

"Mister, put your butt on a bench or get ready to have it kicked down the stairs."

"We're trying very hard to rectify a long-standing imbalance," began the superintendent, overriding a series of angry cries from spectators. "A long-standing imbalance that we can't yet hope to—"

The balloon of stale air in Lang's chest burst with a hiss, and he could no longer sustain the masquerade of civility and reasonableness that had kept him in his skin since the third year of the decade. He manifested. He convoluted above the courtroom floor, unfurling, with all the magnificent grace of a clipper ship spreading canvas, an armor of

metallic blue and iridescent gold scales. His wings and his
cold, ethereal intelligence held him aloft. Eyes of hot im-
placable ruby surveyed the shambles of overturned furniture and fleeing human bodies his metamorphosis had
made of the courtroom. He trod the air with regal impunity. His glinting jade talons, five to each foot, opened and
closed on the invading night wind like those of a hawk in
full expectation of its prey. From the enigma of his jaws
shot a tongue of searching, liquid fire. Neither the courthouse nor the whole of Wickrath County could contain
him. In a nictitating eyeblink he recreated the surrounding
Georgia countryside in the vivid chiaroscuro of the terrains
of undying myth. Meanwhile, and afterwards, he rose like
many raucous birds toward the mute simplicity of the
moon.

But before the part of this manifestation that was Lang
fell forever into eclipse, it acknowledged again how miserably unfulfilled were its good intentions and how tangled
and strange were the ways of men.

A DRAMA OF DRAGONS

CRAIG SHOW GARDNER

ILLUSTRATIONS BY
GINI SHURTLEFF

> "A good magician should always subscribe to
> the highest purposes, and nothing should dis-
> suade him from these lofty goals, except,
> perhaps, that he has to eat, and it is nice to put a
> little away for retirement."
> —from *The Teachings of Ebenezum*
> Volume III

I could no longer bring myself to gather firewood. My
world had ended. She hadn't come.

I sat for far too long in the sunlit glade where we always
met. Perhaps she didn't realize it was noon; she had
somehow been delayed; her cool blue eyes and fair
blonde hair, the way her slim young body moved, the way
she laughed, how it felt when she touched me. Surely she
was on her way.

But I didn't even know her name! Only her interest in
me—a magician's apprentice. She'd once called magicians the closest things to play actors she knew in this
backwater place, said she'd always admired the stage. And
then she laughed, and we kissed and—

A cold breeze sprang up behind my back. Winter was coming.

I gathered what logs and branches I could find and trudged back to my master's cottage.

In the distance I heard a sneeze. My master Ebenezum, no doubt one of the world's greatest magicians until an unfortunate occurrence involving a demon from the seventh Netherhell. My master had succeeded in banishing the foul creature, by far the most powerful he had ever faced, but his triumph was not without its costs. From that moment onward, Ebenezum found that, should he even approach something of a sorcerous nature, he would fall into an immediate and extended sneezing fit. This malady had put something of a crimp in Ebenezum's wizardly career, but my master was not one to accept defeat easily. Just this moment, he had probably made another attempt to read from one of his magic tomes. Hence the sneeze. Why else?

Unless there was something sorcerous in the air.

Perhaps there was another reason besides my mood that the world was so dark around me, another reason that she hadn't met me as we'd planned. The bushes moved on my right. Something very large flew across the sun.

I managed the front door with the firewood still in my arms. I heard the wizard sneeze. Repeatedly. My master stood in the main room, one of his great books spread on the table before him. I hurried to his aid, forgetting, in my haste, the firewood that scattered across the table as I reached for the book, a few miscellaneous pieces falling among the sneezing Ebenezum's robes.

I closed the book and glanced apprehensively at the mage. To my surprise, Ebenezum blew his nose on a gold-inlaid, dark blue sleeve and spoke to me in the calmest of tones.

"Thank you, 'prentice." He delicately removed a branch from his lap and laid it on the table. "If you would dispose of this in a more appropriate place?"

He sighed deep in his throat. "I'm afraid that my affliction is far worse than I imagined. I may even have to call on outside assistance for my cure."

I hastened to retrieve the firewood. "Outside assistance?" I inquired discreetly.

"We must seek out another magician as great as I," Ebenezum said, his every word heavy with import. "Though to do that, we might have to travel as far as the great city of Vushta."

"Vushta?" I replied. "With its pleasure gardens and forbidden palaces? The city of unknown sins that could doom a man for life? That Vushta?" All at once, I felt the lethargy lift from my shoulders. I quickly deposited the wood by the fireplace.

"That Vushta." Ebenezum nodded. "With one problem. We have not the funds for traveling, and no prospects for gaining same."

As if responding to our plight, a great gust blew against the side of the cottage. The door burst open with a swirl of dirt and leaves, and a short man wearing tattered clothes, face besmirched with grime, staggered in and slammed the door behind him.

"Flee! Flee!" the newcomer cried in a quavering voice. "Dragons! Dragons!" With that, his eyes rolled up in his head and he collapsed on the floor.

"I have found, however," Ebenezum said as he stroked his long, white beard, "in my long career as a magician, Wuntvor, if you wait around long enough, something is bound to turn up."

(2)

"Dire creatures from the Netherhells should always be faced directly, unless it is possible to face them some other way, say from behind a bush, in perfect safety."

—from *The Teachings of Ebenezum*
Volume V

With some water on the head and some wine down the gullet, we managed to revive the newcomer.

"Flee!" he sputtered as he caught his breath. He glanced about wildly, his pale blue eyes darting from my master to me to floor to ceiling. He seemed close to my master in age, but there the similarity ceased. Rather than my master's mane of fine, white hair, the newcomer was balding, his hair matted and stringy. Instead of the wizard's masterful face, which could convey calm serenity or cosmic anger with the flick of an eyebrow, the other's face was evasive; small nose and chin, a very wrinkled brow, and those eyes, darting blue in his dark, mud-spattered face.

"Now, now, good sir," Ebenezum replied in his most reasonable voice, often used to charm young ladies and calm bill collectors. "Why the hurry? You mentioned dragons?"

"Dragons!" The man stood somewhat shakily. "Well, at least dragon! One of them has captured Gurnish Keep!"

"Gurnish Keep?" I queried.

"You've seen it," Ebenezum murmured, his cold grey eyes still on our guest. " 'Tis the small castle on yonder hill at the far side of the woods." Ebenezum snorted in his beard. "Castle? 'Tis really more of a stone hut, but it's the home of our neighbor, the Duke of Gurnish. It's a very small dukedom. For that matter, he's a very small duke."

Our visitor was, if anything, more agitated than before.

"I didn't run all the way through Gurnish Forest to hear a discussion of the neighborhood. We must flee!"

"Gurnish Forest?" I inquired.

"The trees right behind the hut," my master replied. "Surely the Duke's idea. Everyone else knows the area as Wizard's Woods."

"What do you mean, Wizard's Woods?" the newcomer snapped. "This area is Gurnish Forest. Officially. As Gurnish Keep is an official castle!"

" 'Tis only a matter of opinion," Ebenezum replied, a smile that could charm both barbarians and maiden aunts once again upon his face. "Haven't we met somewhere before?"

"Possibly." The newcomer, who was somewhat shorter than my master's imposing frame, shifted uneasily under the wizard's gaze. "But shouldn't we flee? Dragons, you know."

"Come now, man. I wouldn't be a full-fledged wizard if I hadn't dealt with a dragon or two." Ebenezum looked even more closely at the newcomer than he had before. "Say. Aren't you the Duke of Gurnish?"

"Me?" the smaller man said. His eyes shifted from my master to me and back again. "Well—uh—" He coughed. "I suppose I am."

"Well, why didn't you say so? I haven't seen you since you stopped trying to tax me." Ebenezum's smile went to its broadest as he signaled me to get our guest a chair. The duke obviously had money.

"Well, this whole situation's a bit awkward," our honored guest said as he stared at the floor. "I'm afraid I feel rather undukeish."

"Nonsense. A run-in with a dragon can unnerve anyone. Would you like some more wine? A nice fire to warm you?"

"No, thank you." The duke lowered his voice even more than before. "Don't you think it would be better if we fled? I mean, dragons. And I've seen other things in the forest. Perhaps if your powers were—" The duke coughed again. "You see, I've heard of your accident."

Ebenezum bristled a bit at the last reference, but the smile more or less remained on his face. "Gossip, good duke. Totally blown out of proportion. We'll deal with your dragon in no time."

"But the dragon's taken over Gurnish Keep! He's immense, bright blue and violet scales, twenty-five feet from head to tail. His wings scrape the ceiling of my great hall! And he's invincible. He's captured my castle and beautiful daughter, and defeated my retainer!"

Beautiful daughter? My thoughts returned to the girl of my dreams. Where had she gone? What had kept her away?

"Only a child!" the duke cried. "No more than seventeen. Fine blonde hair, beautiful blue eyes, a lovely, girlish figure. And the dragon will burn her to a crisp if we don't do his bidding!"

Blonde? Blue? Figure? I had a revelation.

"Come now, man," Ebenezum remarked. "Calm down. It's common knowledge that dragons tend to be overdramatic. All the beast's really done so far is to overwhelm one retainer. I assume you still only had one retainer?"

She hadn't deserted me! She was only held prisoner! All the time she and I had spent together, all those long, warm afternoons, that's why she would tell me nothing of herself! A duke's daughter!

The duke glared at my master. "It wouldn't be like that if my subjects paid their taxes!"

A duke's daughter. And I would rescue her! There'd be

no need for secrecy then. How magnificent our lives would be!

A fire lit in Ebenezum's eyes. "Perhaps if certain local nobility were not so concerned with extending the borders of his tiny dukedom—" The wizard waved his hands and the fire disappeared. "But that's not important. We have a dragon to evict. As I see it, the elements here are quite ordinary. Dragon captures castle and maiden. Very little originality. We should be able to handle it tidily."

The duke began to object again, but Ebenezum would have none of it. Only one thing affected his nose more than sorcery—money—and the smell of it was obvious in the cottage. My master sent the duke outside while we gathered the paraphernalia together for dragon fighting.

When I had packed everything according to my master's instructions, Ebenezum beckoned me into his library. Once in the room, the wizard climbed a small stepladder, and, carefully holding his nose, pulled a slim volume from the uppermost shelf.

"We may have need of this." His voice sounded strangely hollow, most likely the result of thumb and forefinger pressed into his nose. "In my present condition, I can't risk using it. But it should be easy enough for you to master, Wuntvor."

He descended the ladder and placed the thin, dark volume in my hands. Embossed in gold on the cover were the words "How to Speak Dragon".

"But we must be off!" Ebenezum exclaimed, clapping my shoulder. "Musn't keep a client waiting. You may study that book on our rest stops along the way."

I stuffed the book hurriedly in the paraphernalia-filled pack and shouldered the whole thing, grabbed my walking staff and followed my master out the door. With my afternoon beauty at the end of my journey, I could manage anything.

My master had already grabbed the duke by the collar and propelled him in the proper direction. I followed at Ebenezum's heels as fast as the heavy pack would allow. The wizard, as usual, carried nothing. As he often had explained, it kept his hands free for quick conjuring and his mind free for sorcerous conjecture.

I noticed a bush move, then another. Rustling like the wind pushed through the leaves, except there was no wind. The forest was as still as when I had waited for my afternoon love. Still the bushes moved.

Just my imagination, I thought. Like the darkness of the forest. I glanced nervously at the sky, half-expecting the sun to disappear again. What was so big that it blotted out the sun?

A dragon?

But my musings were cut short by a man dressed in bright orange who stood in our path. He peered through an odd instrument on the end of a pole.

I glanced at the duke, walking now at my side. He had begun to shiver.

The man in orange looked up as we approached. "Good afternoon," he said, the half frown on his face disproving the words. "Could you move a little faster? You're blocking the emperor's highway, you know."

The duke shook violently.

"Highway?" Ebenezum asked, stopping mid-path rather than hurrying by the man in orange.

"Yes, the new road that the great and good Emperor Flostok III has decreed—"

"Flee!" the duke cried. "Dragons! Dragons! Flee!" He leapt about, waving his hands before the emperor's representative.

"See here!" the orange man snapped. "I'll have none of this. I'm traveling to see the Duke of Gurnish on important business."

The duke stopped hopping. "Duke?" he said, pulling his soiled clothing back into place. "Why, I'm the Duke of Gurnish. What can I help you with, my good man?"

The man in orange frowned even deeper. "It's about the upkeep of the road . . ."

"Certainly." The duke glanced back at us. "Perhaps we should go somewhere that we can talk undisturbed." The duke led the man in orange into the underbrush.

"They deserve each other," Ebenezum muttered. "But to business." He looked at me solemnly. "A bit about dragons. Dragons are one of the magical sub-species. They exist largely between worlds, partly on Earth and partly in the Netherhells, and never truly belong to either. There are other magical sub-species—"

Ebenezum's lecture was interrupted by a commotion in the underbrush. Large arms with a thick growth of grayish-brown hair rose and fell above the bushes, accompanied by human screams.

"Another sub-species is the troll," Ebenezum remarked.

I let my pack slide from my back and firmly grasped my staff. They would eat my true love's father! I had never encountered trolls before, but this was as good a time as any to learn.

"Slobber! Slobber!" came from the bushes before us. A rough voice, the sound of a saw biting into hardwood. I assumed it was a troll.

"Wait!" another voice screamed. "You can't do this! I'm a representative of the emperor!"

"Slobber! Slobber!" answered a chorus of rough voices.

"Let's get this over with!" Another voice, high and shaky. The duke?

Although the voices were quite close now, it was getting

difficult to distinguish individual words. It just sounded like a large amount of screaming, punctuated by cries of "slobber!" I lifted my staff over my head and ran forward with a scream of my own.

I broke into a small clearing with four occupants. One was the duke. The other three were among the ugliest creatures I'd seen in my short life. Squat and covered with irregular tufts of greybrown fur, which did nothing to hide the rippling muscles of their barrellike arms and legs. Three pairs of very small red eyes turned to regard me. One of them swallowed something that looked a good deal like an orange-clad foot.

The sight of the three hideous creatures completely stopped my forward motion. They regarded me in silence.

"Oh, hello," I said, breaking into the sinister quiet. "I must have wandered off the path. Excuse me."

One of the trolls barrelled towards me on its immensely powerful legs. "Slobber," it remarked. It was time to leave. I turned and bumped into my master, who ignored me as he made a mystic gesture.

"No slobber! No slobber!" the trolls cried and ran back into the heart of the woods.

I picked myself up and helped the wizard regain his feet as well. Ebenezum sneezed for a full three minutes, the result of his actually employing magic. When he caught his breath at last, he wiped his nose on his robe and regarded me all too evenly.

"Wuntvor," he said quietly. "What do you mean by dropping all our valuable equipment and running off, just so you can be swallowed by—"

The duke ran between the two of us. "Flee! Flee! Dragons! Trolls! Flee!"

"And you!" my master said, his voice rising at last. "I've had enough of your jumping about, screaming hysterical

"Smoke poured from the Keep's lower windows, and once or twice I thought I saw the yellow-orange flicker of flame."

warnings! Why do you even worry? You were surrounded
by trolls and they didn't touch you. You lead a charmed
life!" He grabbed the duke's shoulder with one hand and
mine with the other and pushed us back to the trail.

"Come," he continued. "We will reach Gurnish Keep
before nightfall. There, my assistant and I will deal with this
dragon, and you, good duke, will pay us handsomely for
our efforts." The wizard deposited us on the trail and
walked briskly towards the castle before the duke could
reply.

"Look!" The duke pulled at my sleeve. There was a
break in the trees ahead, affording a clear view of the hill
on the wood's far side. There, atop the hill, was Gurnish
Keep, a stone building not much larger than Ebenezum's
cottage. Smoke poured from the Keep's lower windows,
and once or twice I thought I saw the yellow-orange flicker
of flame.

"Dragon," the duke whispered. I hurriedly reached into
my satchel and pulled out *How To Speak Dragon*. The
time to start learning was now.

I opened the book at random and scanned the page.
Phrases in common speech filled one side. Opposite these
were the same phrases in dragon. I started reading from
the top:

"Pardon me, but could you please turn your snout?"

"Sniz me heeba-heeba szzz."

"Pardon me, but your claw is in my leg."

"Sniz mir sazza grack szzz."

"Pardon me, but your barbed tail is waving perilously
close . . ."

The whole page was filled with similar phrases. I closed
the book. It had done nothing to reassure me.

Ebenezum shouted at us from far up the trail. I ran to
follow, dragging the Duke of Gurnish with me.

We walked through the remaining forest without further difficulty. The woods ended at the edge of a large hill called Wizard's Knoll or Mount Gurnish, depending upon whom you spoke with. From there, we could get a clear view of the castle. And the smoke. And the flames.

The duke began to jabber again about the dangers ahead, but was silenced by a single glance from my master. The wizard's cool grey eyes stared up towards the castle, but somehow beyond it. After a moment, he shook his head and flexed his shoulders beneath his robes. He turned to me.

"Wunt," he said. "More occurs here than meets the eye." He glanced again at the duke, who was nervously dancing on a pile of leaves. "Not just a dragon, but three trolls. That's a great deal of supernatural activity for a place as quiet as Wizard's Woods."

I expected the duke to object to the wizard's choice of names, but he was strangely quiet. I turned to the pile of leaves where he had hidden.

The duke was gone.

"Methinks," Ebenezum continued, "some contact has been made with the Netherhells of late. There is a certain instrument in your pack . . ."

My master went on to describe the instrument and its function. If we set it up at the base of the hill, it would tell us the exact number and variety of creatures from the Netherhells lurking about the district.

I held up the instrument. My master rubbed his nose. "Keep it at a distance. The device carries substantial residual magic."

I put the thing together according to the wizard's instructions, and, at his signal, spun the gyroscope that topped it off.

"Now, small points of light will appear." Ebenezum sniffled loudly. "You can tell by the color of—"

He sneezed mightily, again and again. I looked to the device. Should I stop it?

Ebenezum sneezed to end all sneezes, directly at the instrument. The device fell apart.

"By the Netherhells!" Ebenezum exclaimed. "Can I not perform the simplest of spells?" He looked at me, and his face looked very old. "Put away the apparatus, Wunt. We must use the direct approach. Duke?"

I explained that the duke had vanished.

"What now?" Ebenezum looked back towards the forest. His cold grey eyes went wide. He blew his nose hastily.

"Wunt! Empty the pack!"

"What?" I asked, startled by the urgency of my master's voice. Then I looked back to the woods, and saw it coming. A wall of black, like some impenetrable cloud, roiling across the forest. But this cloud extended from the sky to the forest floor, and left complete blackness behind. It sped across the woods like a living curtain that drew its darkness ever closer.

"Someone plays with great forces," Ebenezum said. "Forces he doesn't understand. The pack, Wunt!"

I dumped the pack's contents on the ground. Ebenezum rifled through them, tossing various arcane tomes and irreplacable devices out of his way, until he grasped a small box painted a shiny robin's egg blue.

The magician sneezed in triumph. He tossed me the box.

"Quick, Wunt!" he called, blowing his nose. "Take the dust within that box and spread it in a line along the hill!" He waved at a rocky ridge on the forest edge as he jogged up the hill and began to sneeze again.

I did as my master bid, laying an irregular line of blue powder across the long granite slab. I looked back to the woods. The darkness was very close, engulfing all but the hill.

"Run, Wunt!"

I sprinted up the hill. The wizard cried a few ragged syllables and followed. He tripped as he reached the hilltop, and fell into an uncontrollable sneezing fit.

I turned back to look at the approaching blackness. The darkly tumbling wall covered all the forest now, and tendrils of the stuff reached out towards the hill like so many grasping hands. But the fog's forward motion had stopped just short of the ragged blue line.

There was a breeze at my back. I turned to see Ebenezum, still sneezing but somehow standing. One arm covered his nose, the other reached for the sky. His free hand moved and the breeze grew to a wind and then a gale, rushing down the hill and pushing the dark back to wherever it had come.

After a minute the wind died, but what wisps of fog remained in the forest below soon evaporated beneath the bright afternoon sun. My master sat heavily and gasped for breath as if all the air had escaped from his lungs.

"Lucky," he said after a minute. "Whoever raised the demon fog had a weak will. Otherwise . . ." The magician blew his nose, allowing the rest of the sentence to go unsaid.

A figure moved through the woods beneath us. It was the duke.

"Too exhausted to fight dragon," Ebenezum continued, still breathing far too hard. "You'll have to do it, Wunt."

I swallowed and picked up *How To Speak Dragon* from the hillside where it lay. I turned to look at Gurnish Keep, a scant hundred yards across the hilltop. Billows of smoke poured from the windows, occasionally accompanied by licks of flame. And, now that we stood so close, I could hear a low rumble, underlining all the other sounds in the field in which we stood. A rumble that occasionally grew into a roar.

This dragon was going to be everything I expected.

The duke grabbed at my coatsleeve. "Dragon!" he said. "Last chance to get out!"

"Time to go in there," Ebenezum said. "Look in the book, Wunt. Perhaps we can talk the dragon out of the castle." He shook the quivering duke from his arm. "And if you, good sir, would be quiet for a moment, we could go about saving your home and daughter. Quite honestly, I feel you have no cause for complaint with the luck you've been having. Most people would not have survived the evil spell that recently took over the woods. How you manage to bumble through the powerful forces at work around here is beyond. . ." Ebenezum's voice trailed off. He cocked an eyebrow at the duke and stroked his beard in thought.

The rumble from the castle grew louder again. I opened the thin volume I held in my sweating palms. I had to save my afternoon beauty.

I flipped frantically from page to page, finally finding a phrase I thought appropriate.

"Pardon me, but might we speak to you?"

In the loudest voice I could manage, I spat out the dragon syllables.

"Sniz grah! Subba Ubba Szzz!"

A great, deep voice reverberated from within the castle. "Speak the common tongue, would you?" it said. "Besides, I'm afraid I don't have a commode."

I closed the book with a sigh of relief. The dragon spoke human!

"Don't trust him!" the duke cried. "Dragons are deceitful!"

Ebenezum nodded his head. "Proceed with caution, Wunt. Someone *is* being deceitful." He turned to the duke. "You!"

"Me?" the Gurnish nobleman replied as he backed in my direction. Ebenezum stalked after him.

They were squabbling again. But I had no time for petty quarrels. I firmly grasped my staff, ready to confront the dragon and my afternoon beauty.

The duke was right behind me now, his courage seemingly returned. "Go forward, wizard!" he cried in a loud voice. "Defeat the dragon! Banish him forever!"

"Oh, not a wizard, too!" cried the voice from within the castle. "First I get cooped up in Gurnish Keep, then I have to capture your beautiful daughter, and now a wizard! How dull! Doesn't anyone have any imagination around here?"

I came to a great oak door. I nudged it with my foot. It opened easily and I stepped inside to confront the dragon.

It stood on its haunches, regarding me in turn. It was everything the duke had mentioned, and more. Blue and violet scales, twenty-five feet in length, wings that brushed the ceiling. The one oversight in the duke's description appeared to be the large green top hat on the dragon's head.

I saw her a second later.

She stood in front and slightly to one side of the giant reptile. She was as beautiful as I'd ever seen her.

"Why, Wuntvor," she said. "What are you doing here?"

I cleared my throat and pounded my staff on the worn stone pavement. "I've come to rescue you."

"Rescue?" She looked up at the dragon. The dragon rumbled. "So father's gotten to you, too?"

The duke's voice screamed behind me. "I warned you! Now the dragon will burn you all to cinders!"

The dragon snorted good naturedly and turned to regard the ceiling.

"The game is up, duke!" Ebenezum called from the doorway, far enough away so that the dragon's magical odor would not provoke another attack. "Your sorcerous schemes are at an end!"

"Yes, father," my afternoon beauty said. "Don't you think you've gone far enough?" She looked at my master. "Father so wanted control of the new Trans-Empire Highway, to put toll stations throughout the woods below, that he traded in his best retainer for the services of certain creatures from the Netherhells, which he'd use to frighten off anyone who stood in the way of his plans."

She turned and looked at the dragon. "Luckily, one of those creatures was Hubert."

"Betrayed!" The duke clutched at his heart. "My own daughter!"

"Come, father. What you're doing is dangerous and wrong. Your greed will make a monster of you. I've been worrying what my future was with you and the castle. But now I know." She glanced happily back to the dragon. "Hubert and I have decided to go on the stage."

The duke was taken aback.

"What?"

"Yes, good sir," Hubert the dragon remarked. "I have some small experience in the field, and, on talking with your daughter, have found that she is just the partner I have been looking for."

"Yes, father. A life on the stage. How much better than sitting around a tiny castle, waiting to be rescued by a clumsy young man."

Clumsy? My world reeled around me. Not wishing to be

rescued was one thing, considering the situation. But to call me clumsy? I lowered my staff and walked towards the door.

"Wait!" my afternoon beauty cried. I turned quickly. Perhaps she had reconsidered her harsh words. Our long afternoons together still meant something!

"You haven't seen our act!" she exclaimed. "Hit it, dragon!"

She danced back and forth across the castle floor, the dragon beating time with its tail. They sang together:

"Let's raise a flagon
For damsel and dragon,
The best song and dance team in the whole, wide world.
Our audience is clapping,
And their toes are tapping,
For a handsome reptile and a pretty girl!"

The dragon blew smoke rings at the end of a line and breathed a bit of fire at the end of a verse. Six more verses followed, more or less the same. Then they stopped singing and began to shuffle back and forth.

They talked in rhythm.

"Hey, dragon. It's good to have an audience again."

"I'll say, damsel. I'm all fired up!"

They paused.

"How beautiful it is in Gurnish Keep! What more could you ask for, damsel, than this kind of sunny day?"

"I don't know, dragon. I *could* do with a shining knight!"

They paused again.

"Romance among reptiles can be a weighty problem!"

"Why's that, dragon?"

"When I see a pretty dragoness, it tips my scales!"

They launched into song immediately.

"Let's raise a flagon
For damsel and dragon—"

"I can't stand it any more!" the Duke of Gurnish cried. "Slabyach! Grimace! Trolls, get them all!"

A trapdoor opened in the corner of the castle floor. The trolls popped out.

"Quick, Wunt!" Ebenezum cried. "Out of the way!" But before he could even begin to gesture, he was caught in a sneezing fit.

The trolls sauntered towards us. I bopped one on the head with my staff. The staff broke.

"Slobber!" exclaimed the troll.

"Roohhaarrr!" came from across the room. The dragon stood as well as it was able in the confines of the castle's great hall. It carefully directed a thin lance of flame towards each troll's posterior.

"No slobber! No slobber!" the trolls exclaimed, escaping back through the trapdoor.

"Thank you," Ebenezum said after blowing his nose. "That was quite nice of you."

"Think nothing of it," the dragon replied. "I never sacrifice an audience."

(3)

"The best spells are those that right wrongs,
bring happiness, return the world to peace and
cause a large quantity of the coin of the realm to
pass into the wizard's possession."
—from *The Teachings of Ebenezum*
Volume IXX

"I finally got our good Lord of Gurnish to listen to reason," my master said when we returned to our cottage. "When I mentioned how close to the palace I might be soon, and that I might find myself discussing the region, the duke saw his way to hire me as a consultant."

Ebenezum pulled a jangling pouch from his belt. "The duke will now most likely receive clearance to build his toll booths. Pity he no longer has the money for their construction."

"And what of his daughter and the dragon?" I asked.

"Hubert is flying to Vushta with her this very instant. I gave them a letter of introduction to certain acquaintances I have there, and they should find a ready audience."

"So you think they're that good?"

Ebenezum shook his head vigorously. "They're terrible. But the stage is a funny thing. I expect Vushta will love them.

"But enough of this." The wizard drew another, smaller pouch from his bag. "Hubert was kind enough to lend me some ground dragon's egg. Seems it's a folk remedy among his species; gives quick, temporary relief. I've never found this particular use for it in any of my tomes, but I've tried everything else. What do I have to lose?"

He ground the contents of the pouch into a powder and dropped it in a flagon of wine.

"This might even save us a trip to Vushta." He held his nose and lifted the concoction to his lips. My hopes sank as he drank it down. With the duke's daughter gone, a trip to Vushta was the only thing I had to look forward to.

The wizard opened a magical tome and breathed deeply. He smiled.

"It works! No more sneezing!"

His stomach growled.

"It couldn't be." A strange look stole over the wizard's face. He burped.

"It is! No wonder I couldn't find this in any of my tomes! I should have checked the *Netherhell Index*! It's fine for dragons, but for humans—" He paused to pull a book from the shelf and leaf rapidly through it. He burped again. His face looked very strained as he turned to me.

"Neebekenezer's Syndrome of Universal Flatulence!"
he whispered. A high, whining sound emerged from his
robes.

"Quick, Wunt!" he cried. "Remove yourself, if you
value your sanity!"

I did as I was told. Even from my bed beneath the trees, I
could hear the whistles, groans and muffled explosions all
night long.

We would be traveling to Vushta after all.

SILKEN DRAGON

STEVEN EDWARD McDONALD

ILLUSTRATIONS BY
RON MILLER

"A curse," said Rit Ho-chep. "You *do* believe in curses?"

Suona of Shalin, daughter of the Devil-king Tamien, was silent for a moment, concentrating on the golden symbol that had been worked into the side of the bath. Her long black hair drifted about her semi-submerged head.

Rit was about to ask again when Suona said, "Occasionally I believe in them. I seldom see them bear fruit, though. One's gods are not necessarily those of another person—many *are* imaginary, after all."

Rit swirled the water with her hand, and the tiny, twisting currents thus produced forced water to stroke Suona's skin. Rit Ho-chep was the most expert of the attendants in the palace of Shan Kaang Ur-kef; none of them were poor at their jobs. Suona liked Rit less for her obvious ability to tend to the needs of man or woman than for her conversation.

The tiny woman now attended to Suona's hair with a water-comb, expert and gentle.

"Well?" Suona prompted. "Or shall I tell you of the winters in my homeland?"

"Brrrr!" Rit said, with an exagerrated shiver. She giggled like a young girl, though she was older than Suona. "You would not. I feel my toes dropping off even *recalling* your tales. I am glad to be of Klusos—at least here I might enjoy myself naked, in the fields, and in the rivers—"

"And beneath men too, I don't doubt," Suona said.

More giggles. Suona waited for the woman to quieten, and looked closely at the golden and red dragon that had caught her attention. The dragon's body was worked in gold, the eyes in red, the honor-color of Klusos. The dragon was surrounded by flames; she was impressed by it, though she had seen other representations of the dragon throughout Klusos. This dragon seemed different, malignant, yet tragic.

Rit said, "You are a *vulgar* woman."

"In my home, *that* is polite. Now," she added, firmly, sitting up in the wide bath, "this dragon, this curse." Suona's black hair hung against her back, water sluicing from it. Rit made a sound of annoyance. "Tell me, before I lose my temper and drown you. Or worse."

"Brrrrr!" Rit said, and Suona smiled. "I am *not* a storyteller, my lady. I know my work."

"Stubborn as a tavern wench, that's what you are. Very well, I'll go as I am and find a storyteller and see if he'll tell me about it." Suona started to get up, but Rit, her small hands firm on the Northwoman's shoulders, pushed her back down into the water. Suona could have resisted, and would have won if she had, but that was not the point of the game.

Rit said, "I am not finished with you yet. In your land, it may be proper to run about in breeches and jerkin, waving swords and axes and howling at the moon, but *here*, a woman is a *woman*. We are cultured, thoughtful, and gentle. *Not* barbarous."

"And you wouldn't know a bow from your backside, you little heathen."

"And so I *would*, my lady. If only to avoid the bow. Men, now, *they* are warriors and brutes, and are meant to be, with their muscles and their hairy arms."

"And women to the witchly arts, eh?"

"The *finer* arts, my lady. It is said that the gods keep dragons, and the *women* tend them. A man will inspire a dragon to battle—he is a challenge. But a woman is merely a friend, a companion, and a helper. Children, now, a manchild dreams most *horrible* dreams about dragons, and fears to find them crouching in the dark, awaiting a morsel. But a womanchild, she dreams little poems, and wishes her dragon-spirit with her whenever she ventures out into the darkness—for *she* fears the barbarian and the spirit-of-stone who lie in wait for the unwary little girl."

"Ha! Now I have you. Terrified to walk outside, are we?" Suona sank back into the bath, allowed herself to sink completely, feeling the gentle touch of Rit's water-comb around her head, in her hair.

When she rose up, Rit said, "I fear more the spirit-of-stone, my lady."

"*Hmm.*" Suona closed her eyes. She was unaccustomed to this sort of pampering. "Well, I'm not sure I fear *any*thing—all sorcery tends to spring from one group of laws. With that in mind, and some knowledge of the laws, one can work towards a defense against sorcery."

"I would sooner avoid getting into positions where battle is inevitable, my lady."

"And, of course, you'd sooner let curses and charms do all the work."

Rit released the Northwoman, swimming around to her side. "Of course, that is their purpose. Besides, the curses of the dragon are the curses of women and are *very* effective. The *threat* is often sufficient, but some are brave, and some are stupid, and then the curse must live."

"And this one?" Suona said, touching the dragon.

"An *image* of a curse, my lady, at least here. The curse of the Silken Dragon, which hangs in the inner chamber of the tomb of Nilkir Kon-weh, once Chun; it guards the royal form and its belongings, protecting the Chun's spirit on the journey to the Gardens of Neverwhen."

"Ah," Suona said, smiling. "Yes, I see now—it has a threatening stance, as if it has made ready to attack. Yet it has the look of misery about it—the death of the Chun it guards?"

Rit was obviously pleased. "Very good, my lady. That is what it is meant to say—it is sad, but ready. Should the royal chambers be disturbed, the dragon would live."

"If it was a woman?"

Rit shrugged slightly. "She would merely be cursed to wither—swiftly, of course."

"*Hmm*, a curse of curses, that. I shall have to learn about local curses, in case I need the assistance of dragons, silken or otherwise. I imagine a silken dragon would be good company on those long winter nights when there's no companion handy. It can get to be the death of you, my little friend, that cold can. None of this bare skin then."

Rit answered that by ignoring it; she didn't even shiver. Suona suspected that her reaction to the talk of Shalin's winter weather had been little more than elegant sham.

"One day, my lady," the attendant said, "you must tell me about this." She touched a complex rune that had seemingly been branded into Suona's left shoulder.

Suona said, "I might, but not if you're so afraid of spirits-of-stone and barbarians and assorted curses. That's the mark of Sumak, the ruler of the underworld, and the damned—I have a not-very-secret suspicion that your dragon-guarded Chun is residing comfortably in his world; Sumak enjoys the company of royalty."

Rit looked at her charge, forlornly, and gave a slight shake of her head. "And I am to treat you as the peak of womanhood and a true lady." She sighed and shook her head again. "Impossible. Impossible. Impossible. But I try."

"Poor you," Suona said, smiling.

"Yes," Rit agreed, nodding slightly. Her eyes were filled with a tortured sadness. "Poor, poor, pitiful me."

There was pandemonium in the gardens of Shan Kaang Ur-kef, and it bore the name of Vardret Kovair. The sound of a Midlander as a fury was a sound Suona knew well; this Midlander was displaying the classic signs of Midlander rage.

Rit, walking by Suona's side in the gardens, stopped. She seemed frightened, yet terribly curious; training was the only thing that reined in Rit's curiosity. Suona continued to drift forward, then she, too, halted.

"What is it?" Suona asked.

Rit shook her head. "We must go no further, my lady. This is not a matter for women."

Suona grimaced and plucked at the embroidered finery Rit had insisted she wear; she preferred her own clothes, but the attendant had hidden them. "*That* row," Suona said, "is something I'm quite familiar with. I've shut a few of them up."

"Barbarian," Rit said, before she could stop herself. She blushed immediately. "My lady—"

"Be silent," Suona commanded, her attention half on the noise within the garden. Rit ceased apologising, and stood miserably waiting for rebuke. "I have been called so many things in my life that this excessive politeness is almost offensive. Now come, let's see what's what."

"My lady, *please*—the Shan's personal guard—"

"I assume they'll avoid damaging a lady and her attendant," Suona said, starting toward the source of the shouting. She didn't get very far before there was the noise of a
brief scuffle; the gardens were suddenly very quiet. Suona
halted. "Protocol be damned!" She swung about. "You
too, little Ho-chep. It's *your* fault."

"My lady?"

"I wanted to see what was happening."

"Ladies do not delve into the affairs of men," Rit said,
her words precise, as though she was speaking by rote. "At
least in Klusos, my lady."

It took a great deal of effort, but Suona managed to
avoid comment. Perhaps it was for the best. Tamien would
not be pleased if his daughter wreaked havoc in Klusos,
and, as many a man had discovered, once she began to
cause trouble, she had great difficulty stopping. She might
have begun fighting with the Midlander, and, worse still,
might have won. In Klusos, one hid feuds behind masques
of courtesy and ritual; it only made the losers death more
formal.

They walked into the main gardens, towards the grove
that the Shan used as an informal meeting place. Suona
saw no sign of disturbance, or of the Shan's personal
guard. Hidden from the view of those in the grove, a court
musician was playing lulling airs on a woodflute, no doubt
to calm the Shan. Sunlanterns hung from tree branches,
rocking gently in the breeze; those in direct sunlight shone
like small moons.

The Shan was kneeling by a narrow brook, looking into
the water. He turned his head as Suona and Rit approached.

"Ho," he said, standing. He took a moment to look
Suona up and down, while smoothing wrinkles out of his

"Yes, you look more like royal blood now than the warrior woman you pretend to be."

own silken red robes. "Yes, you look more like royalblood
now than the warrior-woman you pretend to be. Tamien
would be pleased, my dear."

Suona made a small, mocking curtsey. "Your pardon,
oh Shan. My sire would likely cut the clothes from me
before his warriors and beat me until I bled. If I allowed him
to."

The Shan laughed. "Suona, you are spirited. I am
certain Tamien is proud of you, woman or not."

"Women are as useful to a Devil-king as men," she said,
smiling. "They bear the children and provide warmth that
cannot be taken from a fire."

"You are no judge," said the Shan. "Are you not a
woman?" His round, hairless face showed little expression.

"Nor are you a fair judge," Suona said, her tone properly polite. "You were taught to believe all males superior.
The symbol of man, oh Shan, is the mountain: stolid
strength, unbending will, all that a mountain represents."
Her slim, sunbrowned hands moved as she spoke, outlin-
ing, accenting. "The symbol of womanhood is the dragon.
The mountain may stand and resist, and be chipped away
little by little, but the dragon may move, may *avoid* the
onslaught, and thus remain whole. The dragon is flexible.
The mountain is not."

The Shan seemed both surprised and pleased, his face
reflecting both emotions alternately. Suona studied both
sides of his face, found the pleasure to be genuine. Rit, by
Suona's side, was a study in startled womanhood, her
small rosebud mouth open, her brown eyes wide.

"You are certain," said the Shan, "that you are *wholly*
Northblood? Or—" with an accusing look at Rit, who
looked away, fearful, "have you been listening to
philosophers?"

"Neither," Suona said. "The line of reasoning is obvious if you consider the symbols involved. The female attitude is one of flexibility—which is how I attempt to make my living."

The Shan accorded her the honor of a polite bow. "It would be a rare dragon that had either your form or your grace, my dear Suona," he said. "And a sorry dragon that confronted you, though, according to tradition, the dragon does not confront women."

"Rit has told me," Suona said. Rit's pale blush deepened instantly. "She explained the curse of the Silken Dragon."

The Shan said, "My ancestors were great believers in curses, none more so than Nilkir Kon-weh. A very elaborate curse, this, with clauses and convolutions that would madden a master mage. —Indeed, it is occassionaly used to demonstrate cursing to the student of the art."

Suona nodded slightly, smiling. "I hear that the *Chun* had her entourage slain when she died."

"*She* did not," said the Shan, his chin lifting a little. "She was dead, neh? It is tradition. One must have company on the road to Neverwhen; one must be guarded and cared for, neh? *You* might consign the forms of your ancestors to the flame, Suona, but those of Klusos treat their ancestors differently. With kindness."

"The kindness, oh Shan, is in the memory." Suona plucked at the material of her robes, uncomfortable in their too-warm embrace. "And if I should die here, I would consider it kinder to be buried in something a little less smothering."

The Shan chuckled. Rit looked both offended and ashamed, avoiding looking at Suona, and blushing furiously.

The Shan turned and began to stroll towards the edge of

the grove, following the path of the brook. Near the edge of the grove, a bell-tree had been suspended from a tree branch that curved out over the brook. The Shan stopped and played his fingers over the delicate bells, drawing odd chords of sound. The hidden flutist faltered momentarily, then caught up his melody once again, livening it up a little, the notes skirling.

Turning from the bell-tree, the Shan said, "Have you had the . . . pleasure . . . of meeting Vardret Kovair?"

Suona shook her head. "I've seen and heard him from a distance, but no more than that. He was here before I arrived, wasn't he?"

The Shan raised an eyebrow. "Yes. We had an argument of sorts, over trade items. We are, of course, reluctant to allow things of value to leave Klusos—many of the things in this palace alone are as old as Klusos itself, and beyond value. Kovair has an eye for everything, and I assume he knows the preferences of his countrymen—"

"Of Kal-Menelon?" Suona said.

"Yes." The Shan inclined his head slightly. "You know the city?"

"And the accent," she said. "The City of Thieves."

"All cities are cities of thieves, Suona." The Shan fingered the bell-tree again, drawing chimes. "Perhaps you should get to know him."

Suona smiled broadly, almost laughing. "Would a courtesan not do as well to watch him, oh Shan? Why a poor Northborn wench?"

"Because," said the Shan, polite of tone, "the poor Northborn wench is a noblewoman and the daughter of royalblood, and less to be questioned than an overeager courtesan—and, I might add, you would do a better job, with less difficulty." He smiled. "Kin to the dragon must be flexible, neh?"

Her night was shadowed with dreams and broken with thoughts of her homeland; she rarely slept more than an hour or two, and knew more about the night than most. The night, and moon-shadows, and the things that flourished in the damp, dead places that had been abandoned by mortal beings. Things were abroad that could not stand the light of day; the pressure of light and heat from the sun tore them apart like spiderwebs beneath a careless hand.

So she sat, waiting for the night to end, watching the shivering stars, waiting for the sight of something elemental. Her room looked down on an open palace court, and out over beautifully-tended lawns and flower gardens, something she had never seen in Shalin. She had barely had time to notice the city, passing through it to the palace; she regretted that a little.

There was a rasp behind her, from the door to her chambers, and she turned her head, midnight hair slipping over her bare shoulders. Then a slow, soft sound as the door handle was cautiously turned.

She reached to her weapons harness, slipped her longknife free of its sheath, held it dagger-fashion in her left hand, her hand masking the patterns of jewels worked into the hilt. She rose, drifted silently across the room, hung waiting near the door as it was eased open.

It was almost a full two minutes before her cautious visitor gathered the courage to enter. He slipped quickly through the narrow opening between door and frame, taking a step towards the opposite side of the room, looking, it appeared, for her.

She flowed silently forward, grasping, locking the intruder into position, and discovered, without surprise, that she was holding nine inches of steel at the throat of Vardret Kovair. He had tensed instantly in her grasp, badly frightened. Warily, she released him, glanced quickly towards the door that closed off Rit Ho-chep's quarters. The door remained closed.

"You might," she said, "have found it easier to request audience with me."

The trader said nothing; he was still stunned by surprise. Suona crossed the room, knife ready, picked up a lantern that she found little use for unless reading, and lit it, using flint and striker. The sullen light showed the trader watching her as a sorceror might watch a newly-conjured demon. She didn't bother to look for clothes; she would rather be on guard and naked than modestly dressed and lifeless.

She pointed at a couch. "Sit yourself down before you turn to stone. Then you might explain what you were doing sneaking around like someone out of the thieves quarter."

"I am from—"

"Kal-Menelon," she said. "I know. And you trade. Which makes you a thief under *any* judgement. I don't doubt you intend to cheat Klusos out of everything possible. However, I suspect you didn't come here to steal from me."

One side of the man's mouth twisted, trying to form a smile. It gave him a bitter, edgy expression. "No. I thought it best to come at night. Kaang Ur-kef has too many spies about for me to risk ought else. I did not expect to find you awake. Nor armed. I *had* thought, though, that you might be . . . *ah* . . . accompanied—"

Suona's eyes narrowed. "I am not a palace courtesan, Vardret Kovair."

Kovair was hesitant, his apparent gaffe throwing him off-balance. "Excuse me, my lady, I did not mean—"

"You meant what you said," Suona said, evenly. "I am

a woman of Shalin, not a Midlander wench. Please keep that in mind."

Kovair sat, slowly. He put his hands on his knees, kept them there, fingers twitching like the legs of dying spiders. "I shall. You have my apologies."

"I *almost* had your life," Suona said. She sat on the edge of a table, the hilt of her longknife pressed against her bare thigh. The sooty yellow light made the rune at the base of the blade shimmer and shift. Kovair's eyes tracked her form; she ignored the inspection.

"You are a demon," Kovair said, flatly.

"No. The daughter of Tamien of Shalin, nothing more. I might kill now and then, but I never steal souls." She smiled, but her eyes were narrow. "They tend to be too much of a burden."

It didn't seem to make Kovair uneasy. "You carry your weapons left-handed," he said, "which is the way of demonkind. And you carry the mark of a demon—"

"A god," Suona corrected. "Sumak, who is no doubt eyeing you now." Her eyes flashed red, bright little sparks behind the pupils; Kovair flinched, caught unawares. "I am sure you have a reason for saying all this. One usually talks of demons and the like in a hushed voice."

"I wonder," Kovair said, slowly, carefully, "how the Shan would react if certain . . . details . . . were revealed to him."

Suona almost laughed out loud. "Likely he would correct certain of your assumptions. That is, he knows. Why should I conceal my gifts, or my oddities? There is a pact between Shalin and Klusos. I am here by grace of the Shan; I have little to do other than travel, after all."

Kovair slumped slightly. His hands closed into fists. "It seems that I made my move prematurely."

Suona gestured with the longknife, fragmenting the

gloom. "As you say. You should have paid more attention to your information-gathering. Those courtesans you so dread *can* be coaxed into providing little pieces of information."

Kovair's eyes narrowed, giving him a ferrety appearance. "I trust none of them. I have been a trader for too long."

"Then why trust me?"

"I do not."

"Then why bother coming here?" she said.

"I thought I might . . . persuade . . . you." He stood; Suona gestured with the knife, and he sat again.

"You might still *persuade* me," she said. "As you should know, I have nothing better to do than travel; I have no desire to be a wife to those in Shalin. And I dislike formality and protocol."

"I noticed," Kovair said, roughly. "I am no longer certain of my purpose here. I did not expect such a threat."

"I don't threaten. After all, what is a threat but an extension of protocol?" She held the knife up so he could see the rune on the blade. "If there is a need to slay you, Vardret Kovair, I will slay you; I will give no warning. Your intention was to persuade me—to join you in thievery, *hm*?"

Kovair's mouth moved, forming his bitter smile again. "I had thought you merely an intelligent woman, my lady. One does not expect royalblood women to know aught of thievery." His tone became a little sarcastic. "Then again, I believe you would like to be a warrior-woman."

"I am."

"Weaponry does not make a warrior, my lady—that only comes with practice, experience, and spirit."

"And does foolishness come in the same manner?" Suona gestured with the big blade. "It was certainly no polite lady who caught you skulking, *hm*?"

Kovair was silent, watching her. She studied him, watching for any false gesture. His eyes were dark, the irises floating in a lake of white; a tempermental, impulsive man, a careful planner, a man one step from fanaticism.

She said, "What did you intend to steal?"

He remained silent for a few moments more, still watching her, then said, "Do you know the tombs that are built onto this palace?"

"Yes," Suona said.

"They are rarely visited." Kovair stood, began pacing out a small area. "Things taken from there can be smuggled out at night. It would be a long time before such thefts are noticed, if they are ever discovered. Over a period of time, one or two might steal enough to pay for an army."

Suona shook her head. "You would never take Klusos."

Kovair's eyes flashed. "I do not intend to take Klusos, my lady. I have no interest in the country as yet. I would sooner start with territory that I am familiar with."

"Kal-Menelon?"

"Of course. It is a rich state, and might be expanded. A small war with a neighbor, at first, then further. One might thus build quite a kingdom."

"And one might lose control to a band of rather rapacious warlords," Suona said, "thus recarving the kingdom. It *has* happened. One becomes a puppet, *hm*?"

Kovair smiled again. "That is a problem to face then. Without gold, I have nothing."

"And I?" Suona said. She straightened up. "What do I receive in return for my assistance?"

"You could rule with me," Kovair said.

"Indeed I could, and so I would finally be struck down by a stray arrow during a hunt, or might find my throat being cut on dark night." She smiled. "I have different ambitions, and no desire to endanger myself by ruling."

"Then we shall divide the takings evenly," he said.

Suona opened her left hand. The jewels set into the hilt of her knife caught the light, prism-hammering it, flashing. "As you noted, oh trader of Kal-Menelon, I am royalblood."

He glared at her. "All I wish is your help. I will break into the tombs. You need only stand watch. The tombs are guarded lightly, and there will be no danger."

"I value my friendship with the Shan more than I value gold, silver or jewelry." She shook her head. "No, I will not help you. You might court death yourself, for the sake of power and money; I simply will not join you in the courting."

"Death . . . ?"

"The tombs are protected by curses," she said.

Kovair snorted. "My lady," he said, his tone mocking, "curses are hardly more than threats. I thought you had no truck with threats."

Suona regarded him through half-closed eyes. "I don't. But as you wish, oh unbeliever, I've warned you. You may do as you wish. I hope you're possessed of a remedy for . . . *ah* . . . dragon bite."

Kovair snorted again, and walked towards the door. He stopped as he opened it, turned. "I apologise for the intrusion, my lady Suona. I had thought to engage a warrior-woman."

"And, you have found, I'm merely a foolish and superstitious female. Goodnight, Vardret Kovair."

That angered him, she thought. He managed to avoid slamming the door, but his parting look was filled with black flame.

The hidden musician had forsaken his wood-flute for the brittle-glass tones of a stringed instrument, and was playing a lively reel for the benefit of the Shan and whatever guests he might have.

Suona, kneeling by the brook, said, "I feel that it would be to your benefit to expel him from Klusos."

The Shan had taken an ornamental bench at the point where the brook expanded into a pool, and was throwing breadcrumbs into the water, watching them sink, watching the fish as they darted about in the water. Suona envied him his serenity.

He said, "No. We have a trade pact with Kal-Menelon and certain of her sister city-states. I fear it would endanger that pact to simply have Vardret Kovair expelled or done away with." He looked up. One eyebrow was raised. Suona suspected that the Shan had dismissed her conclusion as womanly nonsense, no matter what her background. "Politics, my dear, are insufferably complex, more so than mere social ritual."

"He made one approach to me, directly," Suona said, "which gave me no time to divine his motives more subtly. Or, I might add, to make a fair attempt at discouraging him."

The Shan fed more crumbs to his fish. "You feel that he might be discouraged?"

"Not now," Suona said. "Before, perhaps. He *might* approach me again, though."

"Then you should agree to help him. Observe him, and let him fall to his fate, if need be."

"No," Suona said, sharply.

The Shan looked up, smiling. "What? A warrior who balks at death?"

"The way of my people, oh Shan, is not murder. It's the way, perhaps, of politicians, and of emperors—all politeness rendered, of course. But not the way of Shalin, not *my* way."

"What is your way, Suona? To challenge him to single combat?"

Suona walked to the bell-tree, touching each bell in turn, gently drawing tones from them. Someone had lately hung a series of water-bells beneath the tree; they hummed very softly, hardly audible.

She said, "My way is to prevent the problem from growing worse. If he is killed here—"

"For transgression? We can hardly help it, my dear, if he triggers a curse, or offends a warrior, or even slips and breaks a leg. To expel him or otherwise hinder him, even to murder him, requires active interference on *our* part, neh? What are we to do? Vardret Kovair is my guest, and abuses that privilige at his own risk."

"He might intend to take Klusos," she said. "Eventually."

The Shan sprinkled the last of the crumbs over the water. "But I think not. It would require a large force, and the cost of such a force is beyond him. It would take too many years; he will be dead, I imagine, in ten, fifteen, twenty years at the most. He is no threat to Klusos. His successor, perhaps, or the one beyond him. Much may happen in that time."

Suona closed her eyes for a moment, listening to the water-bells, and the hidden musician. "Then you will do nothing."

"Nothing," said the Shan. "There seems to be no point, my dear Suona. If he insists upon thievery, rather than mere dishonest trade, then let him suffer the consequences."

"And if he has means by which to counter any curses that stand in his path?"

The Shan looked up from the water. "He would have to be a mage, would he not?"

"Those skilled in sorcery are to be found in all places, oh Shan," Suona said. "I have some small magical skill myself, an effect of Sumak's touch. I am not very well trained, but I can do the odd trick or two."

"*Ah!*" said the Shan, rising. "I smell a hint, Suona. What would you have to gain from helping Vardret Kovair?"

"Self-respect."

The Shan chuckled. "You are still young, my dear. You will discover that self-respect entails a great deal more than striking blows against your elders, no matter how stubborn they are. The trader shall remain here, but, please, you must feel free to discourage him, if you can."

Suona made a small, mocking curtsey, her eyes flashing red. "By your leave, oh Shan?"

The Shan pursed his lips, as though he had just bitten into a blood orange, only to find it the painted lemon prank of a spirit trickster. "I am tempted, oh Suona of Shalin, to apply a stout length of wood to your behind."

The moon and the night.

The stars flickered and shimmered. Suona clung to the highest point of the palace, crouching on a narrow ledge, looking out over the palace grounds towards the city. There was hardly a flicker of light from the city buildings themselves; there was a loose curfew in effect in Klusos, and it was observed—with all politeness rendered, of course—by the citizenry. No-one had bothered to ask the peasants who lived without the walls of the city.

At least, Suona reflected, the cities of Klusos were orderly, unlike Kal-Menelon and its sister city-states. She scanned the grounds again, looking for signs of life.

And Vardret Kovair, she thought, what of him now? She could hardly be certain of his true intentions, after all. Perhaps he had hoped to entangle her in his plotting; it

"She scanned the grounds again, looking for signs of life."

might have been his intention to gain a foothold where by
Shalin and the icy nations about it could be dominated.

She climbed down, sliding a little, rough stone striking
tiny sparks of pain from her bare skin while she damned Rit
Ho-chep. There was a mild breeze tonight; it was warm,
and could be ignored, unlike the murderous storms one
encountered in Shalin. Her weapons harness pressed into
her side.

She passed through the palace like a ghost, avoiding the
patrolling palace watch with the ease of a skilled thief or
trained assassin, using all her senses, though she had no
reason to fear the Shan's soldiers. It was good practice; she
could hardly afford to lose her edge.

She drifted silently into the corridors of the tombs, scanning the shadows, but finding no elemental creatures. The
people of Klusos were meticulously clean, and extended
that cleanliness even to the tombs of their ancestors. The
family that bathes together, she thought, and smiled.

She felt the lingering aura of expert curses, quickly
seperated the one feeling into many, some more malignant than others. Her skin crawled, and she began to
move so lightly she feared she might at any moment float
towards the ceiling.

Away, away, away, they seemed to command. *Away!*

She saw many dragons. She stopped near one, ran her
fingers over it. It was ancient in form, a little crude, unlike
the modern stylized symbol that graced certain of the
dresses and cloaks the Shan had given her. Too, there was
a tapestry, small, hanging in Rit Ho-chep's small room,
that depicted a blood-red, glaring dragon. Red was the
color of honor; the Shan had graced her only with the
finest things in his house. Suona doubted she would take
much of it with her.

The tombs were cold, silent, dry, dustless, empty of life

bar the naked swordswoman who prowled the corridors between them, searching. Night after night, she had come stalking ghosts, only to find nothing bar the emptiness and the pulsing afterimages of brilliant, complex curses.

She stopped before a tomb door, leaned against it, touched her forehead to cold stone, felt the power of the curse with her mind, felt it as a malignant pressure at the base of her skull, tried to counter it with her own powers, and felt the pressure grow, breaking out in a cold sweat. The weary breeze that flowed through the corridors made her feel nauseous, made her skin feel clammy, as though she had just woken from a nightmare.

She leaned back, and the pressure vanished, leaving only a dull ache behind her eyes.

She continued her tour of the tombs, running her fingers over the smoothed stone as she walked. There was nothing, not even a rat, no sign at all of the things that prowled the night. It disappointed her.

She made her way back through the palace, tempted to go back onto the roof for a moment, beneath the stars— *ah, for forests!* —and crushing temptation beneath the heel of necessity. She had not slept for a full three days; whether or not she felt particularly tired, she had to sleep. Dull reflexes invited swift death.

Rit was waiting for her when she reached her chambers. Suona closed the door behind herself, padded silently across to the windows, looking out on the night, watching the stars flicker.

Rit said, "Your pardon, my lady, but it is not proper for you to be wandering about without clothes."

"Hm," said Suona, who was absorbed in watching a star that was rapidly crossing the heavens. An omen, perhaps, if you could take the word of sorcerors and other persons of magical extraction at face value.

Rit flapped her arms, helpless. "I try, oh I honestly try, but you *never* listen. It is not *proper,* my lady."

The star winked out. "The clothes you force upon me, little Ho-chep, are rather limiting in a fight."

"Ladies do not fight, my . . . lady."

Suona shook her head. "The daughters of Devil-kings do. If you would be so good as to return my travelling clothes, I might shame all Klusos a lot less. As you refuse—"

"They are disgusting garments for a lady," Rit said, her chin lifting.

"They also wear out a damn sight slower than fancy skirts, and don't get in the way of one's blades." Suona smiled, and her eyes flashed. "You are a snob, you know."

"You are little more than a child, mistress," Rit said. "I am of the palace of the Shan Kaang Ur-kef of Klusos. What you see is not the manner of a snob, my lady, but the manner of one whose pride lies in her work—which is to the welfare of her house."

"Goodnight, little Ho-chep," Suona said.

"Goodnight, my lady," Rit said, a trace of sulkiness in her voice. Her bearing dignified, she turned and went drifting back to her room. The door closed quietly. Suona shook her head, resigned to the fact that they now had this same argument every night, and for the same reasons. Rit was older than Suona by some years, yet seemed younger. The central sign of her greater age was that she was set in her ways.

Little more than a child!

Suona went to bed, and was quickly asleep, not dreaming.

Gold filled her mind, and exploded into a molten vision, a burning, flowing beast of living gold.

Her conscious mind was last to break free of the chains of sleep; when she became fully aware, she was out of bed, sword and knife in left and right hands, her feet well apart, her balance set for a swift defense and attack.

Blazing bloody eyes shifted, stared down at her. Molten claws flickered, shifted, lifted. Great golden jaws filled with slender, deadly teeth parted. Gold flame flickered, surrounding.

Suona's skin prickled and bumped, creeping and cold; there seemed to be ash on her tongue.

Dragon. A symbol shaped into life, drawn in the gold of a sorceror's vision, a dragon sprung from a curse made years before.

Frightened, she backed away, aware that dragons were supposed to challenge only men, yet convinced to her soul that this golden beast had come to slay her.

It screamed, silent, and its long golden tail lashed; it was lovely, yet deadly.

Rit Ho-chep's door opened suddenly, and the tiny attendant came flying out, her half-tied robe flapping about her as she hurried to Suona's side. She had the look of one woken from a deep sleep—Suona estimated they had slept only an hour—yet she did not appear frightened. Suona moved to protect, should the need arise.

She said, "Little Ho-chep, what is it?"

Rit pulled her sword-arm down. "*Please*, my lady, you must not be frightened. The dragon will not hurt women. Too, it is a vision. It is the image of the Silken Dragon that guards Nilkir Kon-weh, the dragon you questioned me about. Do you recall—"

"Why?" Suona whispered. The beast reared again, silently roaring. "Why *here*?"

Rit shook her head, her long black hair flying. "Not here alone, my lady. It will appear to women throughout the palace and the grounds. The tomb's seal has been broken."

Suona bent quickly, picked up her weapons harness. "The guards—"

"No," Rit said, firmly, surprising Suona. "The guards are all male, my lady. If they enter the tombs now, they will be slain, or driven mad—I am uncertain of the effects of the curse, you see. Some of them are very violent."

Suona was silent as she put the harness on, and nervous because of the shimmering image. She sheathed her weapons. "Then what is to be done? Must we simply stand by and allow the curse to do its work?"

Rit did not even shake her head. "Mistress Suona, if the image of the Silken Dragon has appeared, then the curse is not effective. It requires assistance."

"Sorcery?" Suona said.

"A mage might counter the curse, my lady, or might provide the means by which a curse could be countered." She made a slight bow. "We had considered this, of course. Locks may be opened, doors may be broken, chains may be cut, and curses countered." She held out her hand, and there was a shining silver throwing-star in it, completely filling the woman's tiny palm. "We will all go, my lady, to aid the dragon. Your pardon."

And she was off towards the main door, hurrying, but using only the proper steps of a palace attendant. As she opened the door, Suona heard sounds of movement from the corridor, and hushed, nervous whispers.

She stood staring at the golden, glowing dragon that still hung before her, then reached out to touch it, cautious. There was no heat, and her hand passed through the dragon's form. She closed her eyes and still saw it.

She didn't stop to dress; the hell with what the other attendants thought. She gathered her courage and strode into the image, then on through, to the door. Then down the corridor, cat-soft, moving swiftly enough to catch up with Rit and her sister-workers. The women were speaking in hushed tones, hissing, and their small hands clutched polite weapons, from tiny jewelled knives to small silver darts that had been decorated with colorful plumes.

She turned her head. The image of the dragon came behind, walking, proud and graceful.

She continued walking at her chosen pace, leaving the small group of women behind. She floated down the corridors, into the balmy night air, sensing. The scent of night-flowers was on the air, and, distantly, she could hear the brook that ran through the Shan's gardens.

She became aware of a golden glow, a golden image, another dragon-messenger. She walked to it, let it lead her into the tombs. The corridor walls were suffused with a deep golden glow, and the myriad curses resonated in sympathy with the Curse of the Silken Dragon, touching Suona's seeking mind with a pulse that possessed all the rhythm and ferocity of a beating heart. It made her nervous, sensitive; the touch of the breeze was like a cascade of freezing water.

The dragon halted suddenly, and reared, and through its glowing image she saw only a shadowy form, and a sudden silver spark.

She dropped, rolling to the opposite wall. A silver shape passed into the dragon's golden form, and stopped dead, falling, landing with a hushed rattle on the stone floor.

A dagger. Suona picked it up as the dragon dropped back, looked at it. A narrow Midlander weapon, with one edge cut in the sawtooth pattern that the Midlanders favored. A fierce weapon. She hooked it onto her weapons harness, drawing her own knife.

She passed through the dragon's image. The door to

the tomb of Nilkir Kon-weh was half-open, the dragon-seal broken. By rights, Vardret Kovair should now be mad or lifeless, yet he seemed sane enough to fight, to attempt to slay either her or the dragon-image. She pressed back against the wall, slid along it. Shuffling sounds and hushed voices declared the arrival of the women with their polite weapons.

She pushed the tomb door, heard nothing, pushed it again, and crossed quickly to the opposite side, waiting for sword or spear or knife. Nothing came.

Probing with all senses, she slipped into the darkness of the tomb. Here was the smell of mildew and dust, the musty, choking flavors of death and luxury caught in the trap of years, and here hid elemental creatures, little, hairy, skittering things that fled from her as she moved. A long-legged globular thing crossed the tomb's outer room with peculiar bouncing strides, passing without hesitation through a faded curtain. She scanned the room, senses now fully adapted to the absence of light, finding only the wilting remains of the Chun's luxury, and displaced dust.

Outside, the hushed voices stopped, gathering, waiting.

Suona crossed to the curtain, silently, drawing her sword, her hand tight within the weapon's ornate basket-hilt. Standing well aside, she probed the curtain.

Vardret Kovair's sword thrust through the cloth, ripping, seeking soft midline and the heart.

Suona slashed, bringing the curtain down as Kovair withdrew and fled deeper into the tomb. She had him now, she thought, and could disarm him, without hurting him too seriously.

Kovair had other ideas. He continued to fade through the tomb, using all the cover he could find, pushing orna-ments and pottery and carvings into Suona's path, keep-ing the Northwoman dodging his sudden sword-thrusts.

Suona avoided striking back in anger; her weapons were designed for thrusting and stabbing rather than chopping and slashing.

Finally, she managed to back Kovair up against a wall. He glared at her over his sword, his stance defensive.

Suona said, "Lay down your sword, Midlander. The Shan will deal reasonably with you."

Kovair's eyes never left her. He was sweating, close to exhaustion, panting like a fat man after a half-mile run. "Will he? Better he slays his enemies than he extends courtesies to them."

"This is a land of courtesy," she said. "You will be expelled. Now throw down your sword."

Hushed voices appeared behind her.

"No!" Kovair bellowed.

And he struck at her, forcing her to parry and duck. Any training that he might have had in the proper use of his sword was forgotten; he whirled his blade like a barbarian beserker, howling as he ran at her.

She backed away, defending frantically, trying to find cover without taking her attention from the beserk trader. If she could but trip him, or cut his leg or foot to topple him—

—and was toppled herself as her heel caught one of the ornaments Kovair had flung aside. Cursing, she fell backwards, throwing herself to avoid Kovair's whining blade, striking a curtain and falling through, automatically rolling and curling up in case Kovair thrust at her. Kovair plunged through the curtain after her, tearing the curtain down, crashing down before she could even raise her weapons, rising as swiftly as lightning, it seemed, his sword raised to strike.

A silver shape hissed through the air, biting into Kovair's shoulder. Blood sprang out, the color of honor, the color of life, and the color of death. His sword struck stone, sparking as it scraped, a foot from Suona. The hushed voices were excited.

She rolled, rose.

Kovair turned, groping at his shoulder, pulling. Blood flowed freely as he pulled Rit Ho-chep's throwing-star from the wound, hurled it at Suona, who easily dodged.

She faced him now, blades held defensively before her. "Surrender," she said. "Now. Or suffer."

The voices chattered, were suddenly silent. Feet shuffled, and the women entered, all in a tight group, polite weapons shimmering.

Gold exploded within the tomb, and Suona saw the stone coffin that enclosed the long-dead form of Nilkir Kon-weh. Kovair gasped and let his sword drop.

And the Silken Dragon lived.

Suona swung, horrified. The red eyes of the dragon glared down at her, past her, at Vardret Kovair. Golden jaws sprang wide in a silent, angry howl.

Kovair pleaded.

The Silken Dragon reared back, and struck as Suona whirled.

She stabbed, her sword piercing Kovair's throat, slaying him before the dragon struck him. Mercy for a doomed man.

Snapping, the dragon took the physical form of Vardret Kovair. The golden throat pulsed once.

The women watched, silent, awed, their polite weapons forgotten.

The Silken Dragon's jaws parted again. Vardret Kovair was gone, swallowed whole, drawn into some netherworld or other, lost forevermore. The beast backed away, ponderous, gorged. The great discs of its eyes blazed red.

Slowly, it bowed its head, as though begging approval.

Amongst the glowing golden scales there looped a shining thread.

She stepped forward, raised her sword, and parted it.

And the Silken Dragon folded silently to the floor, shrinking, its form flattening and changing—

—until it was no more than a silken tapestry, lying all in a bundle on the floor of the tomb.

"If you had let me have my own clothes," Suona said, as Rit attended to the scratches and cuts she had picked up while dodging Vardret Kovair's weaponry, "I would not require *this*." Rit said nothing, but continued swabbing and cleaning. "At least I believe I have a good reason for never going naked into battle. The scratches are a damned nuisance."

"Yes, my lady, of course," Rit said, cleaning a long graze on Suona's thigh.

Suona swore, not caring whether they were sitting in someone's tomb. As far as she was concerned, it might as well have been a tavern in the worst part of Kal-Menelon. "Will you *please* take time? You are supposed to be gentle, not trying to strip me of flesh."

"Yes, my lady," Rit said, continuing without pause.

Suona gave up. Rit was angry at her. Ladies are sweet vessels strewn about the garden or scattered about court. They do not hurtle about naked, fighting sword battles with madmen in the tomb of royalblood, no matter how long dead the royalblood is. Especially not when a curse is in force to take care of intruders, and the women called by the dragon are present, waiting to politely do the job. Now Rit Ho-chep was greatly upset because the woman in question was in her charge. She was, of course, far too polite to display her anger directly.

Suona said, "I think I slew Vardret Kovair before the

dragon struck, little Ho-chep. He was dead when the dragon took him."

"Yes, my lady," said Rit, rubbing.

Suona sighed. "Little Ho-chep, you are a poor friend."

"Yes, my lady." She went onto another scratch, scraping. Suona thought she might have to wear dresses simply to hide the resulting welts.

"Well?" Suona said. "What happened?"

"The dragon took him, my lady, trapping his soul as well as his body, though you slew him. The trader will make a meal in Neverwhen, you see."

"Oh," Suona said. She looked around the tomb. The small army of women called by the dragon had begun tidying things up, replacing fallen things, sweeping up those things that had been broken during the fight.

Rit finished cleaning Suona's injuries, and sat back for a moment, glaring righteously at her charge.

"Well?" Suona said.

"You are less the lady," Rit said.

"I was never a lady from the start, little Ho-chep, though I *did* have a hope of saving the Midlander."

Rit shook her head. "No, my lady, you had no hope of that, kin to the dragon though you may be. The trader was a doomed man; those who offend the dragon do not escape retribution. We would have slain him, if need be, for the dragon, had you not taken him to the dragon within the tomb."

"*Hm*," Suona said. "Enough of this. You're making me wish I was home, with a blizzard, or a man."

"Brrr," Rit said, smiling.

"Brrr, hell," Suona said. "You *should* freeze, you bloody-minded little witch."

She chuckled as she rose, stretching. She started out of the tomb, then stopped and went back, for a look at the tapestry that had been hung once more over Nilkir Konweh's stone coffin, the tapestry of the Silken Dragon that had been brought to life by Vardret Kovair.

It might have been her imagination, but the dragon seemed rather well-fed. . . .

DRAGON LORE

STEVE RASNIC TEM

ILLUSTRATION BY
VICTORIA POYSER

Suddenly the widow sees dragons,
unnoticed until the husband died,
Ouroboros around the sun.
He'd never have approved.
Seen dancing behind the curtains,
her spangled hands waving, she grew her hair
long, remembered she enjoyed the unplanned
trips and foreign films he detested,
suddenly knew the dance her own body made.

Her children called in doctors
for order and relief. She'd answer
eclipses come from celestial dragons
swallowing the sun or moon. By nature
they assume many resemblances;
mine's a medusa's head, housewife's claws,
tail of a lioness, teats of a sphinx.

Ignorant of its meaning, she travelled
and took new jobs. *They swallow*
pearls for power, invulnerable
to the ordinary. Her last night suffering
she described a raft of Ethiopian dragons
floating out to sea. *I was contemptible*
until they seduced me; in darkness
they burned me. My husband,
he wrestled them all of his life.

EAGLE-WORM

JESSICA AMANDA SALMONSON

ILLUSTRATIONS BY
GLEN EDWARDS

Tamura'nun-pa rose early and went to the longhouse of
Tribal Mother. Many others had come that morning also,
each with a mystic dream. Those men, women, and the
one child who had dreamt upon the preceeding night
ducked into the longhouse. Tamura'nun-pa went last.

There was not much light within Tribal Mother's longhouse. Her several guests sat cross-legged upon the dry,
packed earth. All were silent.

Tribal Mother was old, and lay ill on a bed of moss and
fern. Her hair was long and grey. Her face was very
wrinkled. Tamura'nun-pa thought: How beautiful you
are, Mother, so old and so wise.

Behind where Tribal Mother lay, Medicine Chief leaned
over her. He was upon his knees. There were no more
chants; no more healing herbs; no more dancing to scare
away Owl, Thief of Souls. He had painted one large, silver
tear upon his cheek. It shined in the dimness of the longhouse.

This was the time of waiting. A time of joyous sorrow.
Every member of the tribe was in a heightened state of
awareness. There were many dreams.

Tribal Mother raised herself with an effort and the help of Medicine Chief. There was pain on her face a moment, and then it passed. Medicine Chief continued to hold her up, for she was very weak. Medicine Chief's visage was serene. He never spoke. He had vowed one moon of silence four days earlier.

"Tell me your dreams," her dry, weary voice said. The young man sitting nearest obeyed:

"In my dream I went to fish without a net. I called the fish to shore with a song. It was a fine day for fishing so. As I cut and dried my catch, I found a pearl in the belly of a strange yellow fish. I ate the pearl. Then I was able to walk on the bottom of the sea."

Medicine Chief's face revealed that he, too, was impressed. Tribal Mother said, "Yours is a powerful dream. It means you will be a great fisher for our people. I will rename you Many-Fish, and send you on a quest. You must go North and North until you meet the Walrus King. If he judges you courageous, he will give you wisdom."

Many-Fish stood with his new name, and with wonder in his eyes. He went away. It would be many moons before anyone of the tribe saw him again.

"You have dreamed too, little one?" Tribal Mother asked of the womanchild who scooted closer. The child nodded, reverent. She said,

"There was a big hole in the ground. I was not afraid to enter. I walked through many Countries-Under-the-Earth. Then there was a white forest, white for lack of sun. In a clearing I heard Grizzly Bear and Coyote conversing. Grizzly Bear said, 'Even I am not strong enough.' Coyote said, 'It is too cruel a trick for me to play.' Together they said, 'We will make a new and powerful Totem animal.' Then Grizzly Bear mounted Coyote. As they copulated, they made sounds like a storm."

Everyone was silent in the longhouse. This was an awesome dream. Even Tamura'nun-pa could interpret it: It was the dream of a warrior. Tribal Mother covered her mouth during the telling, and cried long streams of tears. Then she held the child close to her and patted her back. "You must go and play," said Tribal Mother. "You must play while you can."

The child tugged respectfully at one long, grey strand of Tribal Mother's hair. Then she went off to play.

All of the dreams were important ones. One by one, Tribal Mother told each of the dreamers their destinies with the tribe. Finally all had gone away but Tamura'nun-pa, who looked at how tired Tribal Mother appeared after this busy morning and she so near to Owl. Medicine Chief helped her lie down again. She turned her head, and Tamura'nun-pa saw how bright and cheerful were the old woman's clear, black eyes. Tamura'nun-pa imagined she would be happy, too, if her dying brought so much magic to the tribe in a single night.

"One more dreamer," said Tribal Mother, her voice grown softer and far away. "You are Tam, my sister's daughter."

Tamura'nun-pa nodded. She said, "I fear my dream is insignificant compared to the grand ones I have heard told this morning. I dreamed simply that I held a basket in my hands. It was not a very large basket. In the basket was a small world: river, trees, lake. I was very careful with the basket."

Tribal Mother looked quickly to Medicine Chief. Their eyes held one another for a long while. Tribal Mother touched Medicine Chief's hand and patted it. The painted, silver tear below Medicine Chief's eye glistened. Tribal Mother said to the young woman,

"Your quest, Tam-of-my-Sister, is of immediate concern. You must go to the Valley of Firs. There you must seek Eagle-Worm for your vision. If you return, you will be made Tribal Mother. If you fail, we are in the hands of War Child, and she is yet too small to be strong.''

Tamura'nun-pa was badly shaken when she went into the startling brightness of the day. She spoke to no one. She gathered necessities into a basket, which she tied to her back. Then she left, toward the Valley of Firs.

There were many days and many camping places between the tribe's peninsular homeground and the inland Valley of Firs. Along the way, Tamura'nun-pa found much to eat. Near the first night's camp was a swamp. The swamp was demon-haunted, but she shouted them away as she dug roots of cattails. These she wrapped in leaves of swamp-cabbage, and roasted them together. The smell would frighten predators, but the taste was very good.

Another day she passed through a country rich in berries, several kinds. She also captured a large number of tree frogs and swallowed them whole. It was a good season for a quest.

This was the first quest of Tamura'nun-pa. Because it was expected that all among her people would follow dream-destinies and seek visions from Totem beasts, it was not strange to her that the rhythm of her day-to-day life was so altered: no fishing today, no gathering mushrooms tomorrow, no tending the big fire for tribal feasts. No making or mending baskets. In truth, her days would have felt more disrupted had she gone another season without quest or vision. It was part of growing. "It is my time," she said to herself, and that was all.

The hills were rugged. Sometimes she found huge landslides had sealed roads she had heard would provide easy passage. At times like these, she would be forced to climb

over, or try an unproven route. On one of the latter
occasions, she discovered herself on a trail that was barely
wide enough for her feet, a sheer drop to her right.

The ledge was too narrow. She could not go on. She
stopped and clung to the wall, unable to make herself
move. She thought fearfully: If I take one more step, I will
fall.

Then before her was a mountain goat. She had not seen
him come. He stood close enough to touch, though she
was afraid to move to do so. A huge buck, he had a long
coat of heavy white fur and thick, ivory horns curling in
upon themselves. He regarded the woman who stood on
his path, and she regarded him.

"If there is room for his four legs," thought
Tamura'nun-pa, "there is room for my two."

Though she would not have thought it possible, the
mountain goat turned full circle on the ledge. Then he put
his forelegs against the sheer face and began to climb
straight up! Tamura'nun-pa followed close behind. Her
hands and feet used the niches and protrusions the goat's
cloven hooves revealed. Now and then, he would look
down at her with intense yellow eyes. Tamura'nun-pa
knew that Eagle-Worm, too, had yellow eyes. "Are you
sent by Eagle-Worm to guide me?" she asked. There was
no reply.

Her legs were tightly muscled. The dark flesh of her back
rippled with the strength beneath. The heights made her
giddy. Her basket was light as air. She fancied herself
mighty—and her mightiness was tested.

When she reached easier ground, the mountain goat
was gone. She never saw the buck again, but sent
thoughts of kindness and gratitude after him. He had
taught her how to climb.

On the night of another day, she slept in a shallow cavern. Fishhook-shaped formations grew out of the ceiling. Bats clung to some of these. She hung her basket from one. The floor was dirtied with bat droppings, but she found a clean spot. She lay down to rest.

Her slumber was disturbed by . . . she did not know what. There were no bats here now: they were gone on moonlight sorties. She felt the cavern's emptiness, yet knew she was not truly alone. In the dark, she scrabbled for her two knives. She found only one.

"Who is there?" she asked the darkness. Her voice echoed; there was no other answer.

Against the stars which shone at the cavern's mouth, a black shape arose! It was hunched, formless, and ugly.

"Away, Demon!" Tamura'nun-pa commanded, disguising a quaver in her voice. The demon did not obey as did those which lived in the swamp. She raised her short knife against the approaching shape. It loomed nearer, nearer, until she saw . . . she saw her other knife in its malformed hand!

Tamura'nun-pa leapt up from the floor, projected herself against the demon, clung to the arm which bore the weapon. The demon had little substance, for all its bulk. She outweighed it. She was stronger. She wrestled the demon into the ground. Soundlessly, it melded back into the dung of the bats. Tamura'nun-pa reclaimed her knife. She breathed heavily and alone. She had defeated the demon! Were she a shaman, she might have captured it for her magic bag. As it was, she was glad merely to be safe.

The bats woke her the next morning, returning from their night's excursions and fighting noisily over roosts. Uncertain if her own adventure had been dream or reality, Tamura'nun-pa continued on her way, thinking: Dreams *are* reality.

Three days later, she stood on a hillside overlooking the Valley of Firs.

There, the trees were larger than any she had ever seen. However, from above, the perspective was unusual: the valley looked small, because the firs were so large. She could see over the tops of trees, and did not fully imagine their size. Halfway across the roof of trees, she spied a nest. It was so gigantic it used seven of the tallest trees for pillars. It was the nest of Eagle-Worm.

The walls of the valley were steep. She took a hemp rope from her basket and used it to get down, stage by stage. As she descended into the valley, the trees seemed to be rising, as though they were growing at a visible pace. As this was not possible, she thought instead that she must be shrinking.

Smaller and smaller became Tamura'nun-pa, until the forest loomed around her. Soon she was no larger than a hare. Then a vole. Finally, a cricket. "How can it be," she asked of the valley, "that one as small as I has come to stand before Eagle-Worm?" She thought of her simple existence along the sea, of the duties she performed daily with her tribe. She performed each task with pride and self assurance. Those tasks did not seem lesser than the one now set before her. She felt very proud, and brave. Eagle-Worm would welcome her as a friend.

The undergrowth of the forest floor was so thick that there was limited choice of paths. She followed the trail of a deer she had startled. When she looked up, it was like being in the longhouse of all gods. Each brace was an incredible Totem pole.

Although the valley had looked small from above, after a full day's travel she knew the vastness of her environment. Late in the evening, she had traversed barely half the valley's length. She came to the nest's first pillar.

She slept that night at the foot of a fir whose trunk was as big around as her tribe's entire settlement. Were the trees hollow, all her tribe could live comfortably within.

It rained that night, but high above, the nest served as roof to shelter her.

The next morning, she began to climb.

She strapped her basket firmly to her back, and used the two flint knives to climb as would the cougar. The ridged bark provided many toeholds.

Up and up she went. "I will not fall," she told herself. She was half convinced. "I am brave and strong." Only once did she look down. The sight was very frightening. She closed her eyes and clung to the side of the tree with knives and toes, until the dizziness passed. There was still half the way to go.

It was more harrowing than she had guessed. "Perhaps," she considered privately, "I am not so brave." She could not have made it at all but for the lessons of the mountain goat.

Once, there was a wind. Were she on level ground, it would seem scarcely a breeze. But on the precarious climb, even a breeze felt to be a hurricane sent to rip her from her hold and dash her to the ground. The wind went away as swiftly as it had come, leaving her chilled but undefeated.

Later, she was visited by a woodpecker, who withdrew larvae from beneath the bark where her knives had cut. "Lazy bird!" she said to it. "Foolish girl!" it said in turn, and so startled her that she nearly let go of the tree. It flew away in a hurry, chattering laughter, leaving her to ponder its brief lecture. It was a magic valley, she reminded herself. She should not be amazed that birds could speak.

In the stories of her people's origins, it was said that Coyote was the Maker, but that Wolf was a better friend. It was said that Beaver taught the people to fish and make longhouses, and that Grizzly Bear brought strength in war. In those early days of creation, Eagle-Worm taught her tribe to make baskets. But like Coyote, Eagle-Worm could be an enemy. She made lightning and big winds beneath her wings. She made floods with her tears. She was a test of valor to the heros of every epic. She never forgave those who failed her tests.

As Tamura'nun-pa approached the heavenly nest, she could well believe none but Eagle-Worm taught basket-making. Smaller trees had been bent and woven like wicker into an immense bowl. The design was finely planned. White-trunked trees were interspersed with brown trunks and red trunks so that the design was pleasing, although the pattern resolved into a tangle of untrimmed branches as she climbed nearer. Tamura'nun-pa was awed by the thought of a power that could bend trees into baskets.

Now the nest was a roof directly above her head. She could see how it rested atop the other major firs in the distance.

The nest was too tightly woven to climb up between the logs. She would have to climb out to the rim. Limbs had been left on the trunks which would provide hand-holds. It would be no easy task, however. Already her muscles ached to the edge of endurance. Before starting, she sat on a relatively small limb of the giant fir and rested, rubbing her arms. She felt insignificant on her perch, looking at the grandeur of the vast valley; but in another way, she felt supremely important to have survived to this place.

Afraid her muscles would stiffen if she rested longer, Tamura'nun-pa risked cramps and went onward. She climbed through the tangle of branches on the underside of the nest. It seemed they were left on the trunks precisely for mortal usage.

Eventually she met the bottom ridge of the bowl, and began to crawl upward, hand over hand. Here, the limbs had been sheered off. Still, it was easy to climb up logs. It was so easy that she became oversure of herself. A strip of bark pulled loose in her hand. She fell!

One end of the bark remained attached. Tamura'nunpa swung at its end, dangling so far in the sky that the underbrush on the floor of the forest appeared a smooth carpet. The basket fell loose from her back and spun earthward, vanishing to a pinpoint before she could see it land.

Back and forth she swung, sweat bursting from every pore, dripping down her arms, her belly, her legs; stinging her eyes. Her heart threatened to tear a hole in her chest. Above, the bark peeled off a little more and let her drop another arm's length.

The bark made little ripping sounds as she climbed upward, slowly, with slick palms. Finally she regained the solidity of the nest's outer wall, and clung until the air had dried her cold, quivering flesh.

Then, to her surprise, she discovered that her near-brush with death had emptied out the last of her fear. Now her resolve carried her on, certain of her quest. At last she stood at the top of Eagle-Worm's home. Nothing could harm her now!

She looked across the expanse of the nest in amazement. In the nest was another forest. At first she thought it was only the tips of the pillar trees poking through. But there were too many trees for that. The nest looked much deeper than was possible. Far below, within the confines, there was a stream. It ran into a small lake in the distance.

The nest, covering the distance of seven widely spaced giant firs, was as big as the entire peninsula upon which her people lived. There was room within for much life and activity. But she did not enter the world she saw.

She had long known, by the lessons of her elders, that there were worlds within worlds within worlds, all ruled by Totem animals. Some of these worlds were very similar to her own. Others were entirely different. Some of them were one and the same with her own world, only far in the past or future.

It was easy to enter such worlds. But no one could return without the guidance of a Totem creature. Tamura'nun-pa must await permission to enter, and assurance of return. She must await Eagle-Worm.

When she came, Eagle-Worm first appeared to be a large bird over the Valley of Firs. But she was not a bird, and she was not over the valley. She was way atop the mountains, and she was larger than large. With each passing moment, her astonishing size grew more evident. Fearless, Tamura'nun-pa sat on the nest's rim.

When Eagle-Worm was close enough to discern features, Tamura'nun-pa saw that between the feathered wings was the body of a sleek lizard. Some tribes called Eagle-Worm the Lizard of Fire. Others called her Thunderbird. But Eagle-Worm was the most appropriate. The body had silvery scales. The neck was long and red underneath. She had two spiky tails. The wings were white as mountain peaks. Her feet were like a predatory bird's. The head sported horns like a mountain goat.

Eagle-Worm alighted without stirring the smallest of winds. The deity towered over the woman, but somehow was not threatening. Tamura'nun-pa was spent of fear, and did not quake, though her mouth hung open as she peered up, up into one placid, yellow eye. There was something in that gaze that suggested affection, as of a mother for her child. A bright blue tongue, forked at its end, licked out and touched the woman lightly. "I know you," said Eagle-Worm. "It is good to see you again."

This confused Tamura'nun-pa. She had never visited Eagle-Worm before. Eagle-Worm read these thoughts. "You would not remember," she said. The deep, womanly voice was surprisingly gentle to have issued from so huge a being. She explained, "It was lives and lives ago—perhaps in other worlds. But you are the one. You brought law to your people after the creation. You were White Buffalo Woman."

Tamura'nun-pa felt her heart stop a moment. The name gave her a feeling of ancient sorrows, a nostalgia which she could not understand.

"What do you wish of me, White Buffalo Woman?" asked Eagle-Worm. She spoke as though this one woman could command gods. She said, "It is yet many generations before you are truly tested. Meanwhile, I serve you."

"I . . . I am chosen to be Tribal Mother. I have come to you for my vision."

The birdlike lizard seemed to smile, but may only have shown her teeth. She said, "Your vision has already begun." She stretched out a great white wing to sever Tamura'nun-pa's vision from the forest in the nest. When the wing folded again, the forest was gone. There was only the floor of the nest, vacant and woven of logs. The wing moved in front of her view again. This time, she saw a peninsula with a stream running into the sea, and a familiar place of longhouses and friendly fires. The wing blocked her vision once more, then parted like a curtain to reveal the peninsula again, but horribly changed. The buildings were not like longhouses, but were tall as the giant firs, and perfectly rectangular. There were no trees. The sea had changed color.

"I give you a present," said Eagle-Worm. A white feather dropped from a wing. It was thrice as long as Tamura'nun-pa was tall, but it weighed nothing. She held

"Eagle-worm alighted without stirring the smallest of winds."

it aloft. Eagle-Worm said, "Leap, my sister. Leap into the world you see."

"You will bring me back?" the woman asked. The word of Eagle-Worm could be trusted. But the promise must be had.

"You will return to your time and people," Eagle-Worm assured.

Tamura'nun-pa jumped from the lip of the gigantic nest. She hung from the middle of Eagle-Worm's feather. Down she drifted toward the world within the nest. The walls of the nest rose all around her, then vanished in mist. Below, the Forest-of-Great-Buildings loomed, hideous as a dream of doom.

When she reached the ground, the feather had shrunk to the size of any bird's.

Tamura'nun-pa stood on something more solid than ground. She bent to touch it. It was stone: grey, unchanging, and stretching between the buildings without end. "Where is moss?" she asked aloud. "Where are mushrooms and ferns?"

A small, malignant creature stared at her from a heap of garbage, its back hunched and its tail ragged. The woman whispered fearfully, "Where are the creatures of the land?"

No one answered her. The tall buildings glowered at her balefully, their windows like eyes. She could not understand them.

She walked at the edge of the stone road. Over its center, herds of raving beasts roared to and fro. In the belly of each beast sat a terrified, ghostly human.

There were other people on the street, but they did not see her. They were heavily clad in odd clothing. All of them had faces and hands pale as death. Everywhere, she saw death. Everywhere, the people were ghosts.

The air stank. Everything was filthy. One small tree grew like a feeble mockery of vanished forests, from a perfectly and puzzlingly round hole in the stone ground. Was it the sole, pitiable survivor of the verdant lands Tamura'nun-pa had known?

She wandered, stricken of her senses, until she saw a stranger who might have been of a neighboring tribe. One eye was cut and swollen. He dressed like the ghosts. His hair was long and black and dirty. He sat in the corner of a stairwell moaning. He needed to see Medicine Chief. He was half asleep and dreaming. He needed to see Tribal Mother. There was something in his hand, held at an angle so that its content was spilling out. It looked like water but smelled vile. Tamura'nun-pa bent to straighten the container. The man smelled too.

He stirred. He opened his eyes one at a time, the swollen one second.

"Where are our people?" Tamura'nun-pa asked. "Where are our tribes?"

The man pressed himself against the wall, whacking himself on the back of the head in the process. He held up one hand, as against a brilliant and destructive light. He chanted a song Tamura'nun-pa only partially understood. If she did not know all his words, she knew his meaning:

"I am your people
I am all that lives
Go from me, Spirit of All Our Ancestors
Do not gaze on what the people have become."

Tamura'nun-pa ran through endless narrow valleys of concrete and steel. She sped that way, this way, up one blocked corridor—a cul-de-sac—and back again. She stopped. She started another way. Lungs aching, Tamura'nun-pa ran on and on. She could find no way home. Her mind reeled. She was sick.

Metal beasts screamed like wounded, mammoth geese. Behind their ice-sheet eyes sat the swallowed ghost-people, clinging uselessly to medicine wheels. Their expressions were bleary. They were less real than the demon who had risen from bat dung.

Was all she beheld merely one of many worlds, not her own? Or was this what her world was to become? Was this the future of her land and people?

What trials would be set for War Child! What agony for Tribal Mothers to come! How often must Medicine Chiefs lose against Owl! .

This was the trick more wicked than Coyote could conceive.

The foe too horrible for Grizzly Bear to consume.

The rent in the world which only War Child could enter.

The forest white for lack of sun.

White Buffalo Woman ran screaming for Eagle-Worm: "Take back the vision! It is not yet my time!"

She looked skyward in despair—the sky a narrow, hazy band. There, a white and silver cloud had taken the shape of Eagle-Worm. The first red of sunset was the color at her throat. Sworls of clouds made the horns upon her head. Ethereal mountains of mist were her wings. She looked down between the skyscrapers, as from another place in time, her gaze upon Tamura'nun-pa. Eagle-Worm wept bitter tears. But there was no flood to cleanse the land of villainy. There was only a sour rain.

"I am too weak!" the woman cried, arms held upward to no avail. Black hair hung wild across her tormented features. The gift of Eagle-Worm was a white gash in her hair. Her shouting echoed between the unnatural escarpments: "I am not the one! I am Tamura'nun-pa, not White Buffalo Woman!"

The winds in the sky blew Eagle-Worm away.

Tamura'nun-pa fled past people who did not see her. She pushed at people who did not move. She screamed in faces that did not hear. The utter futility of her flight burst torturously from her lungs in a maddened, frustrated lament. She would have cursed the land were it not already done. She thought: I will uncurse it instead!

The white feather of Eagle-Worm hung down the back of her head. It began to glow like a pearly dagger. About Tamura'nun-pa there grew an aura of light. Silence engulfed the whole of a city which the moment before had impinged upon sanity with its constant, self-pitying groan. In the recess of the woman's mind, a voice spoke, and it was her own voice, but deep like Eagle-Worm's:

"I can destroy the world!"

Her aura began to pulse and grow. Tamura'nun-pa knew that the light of her would melt away the dream. The world would cease to be—how many aspects of the world, she did not know, for every world was part of the whole, and the whole was a dream.

"Hold, my sister," Eagle-Worm said, gently and far away. Her voice soothed and cured the madness. "It is yet many lives to come that you will rise and conquer. It must not yet be done."

The light drained out of her, and Tamura'nun-pa stood in the remaining silence, the silence of her own despair. She did not think she would ever go from this spot, but would stand, deathly as the city and the ghosts who lived within.

Then, one agile movement caught her eye—strange amidst the slow, dreamy procession of ghost-people. An old woman leapt from a dark alley. It was Tribal Mother! She was laughing. She was strong. Her arms reached out to comfort.

Tamura'nun-pa rushed into the old woman's arms.

"How are you here, Tribal Mother?" she asked, sobbing, tugging with two fingers at a grey lock. "Have you died?"

"Soon Owl shall take me, for now I dream my last. From our deaths comes great magic! I dream Eagle-Worm sends me to fetch you home. I have never dreamed so mighty!"

Tamura'nun-pa thought: If in our deaths comes great magic, there is hope even here, where death abounds. "Help me, Tribal Mother. I wish to bounce War Child on my knee and pray she finds peace. I wish to see Many-Fish fill baskets with his catch, to know our people will never hunger, to share the wisdom he gains from Walrus. I wish a moon of silence with Medicine Chief to count my griefs. I wish my burden to be small."

"Come, then, Tam-of-my-Sister. You shall have all your wishes but one. I will take you home."

THE DRAGON OF DUNLOON

ARTHUR DEMBLING

ILLUSTRATIONS BY
DILEEN MARSH

> In the Western Islands they believe that the
> magic of fairy music is so strong that whoever
> hears it cannot choose but follow the sound.
> . . . It is a beautiful idea that the Irish airs, so
> plaintive, mournful and tear-compelling, are but
> the remembered echoes of the spirit music which
> had the power to draw souls away to the fairy
> mansions and hold them captive by the sweet
> magic of the melody.
>
> —Lady Wilde, *Ancient Legends of
> Ireland*

There was only one pub in Dunloon—a music pub. Day
and night, rain or shine, there was always a musical session
going on; a fiddle, a tin whistle, even Uilleann pipes if you
were lucky. That's what brought me there with my
notebooks and my battery-run tape recorder and my
membership card from the Dorchester Gaelic Music Soci-
ety: I was out to capture the "real stuff." There would be
no smiling Irish eyes, no overalls in the chowder, no lep-

rechauns, no begorrahs and, under no circumstances, any Danny Boys.

I stumbled on Dunloon by pure accident. The village, less than twenty houses and Russell's Pub, was not on any road map I had ever seen. Intellectually I knew I was on the west coast of Ireland, in the county of Clare, midway between Galway and Limerick, but emotionally I felt as if I'd fallen into a fairy ring or a cave inhabited by the Tuatha-de-Danaan. The cold Atlantic, it seemed to me, was my only link with the outside world and its reality.

Dunloon itself was one mile inland. A narrow road rolled a mile from the village to the strand. Looking south you could see the Cliffs of Moher and looking west, if the day was clear, you could see Inisheer, the smallest of the Aran Islands.

Like a modern Tir-na-oge, Dunloon was inhabited by descendants of the ancient Sidhes, beings midway between angels and men who enjoyed perpetual youth, music and joy, and never knew sickness and death. It seemed to me that the people of Dunloon had just those qualities.

After I'd been in Dunloon nearly a month and had recorded miles of music, I was raised to the strange status of 'inside outsider.' At first I had been made to feel like an intruder, but eventually I found myself completely ignored, which was perfect. I could take the recorder out and prepare to tape a session at one of Russell's tables, barge in on them, hook up the recorder and thrust my arm, with the microphone, in amongst the musicians, and my intrusion was tolerated. Frequently the players were curious to hear what they sounded like afterwards, and I would rewind the tape and play it back for them, but inevitably they were disappointed. My small machine made them sound as if they were playing inside a trash can that was placed next to a hydroelectric turbine. It didn't matter to me. I was capturing the "real stuff," and if it was a little scratchy, well, I had my memory to fall back on.

One afternoon, when the musicians had just finished a tune and I was about to rewind the tape, a man who looked like a kind of withered homunculus flung himself through the front door of the pub. It was old Seamus Killderry, his hand upon his chest and gasping for air.

Seamus Killderry was not only very old, he was also very short, barrel-chested and slightly hunched. On most occasions he was also very drunk.

"I swear I'll never touch another drop! As God is my witness, I'm on the wagon for good. Bejaysus and various saints have mercy!"

Flailing his arms, trying to catch his wind, Seamus stumbled to our table on his spindly legs and collapsed into a chair. His wild eyes bulged from deep wrinkled sockets, his head twitched and he looked over his shoulder now and then, as though he were being followed.

"I swear I'll . . ." Seamus began again.

"There'll be no bloody swearin' in this bloody pub!" warned Billy Russell from behind the bar.

"After what I've just witnessed," Seamus went on, "I'll never let another drop pass these lips! I swear it! Oh, Lord, have mercy on a poor sinner!"

With that he dropped to his knees, begging the heavens for redemption.

"I'm through with drink, if that's the likes of what it puts before a mortal's eyes. Billy! Billy! Pour me one last pint, for Jaysus' sake, I think I'm dyin' man!"

The men at the table got him back to his chair, and it took the better part of three pints to calm him down.

"It was big, the biggest thing I ever laid eyes on . . . A-a-and it was breathin' fire, I tell ya."

Intuitively, I pressed the 'record' button.

"What in blazes are you on about, Killderry?" thundered Billy Russell.

"Right off the strand, I'm tellin' ya. I seen it with me own eyes . . . another pint, Billy!"

"You'll pay for this one . . ."

"A dyin' man, pay for his . . . Ah, the Divil!"

"I'll get it," said Finbar. He put down his concertina and reached into his pocket. "What was it exactly that you saw out there, Killderry?"

"Well, boys," Seamus said. A sly sparkle escaped his eye, and I wondered if anyone noticed it. "Well, boys, I'm not sure exactly what it was . . . But I'd bet me last penny . . ."

Killderry licked his lips and his bloodshot eyes skipped from one listener to the other. I could see he was in deadly earnest as he took off his cap and held it with both hands between his knees.

"I'd bet me last penny . . . it was a sea dragon . . . a monster of the deep!"

Without thinking, I burst out laughing, but it didn't take long for me to realize that I was the only one amused. The whole pub was silent as a tomb, and the odd pervasive atmosphere of fear and curiosity made me feel my laughter was a grave social error.

"What . . . What was its face like?" Billy asked timidly.

"It was the ugliest thing I ever laid eyes on. Its face was all green and gnarled and nasty, and smoke and fire belched forth from the top of its head."

There was nodding and mumbling. The drinkers began to ask more questions and before long Killderry found himself bombarded by serious inquiries concerning the size and the nature of his sea dragon. Seamus was plied with drinks, as if everyone was trying to loosen him up so that his answers would be all the more outlandish. Yet with each response he uttered, his reliability seemed less in question.

The inhabitants of Russell's Pub, wrapped up in their own fear and wonder, appeared deliberately to be trying to scare the wits out of themselves and, of course, for every pint they bought for old Killderry, they each had one as well. It wouldn't do to let the man drink alone.

"Purple scales all up and down its body!"

"Sweet Christ!"

"And three huge fins on its back!" Killderry said, making a nervous arc with his arm before his face.

"Mother of God, what shall we do?"

Billy Russell took charge immediately. Wouldn't it be best if we spread the alarm? Wouldn't it be wise to summon the police, Father O'Neil, and the Guiness representative? Shouldn't every able-bodied man who could bring a weapon assemble at the pub and proceed to the strand . . .

Feeling compelled to say something before things got out of hand, I moved the microphone as unobtrusively as I could toward Killderry.

"Are you sure it was a sea dragon?"

Everyone looked at me as if I had lost my mind.

"Is he sure?" Finbar said to me. "Do you not realize that Seamus Killderry is acknowledged to be one of Ireland's leading experts on sea dragons, deep sea monsters and other amphibious menaces?"

"No, I . . . I wasn't aware of that, I . . ."

"All right," Billy said, dismissing me as an idiot. "I'll ring up the police. I want you men to round up everyone you see and bring them back here . . . Has anyone got any sand bags? Good! Bring as many as you can—by God, we'll make a fortress out of this place if we must . . ."

The pub came alive with activity. When the sand bags arrived, they were piled into barricades in front of the windows and all the doors except the main entrance. The surrounding hillsides were flecked by little carts loaded with men, undoubtedly headed for Billy Russell's pub, and soon they trickled in carrying pikes, shovels and brooms upon their shoulders—a ragged militia, but a determined one.

The assemblage in the pub grew. Father O'Neil arrived, and shortly after him George Harrington, the Guinness representative; they shook hands all around, slapped backs and inquired of everyone's health. A grim nervousness developed, but it was not enough to stop the men from drinking nor to prevent a strong tenor from singing a tragic love ballad. As for Billy, he was behind the bar, as busy as a chipmunk. We would wait, he announced after a time, for the arrival of the police, and then spring into action.

"Seamus," I said, hoping to ferret out some truth, "if you are an expert on sea dragons, why were you so frightened when you saw it?"

He looked at me incredulously, then patiently explained . . .

"Son, the more I learn about them, the more I fear them. Besides, I've never made contact with one so close to home."

A few people had gathered to listen. Killderry, resting the hand that held a brimming pint lightly on his knee and tugging on his earlobe, took on the aspect of the sage, we the disciples. An Irish Buddha holding his lotus blossom, a pint of stout.

"Let me explanetate . . . There are two kinds of sea dragons: the large kind and the not so large—or small— kind. The large sort can usually be found in and around the

Mediterranean Sea, for as you know, in the warmer latitudes things grow larger, on account of the curious combination of heavy rainfall and great amounts of sunshine . . ."

Heads nodded and mouths grunted in agreement. I made sure the microphone was close—I didn't want to miss any of this.

"What with all that sunshine and rain coming together like that, things grow all out of proportion, and it's difficult for those things to get up the energy of mind to do much of anything. Their heads and bodies grow so big, and the bone that encases the brain grows so thick it's quite impossible for them to think straight. So mostly the large sort of sea dragon splashes about, looking very ferocious, but basically he's harmless . . ."

"Is this one of the large kind?" Finbar asked.

"Bejaysus no! That's why I took the fright of the Divil. No, I'm afraid we are in for some trouble, lads. This is one of the small sort."

Seamus' tone was pensive, but his green eyes were dancing.

"Yes, a great deal of trouble. Because the small sort, instead of having a well developed body, has a well developed brain. He's a wiley creature. We shall have to outsmart him or he will surely get the better of us. You see, he's from the northern climates, where they get a lot of rain and wind and cold, but very little sunshine. He's had to live by his wits and that makes him a formidable foe."

I could see the old fool had them right in the palm of his hand. They seemed perfectly willing, even anxious, to believe all his sea dragon drivel. Of course, I never believed for a second that there was anything down at the strand. Old Killderry had to have conjured the whole thing up out of his soused up imagination. His next statement confirmed it to me . . .

"Now, to be sure, I didn't get a close-up look at it, but from where I stood, and from my prior experiences with such phenomena . . . I'd say it was a Scot."

"A Scot?"

"Yes. Probably a relation to . . ." he looked around and seemed to hiss . . . "a relation to the monster of Lock Nessss!"

"Why, the bloody Presbyterian!!" Finbar shouted, rolling up his sleeves and putting up his dukes. "It's how many hundreds of years now, and the damned ghost of King Billy is still after makin' a bloody nuisance of himself, ravaging the shores of Holy Erin!"

At that point a presence was felt in the pub. We looked toward the door and saw that Sergeant Burke of the constabulary had arrived, and he was given a hearty welcome. I, for one, felt it was time to end this ridiculous episode. Now that the police were on the case, I had no doubt it would be cleared up in no time, and I could get back to taping the music, which had stopped completely.

"Afternoon, Officer Burke," Billy said, after coming round the bar to shake hands.

"Afternoon, Billy."

"Fine day."

"Aye, lovely."

"The wife?"

"Coming along nicely, after a bad bout with the sneezes."

"Glad to hear it."

"The pub?"

"Never better."

"So I see."

I tugged Billy's sleeve and whispered that wasn't it time to get on with the sea dragon.

"To everything a time and place," he said pompously,

before turning to Burke. "Ah, the youth today—so impatient!"

"And irresponsibile," said Burke.

"I suppose you see a lot of irresponsibility in your line of work, Burke."

"I do. I'll tell you, Billy, it's getting out of control, the youth situation. Absolutely no sense of values. The concept of truth is not to be found in a one of them. They resort to fabrication at a whim. It means nothing to them to falsify the truth to save their own necks, or just to play a prank."

"Sad."

"Yes."

"The old virtues have gone to seed."

"They have."

"Honesty? You don't find it anymore."

"No, you don't."

Father O'Neil came up and offered his greetings to Burke. He was followed by the Guinness rep who shook hands with the sergeant and then turned to Billy . . .

"You know, Billy, that in times of crises, floods, famines, strikes and natural disasters, Guinness and Company will always be there, serving the populace and seeing to their needs . . ."

"I knew we could count on you, George."

"Well, now," said Burke, rubbing his hands together, "what seems to be the problem?"

"Well, Officer Burke," Billy said, scratching his chin, "I'm afraid we've got a sea dragon on our hands . . ."

Burke listened to the account, but not from Killderry who was by then snoring loudly and drunkenly in his chair. After a period of ale-filled deliberation, the sergeant said he thought it best that we climb into our vehicles and proceed to the strand, that is, after we had awakened

Killderry, as he was the authority. This took some doing, but we managed to get him up, out of the pub and into one of the many carts that stood in the street in front of the pub.

The rag-tag procession began, Burke leading the way in his squad car, the only motorized vehicle there. By that time I realized that music had become out of the question and I, too, thought the best course of action was to go down to the sea and confront Killderry's hallucination head on. I was itching to see the people's reaction when faced with the rational explanation of his delirium. Killderry woke from his stupor moments before we reached the strand. The wagons crept over the last rise in the road and as we headed down to the beach we saw it, about two hundred yards offshore, and Seamus began pointing and shouting.

I had expected to see nothing at all. In fact, what I saw bobbing there in the water was better than nothing, because it was visible proof that there was no sea dragon.

We all piled out of the carts and stood on a little hill above the water. We had a clear view of the thing. It was, in substance, a three-masted pleasure yacht, a big one to be sure, but a yacht nonetheless. Killderry's three great fins were sails and the smoke that belched forth from his creature's mouth emerged from a round pipe which, I supposed, led to some sort of heating system for the craft. Where Killderry had seen the purple scales and the nasty green face was somewhat beyond me. But it was a boat. Soon, I thought, relieved, we would all be back at the pub, drinking, laughing and listening to music.

"My God!"

"A sea dragon!"

"Jesus Christ in Heaven!"

"Whatever shall we do!"

Killderry shrugged. Now that his reports were confirmed, he seemed content to let the police handle the affair. He lay down, all curled up like a hedgehog and fell asleep with his head against a rock. As for me, I waited for Burke to restore some sanity to the business.

"Now, calm down everyone," the sergeant said. "There's no need to panic. We can best meet this threat if we all remain calm and collected."

He apparently meant to break the news to them gently.

"What do you intend to do about it?" demanded Billy.

"Nothing to be done about it."

"What do you mean nothing!!"

"Billy, I'm afraid that it's out of my jurisdiction."

"What is this nonsense about jurisdiction?"

"That's correct. I am only empowered to handle breeches of law and order, disturbances both civil and criminal, on land. I have no authority at sea. Besides, I can't swim."

"Can't swim?"

"Not a stroke."

Billy scratched his head.

"Well, that puts a different light on the matter . . . Is there anyone here who can swim?"

A lot of mumbling and shuffling of feet followed, but no one spoke up.

"What about a boat?" Billy suggested.

"A boat is a possibility, certainly, but as I said before I have no jurisdiction at sea."

"Well, that puts us in a bind, doesn't it," said Billy. "What do you suggest, Burke?"

"I suggest that we go back to the pub and confer. Besides I am concerned about the distinct possibility of a rampant thirst epidemic."

Since no one appeared to disagree with Burke's analysis, we began piling back into the carts. Everyone, that is, except me. With a sense of creeping paranoia, I decided I'd been the subject of a hoax. The whole episode had to have been cooked up for my benefit. So, for a moment, I decided to play along.

"Wait," I said, "who'll watch the sea dragon? Someone's got to stay here and keep an eye out."

"He's right," Finbar said.

"Killderry," Billy said. "He'll have to watch on the creature." Taking hold of him, Billy shook him for all he was worth. I thought the old geezer's teeth would come clattering out of his mouth before he finally came to and pushed Billy away.

"Ah, the Divil! Why don't you let an old man sleep in peace?"

"You have to stay here and keep an eye out while we go back to the pub and decide what to do."

"Oh I have, have I? Why don't you stay. I'm very thirsty. Sleeping always makes me very thirsty."

"Now see here, Killderry," Burke said strongly, "I'm ordering you to stay put here and keep us posted of any strange movements or disturbances that might occur owing to the presence of the monster. Is that understood?"

"Shite and nonsense! If I stay out here in the fresh air, I'm sure to catch a fatal disease, and my health is not the best to begin with . . ."

"Don't talk rubbish! It's your civil duty!"

"I won't stay . . . You can't leave me out here to die! I'm not a bloody Eskimo that you can just turn me out onto the tundra when his time comes. I'm a Christian, and I demand a Christian burial!"

I wouldn't have minded giving him a proper funeral right then and there myself.

"Perhaps I may offer a suggestion," George Harrington said.

It so happened that George, the Guinness rep, had a case of stout in his car. He was, fortunately, willing to donate it for the preservation of the community. Would Mr. Killderry be willing to man the crow's nest if the case of stout were to be put at his disposal? Mr. Killderry at once became quite civic-minded. He would, he stated, consider it an honor and a privilege to comply with the wishes of the majority.

The case of stout was placed next to the rock, which was already being called Killderry's Pillow, and Father O'Neil blessed it, the rock, and Killderry. At that Billy Russell proposed that the first round of drinks was on the house, and the train of carts, led by the squad car, crept off toward the pub.

I kept looking back over my shoulder, at the sea dragon, and at Killderry, who had already cracked the first bottle.

*   *   *   *   *

Billy Russell's barroom was packed that afternoon. Between the people and the sandbags still piled up in front of the windows, the place was unusually stuffy. Cigarette smoke hung thick and hazy, and pint glasses filled with the black richness of stout dotted the tables. Small, scruffy urchins ran in and out of the pub, ignored by their elders who were concerned with the more serious matter of the sea dragon. Finbar had taken up his concertina and was playing a tune. He was accompanied by a man on the tin whistle. Normally I would have trucked out my tape recorder, but it was too noisy and, besides I was just not in the mood. So I sat at the bar, next to Sergeant Burke with Billy on the other side, and poured pints to beat the Devil.

We drank slowly and quietly, there at the bar, mulling over the situation. Of course, I knew what the problem was: a boat had been mistaken for a sea dragon. To this day I don't know why I didn't make an issue of it and why I held my tongue. I was experiencing a disturbing sense of vertigo; my notions of logic were no good in the face of the people who sat there and discussed the matter in the pub, going right ahead with the assumption that a sea dragon was in their midst. They emulated a concerned group of citizens, interested in the welfare of their community . . . But it was a boat! I knew it was a boat. Their reactions made no sense . . . I got the feeling that if I told them it was a boat, my story would seem more ridiculous to them than their story seemed to me.

Perhaps it was I who had mistaken a dragon for a boat . . .

The ground seemed cut away beneath me, my foundations were crumbling and I began to feel dizzy. I thought a whiskey would settle me down, but it was no good. The only way to get through this was to go along with it. The weight of public opinion, I'm afraid, was too much for me. I felt irritable. The whole thing had lost its sense of delightful absurdity. I thought about the arrival of Officer Burke and his willingness to go along with the perceptions of the villagers, and there gradually crept up in me a feeling of isolation. Obviously, my sense of humor was wearing thin.

Billy leaned across the bar and directed a question to Officer Burke. I pressed the record button, as I had done frequently all day. When the whole thing had blown over, at least I would be sure that it had not been a dream—that it was the "real stuff"—I didn't wholly trust my memory.

"Then, there's nothing the police can do?"

"Nothing."

"But what if the dragon comes on land?"

"A whole 'nother kettle of fish."

"Fish?"

"In that case, I could arrest it."

"On what grounds?" I asked desperately.

"Why, disturbing the peace, creating a public nuisance . . . any number of statutes. But I can do nothing until it comes out of the water . . ."

"By which time," Billy cut in, "we may all be dead. Our homes destroyed!"

"But, but, what if it's not a sea dragon?" I blurted out.

"Don't confuse the issue, young man. We have enough problems as it is without getting into metaphysics."

"Burke," Billy said firmly, "frankly I'm not very satisfied at the manner in which the police are handling this. I want to hear what you propose to do about it."

"Why must I do anything about it?"

"Because if you don't, we'll form a Citizens Committee that will!"

"Just a minute, now, Billy Russell. Just you hold on there! There'll be no talk of taking the law into your own hands, not here. Not while I've got a breath left in me."

Burke turned to me for support.

"Where would we be if everybody thought he could take the law into his own hands? Why, we'd be nowhere—or worse! Everyone would have their own set of rules, their own ideas about morality, truth. And where would we be without truth? We would have anarchy, chaos, socialism! Why, we'd be in worse shape than England!"

"Do you at least have a suggestion?" Billy demanded.

"I do."

"Then let's bloody-well hear it!!"

"All right," said Burke, finishing off his pint. "I propose that we send for the Irish Navy . . ."

There was silence at the bar. Burke searched the men for a response.

'There'll be no talk of taking the law into your own hands . . .'

"Well?"

Billy thumped his fist down on the bar.

"We'll blow it out of the water! By Christ, we'll smash it to Kingdom Come!"

The Irish Navy. It was a marvelous idea. I felt my senses coming back to me. If anyone could spot a boat and tell the difference between it and a sea dragon, it had to be the Navy. I ordered another round for all of us at the bar, sanity and gravity creeping slowly back into my soul.

"How can we reach the Navy?" I asked eagerly.

"Billy has a telephone here. Who's got the correct change?"

"I do!" I shouted joyously.

"Then give him a call."

"Give whom a call?"

"Why, the Irish Navy, you twit!"

"*Him?*"

"Of course, and who else? He'd be in Dublin this time of year, I suspect," said Burke.

The officer took out his pocket watch.

"This time of day . . . I'd say you'll find him in Mulligan's Public House. Why don't you give him a call?"

Like a zombie I walked over to the telephone, my tape recorder hanging by its straps over my shoulder. I dialed the Dublin operator and asked for Mulligan's. I heard little clicks and connections in the receiver, and they signaled the crashing of empires, the fall of Reason, the demise of Science and Civilization. The Apocalypse!

"Is this Mulligan's Public House?"

"It is!"

"Could I . . . eh, speak with the Irish Navy?"

"Well, now, you'll have to hold the line while I check to see if he's still here."

I waited for what seemed like hours, and then . . .

"Hello! Hello!"

"Ah . . . Is this the Irish Navy?"

"Speaking. What can I do for you?"

"Eh . . . I don't know exactly how to put this, I . . . hah! hah! . . . but, you see . . ."

"Out with it, man. I haven't got all day. Me pint's going flat."

"Yes . . . well . . . I'll come to the point, then . . ."

"I wish you would."

"I'm calling from Dunloon, in western Clare, just a little south of . . ."

"I KNOW where the bleeding place is, you soppy bastard!"

"Oh . . . yes, of course . . . well, it seems we've sighted a . . . a sea dragon off Dunloon Strand and we were wondering if you might lend us a hand with it."

"You'll have to be more specific. What do you want me to do with it? Interrogate it? Chase it? Kill it? Go ten rounds with it?"

"Well, we thought that when you got here, you'd be the best judge of that. There seems to be some concern . . ."

"And why wouldn't there be? I suppose this is an emergency, then?"

"You might say that. How soon can you get here?"

"I don't know. I'm just after getting a fresh pint. And I'll have to check the train times to Galway . . ."

"Train?"

"Yes. The boat is in for repairs."

"THE boat?"

"Yes. The boat."

"I see. Sort of, one man one boat, eh?"

"You've got it . . . Look, I'll try to get the next train out of Dublin tonight. Then I'll have to thumb a lift from Galway. Say . . . tomorrow, noontime."

"Fine. We really appreciate this . . ."

"Never mind that. How is that old rascal, Billy Russell?"

"He's well."

"You give him my regards, now, and you tell him I'll see him tomorrow noontime."

Click! And that was that.

"Well?" asked Finbar.

"It's done," I announced to the pub. "He'll be here tomorrow noontime . . . I'd like a double whiskey, Billy."

*   *   *   *   *

I got to the pub before noon with my tape recorder. I wanted to make sure I was there before the Navy arrived. The barroom was in a complete commotion. Everyone in Dunloon was there, and someone had even hung up a banner: Dunloon Welcomes the Irish Navy. Officer Burke sat at the bar next to Finbar, and Billy Russell was a bundle of energy behind the bar, barely keeping up with the volume of business. Cigarette smoke swam heavy in the late morning air of the pub, and people were chattering away in a state of high expectation. Father O'Neil bustled from table to table cautioning moderation, but at times accepting snorts of Jameson when they were offered with wishes for good luck and good health. When the people standing nearest the door began to push back towards the center of the room, we knew the Navy had arrived.

He was an imposing figure, coming in right on time, and standing nearly a head taller than anyone else in the place.

The Irish Navy—in white cap, braids and epaulets, broad as the doorway itself. A smile brilliant and full of confidence peered out beneath a bushy red beard and handlebar moustache, which he twirled roguishly in his fingers; his eyes shone in anticipation of adventure. Swing-

ing his duffle bag off his shoulder and on to the bar, he
roared out at the top of his voice. . . .

"Billy! Billy Russell! How the hell are ya keepin'?"

"By Jaysus it's good to see you!"

Billy began to pour out a pint of stout while we all
crowded around the Navy who laced into his pint while
Billy questioned him about his plans for dealing with the
sea dragon.

"I've got it all figured out, gentlemen," he said. "We
round up five small boats, sail out, meet the bloody bastard head on . . . and harpoon it! Some of us may go
down, that's almost certain, but it can't be helped. There
you have it."

"But, but what if it's not a sea dragon?" I asked meekly.
"What if it's just a little boat?"

The Navy glowered as he looked me up and down and
scratched his beard.

"Well now, young fellow. If it was only a boat you
people wouldn't have called me down here all the way
from Dublin, now would you?"

"No."

"All right, then! Let's not confuse the issue, and let's not
waste any more time. Get those boats assembled. I want
every able-bodied man down at the strand armed with a
weapon he can throw. Is that clear?"

Finbar collared the fisherman who were there, and he
was soon assured of the five boats. Billy organized the men
and their weapons. Father O'Neil blessed our endeavor
and wished us good luck.

Within an hour we were ready to march: twenty-five
stout-hearted warriors with pikes, shovels, rakes, sharp-
ened broom handles, facing the road ahead with grim
determination—Burke, Billy, Finbar, myself and the Navy
leading the column. Suddenly the Navy broke out into
song to lift our hearts and carry us into battle:

Oh, we're off to Dublin
   In the Green, in the Green,
With our helmets glistening in the sun . . .

Soon everyone was singing:

At the rising of the moon,
   At the rising of the moon,
With your pikes upon your shoulders,
   At the rising of the moon.

By the time we hit the last rise in the road, we were ready for anything. The Navy called for the column to halt and was about to issue directives when Billy cried out.

"Where's Killderry?"

We all looked over at the rock, now known as Killderry's Pillow, and sure enough, he was nowhere to be seen. The case of Guinness had been finished and empty bottles were strewn about in every direction.

"We'll worry about him later," said Burke. "To the business at hand!"

As he started forward, a strong arm held him in place.

"I'm running this operation, Burke," said the Navy. "It's not in your jurisdiction, I believe."

Burke's jaw tightened but he said nothing.

"Now," the Navy commanded, turning to the men assembled, "to the business at hand!"

We marched down to the beach where the five boats were awaiting us. The Navy spoke with authority.

"In each boat I want four men at the oars and one harpooner. I shall be one of those . . . Billy, Finbar, Burke will be the others. That leaves one more harpooner needed."

He turned to me.

"Since you seem to think that beastie out there is a mere sailing vessel, you must feel there's no danger whatsoever in attacking it. Here!"

He pushed a pointed broom handle into my arms.

"You'll have command of the fifth boat . . . and I'd advise you to take care of that little machine. There's liable to be some rough action ahead."

The crews arranged, we climbed into the boats and headed out to sea. It was slow going at the outset. No one really relished the thought of reaching the dragon first. Chagrined at the lack of enthusiasm, the Navy began to berate his crew.

"Come on, ya soft-bellied bunch of swabs! Put your bleedin' shoulders into it. Me old grandmother, God rest her soul, could lift an oar better than the four of you! Show a bit of spirit, lads! Show a bit of life! Let's heave to! A sorry bunch of excuses for men you be. We should have asked your wives to row instead. Come on lads, put a shoulder into it!!"

His boat picked up some speed, but it seemed the rest of us were intent on running a race to see who could get to the dragon last. However, the enthusiasm of the Navy was contagious, and though none of us really wanted to reach the creature, a strange spirit of competition overcame us. Because no one enjoys coming in last in a race, the harpooners began to urge their crews on, even against their will.

"You lazy bunch of yarbos!" I screamed. "Why, none of you Clare men are half a match for a Limerick man! Pull those oars, now boys, pull! Pull!!"

Before I knew it, my boat was out in front. Then Burke's boat pulled ahead of mine and led the charge. He was yelling and threatening to put his crew behind bars on various charges if they did not put some muscle into it. All the men at the oars, in all five boats, straining and stretching every muscle and nerve, were at the same time screaming and shouting and cheering, setting up such a wailing that it was difficult to think straight.

Finbar's boat pulled even with mine, and I heard him threaten to beat the living daylights out of his crew if they didn't prove the best crew in the water. But coming up alongside and rowing furiously, Billy's crew overtook us; the promise of free whiskey had given them the strength of demons.

Billy was in the lead, a half length ahead of me, the Irish Navy was closing in behind us both and, by God, it was a race!

"Harpoons!! At the ready!!" came the cry from the Irish Navy.

The boats were almost even now. And we weren't twenty-five yards from the dragon. The moment of truth was upon us, and at any time we expected the monster's anger to flare up and send us all to our doom. But we did not let up. The men, in spite of their fear, split their throats with cries and curses aimed at the dreaded creature of the deep.

"Harpooners!"

Ten yards from it now.

"Throw your harpoons!!!"

The five of us heaved with everything we had . . .

Thud, thud . . . thud thud thud.

Still cursing and shouting, we picked up our second harpoons and let fly another broadside . . .

Thud, thud . . . thud thud thud

We were about to pick up our third round when a figure suddenly appeared on top of the creature, dressed in white cap, blue blazer, white shoes, blue trousers and spotted ascot.

But we were not, it appeared, about to receive an invitation to tea . . .

"What the bloody hell is all this racket??!!"

We were stunned.

A mighty tail flailing at us; a fin sweeping us overboard; fiery breathy enveloping us in flames; even jaws splitting our boats in half. All that would have fit our expectations. Yes. Mine too. By that time I was as crazed as the rest of them.

"You there! Put that bleeding stick down before I ram it up your bloody arsehole! What the devil do you mean disturbing a subject of the Queen in the middle of his Tanqueray and Schweppes? This is an outrage!!"

The chastened men were silent, and their silence served to reinstate my temporary loss of sanity and humor. I had all I could do to hold a belly laugh inside, and in an effort to distract myself, I switched on my recorder.

"Will someone please explain to me just what you ragged bunch of ignorant bumpkins hope to accomplish by yelling and screaming and beating upon my ship? Is this your idea of a Polynesian welcome? Well? What is the meaning of this?"

It occurred to me that we'd asked Killderry, we'd asked the police, and we'd asked the Navy how to deal with this sea dragon and had gotten nowhere. The only thing we hadn't thought of was to ask the dragon itself. I had to look away because there was a very smug smile on my face.

"I'm waiting for an answer!"

The Irish Navy spoke up sheepishly.

"We thought we were attacking a sea dragon, sar . . ."

"A sea dragon? A sea dragon!"

"Yes, sar . . ."

"My good fellow, I have been sailing and navigating for twenty years. Do you think I would be foolish enough to

"A strange spirit of competition overcame us."

anchor in the vicinity of a sea dragon? What do you take me for, an imbecile?"

"No, sar!"

"I should hope not! We waited until the dragon moved on to other waters before we anchored here."

"Are you trying to say," I asked, choking on my words, "that there *was* a sea dragon here?"

"Of course there was! Why do you think I waited until late last night to anchor . . . I laid out at sea till it was gone. Do you think I'd risk this ship—dead expensive, mind you—and the lives of my crew?"

Desperately, I pressed on.

"B-but we saw the dragon yesterday. It looked remarkably like your boat . . ."

"Ah, yes! Clever bastards, sea dragons—especially the small sort. Full of tricks and disguises. Never know what they'll resort to."

I sank back down into the boat and hung my head in my hands.

"Who, may I ask, is the leader of this, this, expedition?"

"He is," said Burke, pointing to the Irish Navy.

"He is," said the Navy, indicating the police officer.

"Well, whoever it is, one of you must take responsibility for the sabotage attempt upon my ship at approximately four o'clock this morning."

"What? What sabotage?"

"It'll do you no good to evade the issue. I am Captain Wesley Lovemore Smith-Smythe, O.B.E., sailing out of London, and unless I receive some explanation I must warn you of grave international repercussions."

"What happened?" asked Burke.

Smith-Smythe turned to speak to a crew member who immediately disappeared below deck.

"If you wanted to sink this boat, the least you could have

done was to send someone reasonably sober to do it, someone with at least a modicum of intelligence . . . You show gross incompetence, if you ask me."

That was when old Killderry appeared, locked in irons that dragged along the planking.

"I've been swallowed by a sea dragon," he shouted with a crazed, glassy look in his eyes. "Like Jonah of old, I have been eaten by a monster of the deep, and now I am spewed forth! I have lived! God be praised!"

"This idiot," explained Smith-Smythe, "attempted to bore holes in the hull of my ship early this morning. He came out in a small boat, like the ones you have there, but before he could bore one hole he lost his balance and fell into the drink. Nearly drowned and made a damn bloody racket doing it. The man was reeking of alcohol."

"No harm done," said Billy.

"No harm! The man tried to sink my ship!"

"He's just a crazy old man," pleaded Burke.

And a renowned expert on dragons and sea monsters.

"We set him to watch the creature," Burke explained. "I guess he got carried away . . . tried to take matters into his own hands . . . I was just telling the lads yesterday about the dangers and pitfalls of taking the law into your own hands."

"I see."

"I'll take full responsibility for him. I'm a police officer."

"Oh no you won't! I am the Irish Navy, and I have jurisdiction over events occurring at sea. I say the man is my prisoner."

"It is plainly obvious," Burke insisted, getting heated, "that Seamus Killderry is a land animal. My authority is on land, and he is, therefore, my prisoner."

"With all the liquid the man consumes," argued the Navy, "I think it highly debatable whether he is a land animal or a sea animal. I'll take charge of him."

"Over my dead body!"

"That's fine with me!"

"Just a minute, you two," counseled Smith-Smythe. "The chap who has jurisdiction at sea will be responsible for the prisoner until you reach the shore. Then the chap who has jurisdiction on land will assume charge of the prisoner."

"The wisdom of Solomon!" Billy said with admiration. "Sar, I would like to extend an invitation to you and your crew to retire to my pub where we may better arrive at an understanding."

"One sensible man among you," said Smith-Smythe. "I accept."

"I've been saved!!" cried Killderry. "Swallowed by the sea dragon, I have survived to see the truth. It's a miracle! I am Jonah, of old! I am spewed forth and have seen the light of the Lord!! God be praised!! I am . . ."

"Shut that eejit up," demand the Navy, "and get him down into the boat."

When we reached the shore, I decided not to return to the pub, not just yet. I told them I'd join them all later and watched them shamble up the road, over the rise and disappear. I climbed the small hill above the beach and sat down facing out to sea with my back against Killderry's Pillow, my tape recorder at my side. I was glad I had the recorder along. Pressing the rewind button, I fixed my eyes on the craft gently rolling on the water. As the tape rewound I found the hum of the machine, with its periodic clicks—like a train rushing along the tracks—strangely comforting. I felt the need to review the snatches of conversations I'd recorded over the last twenty-four hours because I didn't trust my memory.

The machine stopped suddenly, and the rewind button snapped loudly upright. I pressed the play button and

settled back against Killderry's Pillow. There was the tune
I'd recorded just before the old souse came barging
through the door. Now, that was the "real stuff" I was
after, even with all the noise and scratch that always accompanied it—the pure Irish tradition. So solid, so steeped
in the ancient lore of the race. With the end of the tune, I
leaned forward to better hear what came next. When the
scratchy trash can noises stopped I pressed the fast-
forward and listened to the gabble until I gauged I had
reached the point at which the battle had begun. The tape
ran with a slow, electric breathing . . . It was fifteen minutes before I realized that there was nothing on the tape
but the breathing, like the sound of the sea in a conch . . .
I sat there watching the revolving tape and listened to the
breathing getting louder. At first a kind of emphasymic
wheezing, it gradually developed into a low growl, with the
lapping and splashing of water coming through as
background.

When the roaring began I knew it wasn't the tape and I
raised my eyes to the sound coming from the sea.

A powerful tail lashed the water and I looked away from
eyes that glistened feverishly.

I gathered up my equipment and ran the mile to Billy's
pub, determined to warn the people of Dunloon.

IF I DIE BEFORE I WAKE

GREG BEAR

ILLUSTRATIONS BY
GREG BEAR

Herbert was a year older than Carl Weber and wasn't afraid of the dark anymore, but that didn't make Carl feel any easier. Herbert had changed in other ways, too. Maybe that was because he was five. Carl didn't want to think about the alternative.

He sat on the back porch, looking out across the yellow grass and weeds of the back yard, chin in hand. He was usually too full of energy to sit still so long. There was always paint to peel off the fence, or mud balls to throw at the wasps under the eaves. (His father had said, "Let him do it! He'll learn soon enough.") There was the river that ran behind the small trailer court, rippling lazily with foot-long suckers or an occasional trout. Carl swatted a mosquito and looked at his short, stubby fingers before rubbing them on his pants. Always something to do. But today he was afraid.

Today always turned into tonight, and when he went to bed, there it would be again.

The dream.

It was like somebody breaking down a door, or trying to. Carl wasn't sure whether the door had come down yet.

Every night, *SLAM!* He punched the air with his fist. He would wake up in bed, half-asleep, not sure where he was, still mired in that terrible darkness and pain, and there it would be again, even when he was awake.

What came in the Dream.

Herbert and Carl used to talk about such things, but now Herbert wouldn't listen. Not that it had been easy, with their beginner's grasp of language, to tell each other exactly what they had seen or felt. Carl had known Herbert ever since he could remember—when both ran around in hang-dog diapers with bottles clutched in pudgy fists—and still it had taken a long time (Years and Years, maybe) to get across to each other what they were so scared of, at night.

Carl watched the sun on the tall granite mountains that rose on the eastern side of the valley. The shadow of the western mountains was creeping up the slabs, turning orange and burned brown into cool grey, so fast he could see it. Soon the valley would be in twilight, but the sky above would stay blue for a few more hours. Then the stars would come out, watching him.

He and Herbert didn't play together now. There didn't seem much point. Carl scrunched his face up and spat on the grass. Before long it would be twilight and he felt he had to get something done before his mother's curfew took effect. He stood up, brushed off his pants like he had seen his father do, then ran stumpy-legged around the corner of the house. It had been cool today, so the flatulent smells from the trailer court dump stations weren't strong. He dragged his feet through the dust, shoelaces flapping on his edgeworn tennies, and looked down as he went past Mr. Hobson's trailer. Normally he liked talking to the old man and his wife. They were the only permanent residents in the court. Mr. Hobson helped Carl's father with some of the duties, in return for a free spot, and Mrs. Hobson worked with his mother in the office. But today Carl just wanted to do something before twilight. That way, if this was his last night—

Now, what exactly did that mean? He could only vaguely guess. Carl could almost remember a time when he *wasn't*. Maybe after he was through being a little boy—or after tonight—such a time would come again.

The orange cat his father called Dandelo floated on four pumping legs around the corner of the one-car garage and stopped square-footed to survey Carl. Carl mewed and the cat blinked down to slits. Carl was okay. Dandelo allowed himself to be petted, then looked over his shoulder in wide-eyed surprise as Carl abandoned him and walked toward the gravel drive. Dandelo plumped down in the short dusty grass and rolled back and forth.

Dinner would be in an hour. Before then, Carl was free to play wherever he wanted, so long as he didn't go out onto the highway or get close to the river—close being beyond the barbed-wire horse fence which followed the bank behind the house and court.

His sister, Janet, was working in the store. She was twelve and he couldn't talk to her straight because she thought four-year-olds talked silly. Usually he did talk silly, but now . . . Who could he talk to, then? Oh, he remembered. He wasn't out to talk. He was out to *do*.

He snuck up beside the service station and peeped through the boards into the garage. Lanny Carson, the smooth-faced curly-haired fellow Mr. Jansen employed to fix cars and run the pumps, sat in the shadows, chewing on a pencil. Carson didn't like kids and had once chased Carl out of the garage, swinging a credit-card pad at him. Carl was afraid of him, and walked behind the garage.

He sat on a bench in front of the store. His time was

almost up. There were maybe one or two fingers of orange
rock left on the top of the eastern peaks. The cottonwoods
and diseased old elms with their wire and board props
were beginning to rustle in the dusk breeze. If Herbert had
been there, they could have done something together,
even if it was something naughty. They could have looked
through the trash barrels behind the cafe, or—

He sniffed. For a moment he hoped it might be the
breeze making his nose run, but then his eyes spilled over.
He was fully into a good cry when he saw a small figure
staring at him from the other side of the gasoline pumps. A
car had driven up and a tall man with long black hair was
filling his own tank. Inside the car was a thin-faced woman
with a kerchief tied around her head, and looking at Carl
was a little girl, no more than three. Carl wiped his eyes
quickly.

That was all Carl got to do before twilight. The rocks
were dark grey, like his German army tank model. His
mother called from the house. Come to dinner. After
dinner, TV for an hour. That cheered him up a little.

But after TV, bed.

He got up and ran, but not straight toward the house.
He was being bad, but he had to do something before
night fell completely. He decided the quickest thing was to
look at the river behind the house, then go in to dinner.
Maybe his mother wouldn't even notice he took a bit
longer. He answered in a thin, clear voice that he was
coming, but he skirted off behind the wooden horse stable,
stumbled on a hummock of grass, got up, and finally stood
by the fence, small fists gripping two clear spots on the
second wire up, looking out across the widest stretch of the
river in this area.

Here, the river was fast and deep—over his father's
head—like a separate place under the surface, a long

house of water where fish lived but little boys didn't dare go.

In the fading blue sky light, Carl saw the concentric circles where fish sucked air or bit at bugs, lots of little circles spreading now because it was feeding time, just like at home. His mouth hung open and his tongue played in and out with a will of its own. His tongue always went free when he thought real hard. How come you didn't see fish in the water where ripples started? Because the sky or rocks were all shiny on the surface, maybe. But sometimes he could see fish anyway. Why not all of them?

Maybe fish were down deep, sending up bubbles. He had seen a picture in one of his father's magazines of a big fish, bigger than Carl by two or three times, a catfish. There weren't any big catfish in the river, his father said, and it was just as well, because they could swallow things as big as Carl. (His father had laughed and his mother had said "Oh, Sandy, the boy'll have nightmares now.") But Carl knew better than to be afraid of things in the river, unless you went in with them. Still . . .

He imagined a big fish at the bottom of the deep, fast water, shiny black with tiny marble eyes and big feelers, slick, with a wide under-turned mouth. Was that what It was like—a big fish that could swim through air, look through his bedroom window at night? No—something else. Formless. Waiting, like the fish, but with no eyes at all.

He shook his head. He was bringing It on before dark now. Best not to think about It at all.

He started to turn away from the fence. A fluff of cottonwood caught his eye, drifting past. He watched it, craning his neck; saw it light on the river and bob along.

There was a wide, violent ripple in the middle of the river. Until now, the river had always seemed fairly innocuous—as long as you behaved—even friendly, chat-

tering and gurgling. It didn't seem very friendly now. Carl
wanted to run but couldn't. The ripple in the middle was
bigger than any ripple he had ever seen, and something
dark and shiny was surfacing.

Carl's mouth went round and the pee started its journey
to his pants. He could vaguely see several humps under
the water, not green-black like a catfish, but deep metal
blue like his father's old Chevy. Two gold cat-slit eyes
broke the surface and stared at him, unblinking.

It twisted its head around slowly, the eyes turning from
gold to red-gold. Then it sank and disappeared.

"Carrr-r-r-l!"

He stood by the bank, shivering. The pee had stopped
before coming out, but he was still scared. Dark was
gathering under the trees and the river was almost black.
Cold air and the distant smell of burning wood poured
down onto him. "Got to go away," he said to the river.
"Go to the bathroom. Don't follow me, now." And he
backed away slowly, turned and ran, breath hissing with
fear.

He barely made it into the house. "Carl, I've been
calling you for five minutes," his mother said. She was
wearing denim slacks and a checkered blouse, just like
Annette on the Mouseketeers. Her hair was done up for
cooking, but a wisp had gotten loose and fallen in her face.
She mother-eyed him and he looked back over his shoulder, biting his lower lip as he walked stiffly to the bathroom.

"I came!" he said, and shut the door. He pulled out the
step-stool, lowered his pants, lifted the potty lid, and went
just like a grown-up. When he was done, he pushed the
stool over, washed his hands, and blew his breath out.
There—ready for dinner. He walked into the dining room,
sat on his special chair and took the napkin down from the
table. His sister was talking about new clothes in the store.

"Janet, they're too expensive even with discount. We buy all our stuff in town. They get it with bulk discounts and sell it for less than we pay wholesale, you know that."

"But there's some cute stuff in there," Janet said, not looking too hopeful. Their father came in and settled the matter. "We don't take out of the store now, except for food and hardware."

"You got my radio in the store," Janet reminded him.

Their father was two years older than their mother, about thirty-seven, with brown tight skin and curly black hair. He had changed into a white long-sleeved shirt for dinner. "That was for Christmas," he said. "Electronic stuff isn't much cheaper anywhere you go."

"So you find an electronic dress and we'll think about it," their mother said, putting the main casserole dish on the table.

Janet awmommed under her breath and they started passing things around. It was all very familiar. Carl had heard this sort of thing all his life. But now he watched them owl-eyed. *What would Dad say?* When he had told him about the lion that looked in through the window, and spoken to him, instructed him to go hunt zebras and lizards, Mom had laughed and Dad had said he was dreaming. And Carl, now, was pretty certain it had been a dream. But what came at night—The Dream—wasn't the same sort at all. And he had seen the thing in the river while he was wide awake.

They all said he had a big imagination. That wasn't bad—it just would make it harder to explain what he had seen. Janet would titter, Dad would grin. Mom would shake her head and smile.

The television came and went, snowy as usual, lulling him unwillingly to sleep. His father gathered him up in wide brown arms and carried him into the dark bedroom,

turning on the light with an elbow. "Sleep tight, sport."
Under the covers, Carl opened his eyes and looked
around. The night-light was on, a pale milk-glass silver-
moon with hooked nose and broad, benevolent smile. It
should have been very comfortable.

But he was afraid. The drowsiness was inescapable,
holding down his arms, his legs, dragging his eyelids shut.
Curling up and drawing the covers tight around his head,
wrapping himself in a ritual cocoon, he reluctantly allowed
the dark into his head.

For Carl, early sleep was a succession of memories. He
relived the events of the day, seeing them as if through a
topaz-colored filter, with brilliant flashes of light announc-
ing scene changes. Indistinct shapes and shadows flitted
through the scenes, making him uneasy, but not really
frightening him. They were the reflections of his growing
mind, memories finding their way home, new schedules
being established. Over them all watched sleep-Carl, not
the same as waking-Carl, wise in the ways of slumber.

The topaz dimmed, the scenes became smoky, and
sleep-Carl gradually faded into a background murmur.

Then he came partly awake. Opening his eyes half-way,
he looked around the dimly lighted room. He hadn't been
alive long enough to accumulate a lot of things, but the
room had its own character, and something was in the
middle of the room, moving things about, changing them.
Preparing to take over. It didn't seem to know he was
watching. Then It saw him—or whatever It did that was
like seeing. It was a great black cloud, not the size of the
room but much larger, and yet contained within the walls.
Whatever It had that passed for breath stank like Carl's
training potty, or worse. This was The Dream.

It didn't take Carl long at all to realize that he was still
seeing things through the eyes of sleep. He was familiar

with the tension in his whole body, and the incredible ache in his throat, as if he were being strangled. Sleep-Carl didn't know how to scream, but wake-Carl wasn't yet fully in control.

This was The Dream that Herbert no longer had.

Carl opened his mouth and moved an arm. The cloud seemed to hear. Suddenly It was hovering over him, looking down without eyes, running itself over his legs, his body, like Mom when she squeezed fruit at the market, but gleeful.

Without a mouth, without a voice even, it said to him, There is no Carl I am Carl soon *I will eat you.*

Now Carl was awake. It still hovered, felt him, spoke, repeating itself without inflection. Carl let out a high, siren-like wail, piercing the walls, dragging his father and mother and sister out of bed as if they had been lanced. They ran from their rooms and his father opened Carl's door, fumbled for the switch. While he fumbled, the cloud hovered, unafraid, still talking. Carl could hear it over his scream. The light came on, blinding, and Carl stared up at the empty ceiling.

"Jesus, Carl, again?" Janet moaned sleepily.

"Janet, don't profane—" their mother began, but she cut herself off to go to Carl, who was sobbing as if he would die.

The Dream only came once a night. Carl went back to sleep quickly, exhausted, and gladly heard the morning sounds, it seemed no time later. He ate breakfast, did his few assigned chores—making his bed as best he could, dressing himself, feeding Dandelo dry catfood—and then went into his parents' room to look at himself in the full-length mirror.

It hadn't been so long ago that Carl hadn't thought of

himself as Carl Weber age 4. He had been everybody and
everything, with incomplete control over those distant
limbs and outcroppings known as Mommy and Daddy
and Janet, pinching car doors, butterflies and water
faucets. When he couldn't shut off a water faucet, was it
really different from going in his pants? Just lately, he had
come to see that Carl Weber was a distinct unit and that the
world did not revolve around him and his wishes. It had
been a hard time—more spankings than ever before or
since. Now that he had fought his way through to that
awareness, it was about to be taken from him.

He knew that for certain. He looked at himself in the
mirror, and there were dark circles under his eyes. His
throat hurt. Pretty soon Carl Weber would be somebody
else.

To his parents and sister, he was just having things called
nightmares. Everyone had nightmares. What Carl wondered was why did little kids have more nightmares than
other people?

It was pretty clear.

Something out there wanted to be Carl Weber. When It
became him, there'd be no more need for dark clouds and
night frights. No more screaming.

His four-year-old's judgement was that he didn't look
too well, but his parents attributed that to a disturbed
night's sleep. They didn't look too well, either. They talked
about preferring changing diapers and late-night feedings.

There was no help. So he played as hard as he could,
played alone because Herbert was too old and changed to
even talk to, and it was a small community. Only Herbert
was near his age.

He laughed at the horses. They nuzzled his hands until
he picked up straw for them from the stable rick. He
chewed clover while watching ants. Ate lunch, but not very

much—a dry cheese sandwich and High-C. Scribbled on a chunk of white concrete with some campfire embers from a pit in the trailer court. Sat. Ran. Looked up at the clouds and the mountains. The sun, coming down again. Felt the chill of early evening. Mother put his sweater on him one arm at a time then hiked him into it and buttoned up. Back to the horses.

And then to the wide spot in the river.

Herbert was there, sitting on a rock by the fence.

"Hi," Carl said. Herbert stared at him.

"Still an old scaredy-cat?"

"Huh?"

"I heard you scream last night," Herbert said. Herbert's house was across the highway and the nights were quiet in the valley.

"Did not," Carl said ineffectually.

"I heard." Herbert smiled.

Carl looked deep into Herbert's eyes. There was a distant smell of the trainer potty mixed with something worse, and blackness.

"You lost," Carl whispered, eyes wide. "You don't scream no more."

"What?" Herbert asked, still smiling. Then he jumped down from the rock and shoved Carl. "Just an old scaredy-cat. Stupid old momma's boy." Carl didn't push back. Herbert had been nice once, bright, and they had done lots of neat things together.

"I saw something scary in the river last night," Carl said, searching for some spark of sympathy and trying to find an excuse.

"There isn't anything in the river."

"Then you go in and see!" Carl said, getting angry.

"You just have nightmares, like a little baby," Herbert said, reaching out to push him again.

"Stop it!"

"What's up with you boys?"

Herbert backed away and stopped smiling. Mr. Hobson walked up to the fence, followed by the little girl Carl had seen at the gas pumps. She negotiated the rough ground carefully, dressed much like the boys, in pants and tennis shoes, but with a flowered cotton t-shirt top.

"If you two can stop quarreling, I'd like to introduce my grand-daughter," Mr. Hobson said "Georgia, this is Carl and Herbert. And this is Georgia Kemper." The girl looked them over with one finger to her lip. "I'd like you fellows to watch out for her if she should ever get away from the trailer. Which won't be often, I think—her mother'll paddle her britches. But just in case." Mr. Hobson bent down and started to talk to Georgia about the river and the fence, and how the fence was to keep away horses and little girls from this part—"And little boys, too," he added meaningfully.

Herbert began to edge away, then ran. Carl stayed and looked at the little girl for a while, talking with Mr. Hobson. He wondered if he should tell the old man about the river thing, but decided against it. Mr. Hobson had been a car mechanic and was level-headed, or so Carl's father said. Down to Earth.

But at least they had made Herbert go away. Carl said good-bye and walked back through the trees to the trailer-court. Halfway between the river and the court, he noticed the trees were very quiet. He couldn't hear the river and he couldn't hear the court noises. He stopped and put his hands in his pockets, waiting. The leaves above blocked the sun and dappled the dirt and grass, making little coin-like sparkles of gold on the ground. Carl remembered a movie on TV where all the little people had played around a big potty full of gold, and he felt like that now. For a moment, he forgot his troubles, kneeled down, and looked at the lights, blurring his eyes to make them prettier. He stood up quickly and almost fell over backward when the leaves rustled overhead. There was no wind. He looked up, expecting to see Dandelo high up on a limb, but at first there was nothing. His gaze wandered and out of the corner of his eye he saw a glint of green and gold, not exactly leaf-colored. Mouth open, tongue playing in and out between his teeth, Carl followed the outline of off-color. All at once it seemed to jump into focus.

It was crawling through the branches—a snaky thing, speckled green and yellow and gold. It moved a clawed foot onto another branch, and slithered a few inches forward, staring down at him. Its eyes were smoky topaz and green, like the filters on sleep-Carl's vision. Just staring into them made him drowsy.

Something else moved in the grass behind him. He turned but didn't see anything. Rocks seemed to shift. He looked back up but the tree-snaky was gone. Squinting didn't help him find it. "Where are you?" he asked, hands shaking. He almost didn't dare move. It had looked at him the way Dandelo looked at prey. "Do you want me?" He held his hand to his mouth. If they were friends of the cloud.—

But he couldn't see anything now, except ordinary trees, rocks, grass.

Mr. Hobson returned from the river with Georgia and they passed Carl. Mr. Hobson tipped his hat and Georgia smiled shyly. "Be careful now, Carl," Mr. Hobson said.

"Be caewful," Georgia repeated.

The coin dapples faded as the shadow of the western mountains advanced across the valley. Carl went home an hour early and watched his mother put biscuits in the oven for the creamed chipped beef they were having for dinner.

Then he went to his room and sat by the side of the bed on his play stool, holding his plastic saw and rubber screwdriver. It seemed a long time since he had really wanted to play.

The television was over and Carl lay in his bed with the glass man-in-the-moon glowing beside him. He wasn't very sleepy. He held his thumb to his nose, much better than keeping it in his mouth, and tried to see how brave he was. He wondered how long he could keep from wrapping all the covers around his head.

He lasted about three minutes. Then he carefully cocooned himself and shut his eyes. There wasn't long to wait before sleep-Carl started taking over, but the change wasn't obvious. He didn't really know he was asleep, even as the events of the day started rewinding before his eyes.

This time, wherever he looked in the topaz-colored light he saw snaky things. There was one for the living room in the house, looking very much like the flowers in the old hand-woven carpet. There was an odd grey one that looked a lot like a vacuum-cleaner hose. In the rose garden out back was a dirt-snaky with rose-colored eyes, all mellow with the topaz. Sleep-Carl presided over the investigations, and then faded. Warm, humming dark followed.

There was a tapping at the window. Carl sat by the side of the bed, blankets wrapped around his feet, and opened his eyes. Herbert was peering through the window, standing on the gas-meter cover just outside. "Come on!" Herbert whispered harshly. "We got to go!"

It looked like the old Herbert, friendly, full of adventure and play. Carl smiled. "Go where?" he asked.

"Go out and catch frogs! Fish!"

Carl had never gone fishing with Herbert before, but it was an inviting suggestion. He felt a lot older, ready for such things. Then he remembered he was in a dimly lit room, outside his covers. "No," he said.

"Why not?"

"It's night."

"You afraid?"

For a moment, the old Herbert flaked away and the new Herbert seemed about to take over. "It's dark," Carl said, holding his fist to his mouth. Chewing. Uncertain.

"Look, there's a moon! We can see. Frogging and fishing!"

Carl thought for a moment.

"That girl's out here with me. She's younger than you and *she* isn't scaredy-cat!"

Carl frowned.

"I'll go with just her if you want," Herbert said.

"Mr. Hobson wouldn't like that."

"He doesn't know!" Herbert said. "Come on!"

He didn't like the idea much, but it was better than waiting in bed for The Dream. Besides, Mr. Hobson had told him to keep an eye on the little girl, and he didn't trust Herbert to do a good job of that. He left his pajamas on but put pants and coat over them. His shoes barely fit over the pajamas' closed toes. The living room was dark and empty. Carl made his way to the front door, unlatched it, and opened it carefully. Herbert had told the truth—the moon was full and it was bright outside.

Herbert and Georgia waited for him on the path to the river. Carl looked at Mr. Hobson's trailer. All the lights were out. It was about eleven o'clock. Almost everybody went to sleep by eleven here.

Herbert held up a bag and a small wire-loop fish net. "We can catch suckers in this," he said. "Come on!"

Georgia waddled after and Carl followed, walking slowly to keep pace with the girl. He could hear the river in the quiet. There was no wind and the trees didn't make a sound. Carl couldn't see any of the snaky things in the branches or in the grass, but it wasn't bright enough to be sure they weren't there.

The river was black, with little racing glints and eddies of foam which showed the speed of the water. It had snowed early in the mountains and now the snow was melting and running off, raising the water level almost up to the fence. Herbert stepped through the wire, snagging his shirt for a moment on a barb. Carl unhooked it for him. "Now we can fish!" Herbert said, enthusiastic. Georgia giggled.

Carl lifted up the wire and crawled under, getting his pajamas dirty. He'd be in trouble for sure. "Stay on this side," he told Georgia.

"Why?" she asked.

"Just stay here. We'll fish, you watch."

She didn't seem convinced, but she didn't try to cross under the wire, either. Carl stood beside Herbert. The five-year-old gave Carl the bag. "I'll fish first, and you put them in the bag."

Carl nodded solemnly. Everything was ghost-grey or black in the moonlight. He squinted to see more clearly, but details escaped him. Herbert was a blur kneeling down and dipping the small net in the water. Carl didn't see how the boy was going to catch anything, but after a few moments—after Georgia giggled—Herbert brought the net up and something was in it.

"See?" Herbert said softly. "Caught something." It looked like a piece of mud to Carl, but he held out the bag and Herbert flipped it into the bottom. It squirmed slightly, then was still. Herbert dipped his net again.

Clouds were moving across the sky. A small one passed in front of the moon and Carl could hardly see. He heard Herbert stand up. "Caught something again," the boy said. Georgia asked if she could see. "In a minute," Herbert answered. Carl held the bag closed tight.

"Now your turn." Herbert handed him the net.

"I don't want to fish," Carl said.

"I caught a couple, now you have to."

"No," Carl said. "I'll watch."

"Why not?" Herbert's eyes glinted at him. "Because you're scared?"

"We're not supposed to be here."

"Now's the best time for fishing."

Georgia asked to see the bag. Carl held it away from Herbert's reaching hand. "Show her," Herbert said.

"No."

"Show her!"

Carl felt the bag move. He let Herbert take it from him. Herbert went to the fence and opened it for Georgia to see.

"Nothing in it," the little girl said.

"Look closer, in the bottom."

"Oh." She gasped. "It's all gooey."

"Touch it."

"Go home, Georgia," Carl said. "Mr. Hobson wants you home."

"Shuttup!" Herbert demanded in a high-pitched voice. "You little coward!" He approached Carl and shoved him. "*You* go home! Afraid of everything!"

"I am not!" Carl protested. Herbert shoved him again. This time Carl had had enough. He knocked the boy's arm aside and shoved back. Herbert threw the bag away and struck out with his fist, catching Carl on the side of the nose. Carl spun back and landed on the bank. One arm hit water.

"There!" Herbert said. Carl smelled potty-smell. Herbert reached down to hold his leg. "Now try and get away."

From out of nowhere—from all around—came the
cloud and the unspeaking voice. At first Carl couldn't
understand. It was mumbling. Then he felt its touch.
"Georgia!" he screamed, but his words seemed muffled.
He could hardly hear the river, or feel his hand trailing in it.

There is no Carl I am Carl soon soon.

Now.

And he was in a walled place, surrounded by dead, dry
things, shells like cockroaches or dead spiders, twitching in
a dry, dead breeze. The dust was thick and much, much
older than Carl or anyone he had ever known. This was
where people like him waited forever while nightmares
lived their turn. He squirmed and heard Herbert shout for
him to stop. He squirmed again. His hand felt the water.
He tried to get up, but the ground under him shifted and he
was in the water. Herbert held on to his leg and fell in after.

It was fast and wet and Carl held his breath, but it was
better than the dry husky place. He could see Herbert
dimly, floating along beside him. Being in the river was like
being wrapped in Slippery-Slide plastic.

Above all, it was peaceful. Carl couldn't feel the black
cloud. He regretted having disobeyed his parents, and he
worried about Georgia, but for himself he didn't worry at
all.

He was in the long house filled with water.

Then he felt Herbert's hand. Carl landed gently in the
mud and river-grass and Herbert came down beside him,
wide-eyed, cheeks puffed out. Herbert held on to Carl's
leg, eyes squinched tight. If they opened their mouths it
was all over. Carl's chest ached, but it was best that it
ached, for now, anyway.

Herbert opened his eyes. From behind him, like a cloud
of ink, came a deeper blackness. It seemed to struggle
against the river, but held on to Herbert around his neck

and head. It reached down into the five-year-old and together they tried to drag Carl to the surface. He resisted. He wanted anything but to face the Dream and lose.

Above them, the surface of the river was sparkling with rings of light. Carl thought he saw a few eyes, but he wasn't sure. Something sinuous and skinny rippled into view. It floated steady in the current, treading water with a long, flat tail. It was blue, but translucent like Aunt Patty's aquarium fish. Carl could make out the arrays of thin black bone under the skin. Scales sparkled like a rainbow along its flanks. It had a long, spiky fin from the crown of its head to the base of its tail. The fin bristled, stretching folds of skin like dark patches of stained glass. The eyes were large and gold, cat-slit pupils looking around sharp in the dark water, then staring down at Carl. Turning away, turning back. Treading water, underwater. Carl could see through the long, pale snout, like a dog's but with flaring horse nostrils. He could make out patches of veins with blood coursing through them. The thing glowed all by itself, like the dead mackerel from the bait shop that Dandelo had turned his nose up at and had sat out in the dish for days.

The tail twitched and began to flush deep red.

He felt a stronger tug on his legs and saw Herbert struggling toward the surface, clutching one foot. The cloud had the other foot.

The red flush sped along the snaky's body. Behind it, he could see other snakies, curling up and forming signs in the water, curley-ques and ins-and-outs like the patterns on his mother's sweaters. The whole surface was covered with glowing, twisting snaky things. Their eyes were like bloated stars. The cloud and Herbert pulled harder.

Carl's vision narrowed. His lungs ached horribly and he could feel his legs and arms going numb. There was a familiar, rasping voice in his mind, triumphant. And then, rising around it, came another voice, very faint, calm and distant, like the noise of the river grass. It did not use human words, but Carl understood. It wavered like the river running along stream banks.

Which do you choose? the other voice asked. *Live and be like Herbert? Or stop it all here—take a breath . . . ?*

What will Herbert be? Carl asked.

Herbert will never do anything quite right. He will always lie to others, grab for what they have. He will be loud but have nothing to say. He will use people and never like them very much, unless they are the same as he—and he will use them anyway. Which do you choose?

Can he come back, be like he was?

Herbert has been hunted, and caught.

Are they—have they got me?

You choose . . .

It was a very hard decision for someone as young as Carl. He could see some of the dull-eyed, cruel people he had met in his short life—people like Lanny Carson— could see how the world was so full of them—chasing him out of the gas station, snarling—and now Herbert was one of them, and never coming back. Now he knew how they had come to be that way. They had been hunted and caught. They had stopped being afraid of the dark because they *were* the dark, finally.

Carl didn't want to be like them. Best to let it all go rather than be like that. He still wasn't sure which choice he was making. Herbert and the cloud were tugging him to the surface. He broke away from them, clinging to the grass on the bottom. Above the water, they would have him. He could hardly think, his lungs hurt so bad. Then he chose, and opened his mouth to breath in.

On shore, Georgia saw the river thrashed into a white foam. All around her, the grass was filled with lights. She laughed with delight, then began to cry; she couldn't make up her mind which was more appropriate.

The dirt-snakies and tree-snakies watched with their cat-slit eyes, and somebody bobbed up in the middle of the foam. Georgia was about to go down and see who it was when Mr. Hobson grabbed her arm, squeezing it painfully.

"What in the name of God are you doing here, child?" he demanded. He looked into the river. "Oh, my God . . ."

He let the girl go and ran back awkwardly over the hummocks of dirt and grass for a stick. He knew better than to go into the river himself; it was much too fast and deep. He found a forked branch and broke it off with a strong, gnarled hand. Then he returned to the river and hooked what was caught on the bubbling rock about six feet out from the bank. He dragged it ashore. Hair was water-slicked over the features. He grabbed the boy up and held his ear to the little chest.

"Jesus, Jesus," he moaned. "He's still with us." Mr. Hobson ran up the path, clutching the boy and breathing into his mouth. He forgot about Georgia. She stood by the fence for a while, looking at the lights in the grass. After a moment, with great sincerity, she said,

"Yes, I be a good guwl. Won't get *me*."

Then she followed her grandfather into the trailer court.

Carl awoke in a big white bed in a green room. His chest still ached, and he had bandages on his head, but he didn't feel too bad. His mother and father were sitting beside the bed, which was much too big for him.

"You awake, honey?" his father asked. His mother looked up. Janet was sitting behind her, eyes red and puffy.

Carl nodded.

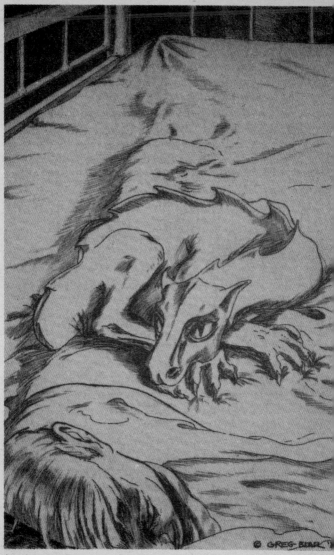

"A dim, long white form came out from under the bed and lay on the counterpane . . ."

"You're going to be okay," his mother said, smiling and crying at once. "We were really worried. You nearly drove us out of our minds."

Someone else was standing by the bed. He was dressed in light brown with a big black belt and a badge. A smaller man dressed just like him whispered in his ear.

"Carl, honey, we need to know—where was Herbert?" his father asked.

Carl looked around, disoriented.

"That's okay, Mr. Weber. We found the boy." The big man with the badge shook his head.

His mother began to cry harder, but with a note of relief mixed in. It hadn't been *her* son, at least. Carl felt sad, but the cloud had gotten Herbert anyway. It wasn't really any different. He didn't think he could tell the grown-ups that, however.

And even if he forgot all about this, by the time he was grown-up, he would remember he had made the choice.

They all left the room. A little night-light remained on after the ceiling lights were turned off. Carl closed his eyes and let everything flow smoothly over to sleep-Carl, but there was no rewinding of events this night.

Instead, as the boy slept, a dim, long white form came out from under the bed and lay on the counterpane, staring at the boy's peaceful face with pale, cat-slit eyes.

Then it began cleaning its claws delicately, one by one.

"The Count looked at the dragon's head, twice Owen's own height, and
behind it the hunched scaly back and thick hind legs."

AS ABOVE, SO BELOW

JOHN M. FORD

ILLUSTRATION BY
JUDY KING RIENIETS

Owen III Count XXI Hanowald watched his sea-captain stump and jingle away, and drummed fingers on the chart upon his dark oak desk. He looked over the inked outline of the Gold Coast. A wondrous profitable voyage, he thought, if the ships return . . . but then they'll not sail if they're not to return, will they, Sherez?

He rolled the map tight and put it in the white sash of his green silk robe. Did it matter to Sherez, that now he wore fine clean silks to visit the dragonium? The Count doubted that it did. He did not doubt that, should it make a difference to Sherez, Owen would put on salty burlap again. And chains, yes.

He walked the corridors of the Serpent Wing: Two turns left, one right, sharp left, up and down a ramp, ignoring the dozens of false passages. A rumble and whine coming from the Artificers' Tower, where they prepared some marvelous and expensive experiment, distracted his thoughts, but his feet knew the way. Owen could walk these halls blindfold, literally. His father had seen to that.

As he opened the door to the dragonium, Count Hanowald heard Sherez greet him. Smiling faintly, the

Count went down the black iron steps, his boots making hollow sounds of doom, the jangle of the grip-chain echoing in his memory.

"Watch your sstep, Owen," Sherez' voice came from the pit, and a moment later the Count stumbled, grabbing the chain with both hands, scraping a heel-tendon on the leading edge of a step, on the iron rasp put there to gash the dragon's belly should he try to ascend . . . escape . . . from the dragonium.

Owen laughed at that, and at the pain in his ankle. Four Counts Hanowald had died mangled on these stairs, Owen's father one of them, all the same way—descending in haste to see Sherez. None had ever fallen while climbing. Who indeed could, with a dragon's counsel upon him as he departed the pit?

I keep the dragonium as have twenty Hanowalds before me, Owen thought, the maze and the stair and the catacomb, and yet if Sherez sprawled on my chair and held my wand in his teeth, would he rule any more than now?

The Count reached the foot of the stair. A shaft of yellow light from Sherez' left eye picked out the lantern on the wall. Before Owen struck the flint, he noticed a small glimmer near the bright beam.

"Your right eye is healing," he said.

"Ssslowly," said Sherez. "I can tell light from dark, now. The blow was well sstruck, Owen. Your grandfather's arm was sstrong."

The lantern blazed up, and the dragonlight was lost. Owen saw a yellow sphere the size of his head, bloodshot and diffuse. The old split in the closed lid beside it was a mere green groove now, the flake-gold luster of dried dragon blood that Owen's brush could never erase nearly gone. Sherez' ropy arms, thinner than Owen's own, were stretched out before the dragon's head, holding a piece of chain. Rust was scoured from some of the links.

"What, Sherez, must you polish your own teeth now? I've given Emael orders that you're not to go three days without a filing."

"Your sson fears me," said the dragon. "He thinkss I sshall ssnap him up."

"So did I, when I was no bigger than your fang. Emael wears a sword now. He can wield a rasp."

"But you will not chain your sson to the stair, as your father did you, will you, Owen? He iss no coward, your sson. Only young, and uncertain."

"He will be Count one day, Sherez, and he must know you."

"No."

Owen stared. "What do you mean by that? What is going to happen to my son?"

"I do not know, Owen."

"Not . . . know?" The Count looked at the dragon's head, twice Owen's own height, and behind it the hunched scaly back and thick hind legs. The vestigial wings were folded flat, fanning open and shut slightly as Sherez breathed. *What a creature is dragon,* the poets sang, *though for his wisdom he resigned the air to crawl* . . . Years ago, a traveling artificer had displayed a whole dragon brain, preserved in smelly liquid. The arms of three men could not span it round. How could that brain—

As the mazes of the dragonium wound above and below, that brain coiled through time; time past, time future. All moments were one to a dragon, tomorrow as real as yesterday, this very instant the same to it as last year or next generation. Sherez could tell Owen the hour of the Count's death, had he only the courage to ask.

How could that brain *not know?*

"Emael is no less healthy than you were at his age—nor less brave," said Sherez. "But I do not know what will happen to him."

"You mean that you are going to die."

"We do not die, as you know."

"Then tell me who will kill you. I'll put the tongs to him. I'll roast him in an iron box!"

"Even if it were your son?"

Owen lost his voice. After three hard breaths he said "Yes, even so," and thought oh gods old, oh God new, what have I said?

Sherez closed his eye. "It is not," he said. "It is no such blow at all. But I wondered. . . .

"Do you know what your artificers do, even now?"

Again Owen could not speak. The dragon *wondered.* Owen had knelt down here with a file and a brush and pans of salt and fresh water—and his own weight of iron on his feet—and cared for Sherez' teeth and blind eye, and the small wounds done by the stones and the deep creatures. After not too much time Owen remained in the dragonium of his own will. Yet though Owen loved Sherez, and knew he loved Sherez, still there were times when he could have raised his hand and put out that other eye.

The wind in his soul subsided. Voice came back. "The artificers are raising some new assemblage. It's consumed pounds of silver, and good steel, but I don't know what it's meant to do."

"They mean to examine causality," said the dragon. "The silver goes for mirrors. The springs hurl pellets, and divide off time, and smash vials of prussic acid so that cats die horribly."

"Cats?"

"It is all in a good cause, the furtherance of knowledge."

"What is 'causality'?"

"They wish to know if the cause of an action must happen before the action, or if perhaps the action may precede the cause."

"For this they use steel and silver? To find if, perhaps, a man may cut down a tree after it falls?"

"It is subtler than that. Ancient philosophies are involved, concerning the nature of light."

"Light or falling trees, who cares? A thing is done; its consequences follow."

"Yet if a dragon said your son was to slay him, you would have put hot iron to the boy to prevent the act. How may I be killed tomorrow by a man who dies today?"

"Then . . . there is no . . . causality."

"Oh, but there is. And the artificers will prove so. It is dragons who are wrong."

Owen pulled the map from his sash. "I would all my advisers were wrong so perfectly."

Sherez clapped his weak hands. Dragons could not laugh. "Count Owen, how exceptional you are. Any of your artificers would be confounded for days by such a paradox, but you deny that paradox can exist in a rational world."

"Can it?"

"Only as long," said Sherez, "as no one notices there is a paradox. I think one day the artificers will prove two objects cannot occupy the same place simultaneously; but until then, who knows? Perhaps they can."

"You are saying that, as a result of these mirrors and levers, all dragons are about to die."

"No. No. Dragons cannot die . . . because it is inherent in the concept of dragons that we shall live forever."

"You can be slain by men."

"Because *your* concept of dragons so strongly demands

that we can be slain. We were here before your evolution, O man; would you believe me if I said, before that time, no hand could kill us?"

"Then what is to happen to you, if not death? What else is there but death at the end?"

"Many things," said the dragon, "an infinity—but for us, oblivion. It shall I think, be as if we never were at all."

"I'll remember."

"Perhaps not."

"What of this pit? I'll put up a plaque in gold on silver, that here were dragons."

Sherez applauded, patter-patter-pat. "A worthy gesture, Owen Hanowald, but perhaps not. You will probably recall this place as having been built for human pain and the confinement of those who frighten you or have information of value. Which—pardon me, Owen—is true."

The Count moved near Sherez' right second fang, the one with the bit of ivory-cementum in it, and crouched, not caring a damn for his robes or his dignity. "I will remember," he said. "Is it not in our concept that we remember our friends?"

Sherez rolled his eye. The split lid creaked a little open. "Exsseptional," the dragon said softly. "Yesss, Owen . . . there may be . . . legendsss."

"What should I do without you, dragon?"

"Substitute reason for prophecy."

Owen stood. "Like an artificer? Then it is the end of life." He looked at the map, crumpled in his white-knuckled hand. "How can I send out ships, men, not knowing if they will return?"

Sherez growled, though Owen did not think it was with anger. "It endss nothing. You will send shipss, and ssometimes they will return, and ssometimes they will not, and ssometimes they will be blown off course and disscover new worldsss . . . Owen, I think this is a good thing, for men."

"To live like artificers? Without faith, except in what hands can touch and measure and take apart?" Owen looked up the stairwell, put his hand on the chain. "I'll smash every one of their mirrors. I'll drive them out with iron and fire!"

"No. There is not even time left. I have thought of a good joke, Owen . . . Ssuppose this experiment itsself contains a paradox? Ssuppose that, succeeding, their success vanishesss too, matter and memory?" Sherez clapped. "Owen, Owen, be sstill. I tell you, there iss no time to make a differensse."

"Will may do what time might not," the Count shouted. He shuttered the lantern with a blow, and ran up the steps, his boots making them ring like a cathedral full of bells.

"*Salt-Owen!*" roared the dragon, and Count Hanowald . . . *had to* . . . stop.

Eyelight spotted him. "Owen, Sssalt-Owen . . . be careful, on the stairsss."

As he neared the top, climbing as fast as care would permit, Count Hanowald heard sounds from the Artificers' Tower: the grate of a steel mainspring, a crash of glass, the yowl of a cat.

As he stepped from iron onto stone, there was a sucking wind behind him, like the breeze that follows a departing army.

The Count turned round and looked down at the black cold dungeon, and wondered why the Devil the door was open.

COCKFIGHT

JANE YOLEN

ILLUSTRATIONS BY
TERRI WINDLING

The pit cleaners circled noisily, gobbling up the old fewmets with their iron mouths. They spat out fresh sawdust and moved on. It generally took several minutes between fights and the mechanical clanking of the cleaners was matched by the roars of the pit-wise dragons and the last-minute betting calls of their masters.

Jakkin heard the noises through the wooden ceiling as he groomed his dragon in the under-pit stalls. It was the first fight for both of them and Jakkin's fingers reflected his nervousness. He simply could not keep them still. They picked off bits of dust and flicked at specks on the dragon's already gleaming scales. They polished and smoothed and polished again. The red dragon seemed oblivious to first fight jitters and arched up under Jakkin's hands.

Jakkin was pleased with his dragon's color. It was a dull red. Not the red of the hollyberry or the red of the wild-flowering trillium, but the red of life's blood spilt upon the sand. It was a fighter's color, and he had known it from the first. That was why he had sneaked the dragon from its nest, away from its hatchlings, when the young worm had emerged from its egg in the sand of the nursery.

The dragon had looked then like any lizard, for it had not yet shed its eggskin which was wrinkled and yellow, like custard scum. But Jakkin had sensed, beneath the skin, a darker shadow and had known it would turn red. Not many would have known, but Jakkin had, though he was only thirteen.

The dragon was not his, not really, for it had belonged to his master's nursery, just as Jakkin did. But on Austar IV there was only one way to escape from bond, and that was with gold. There was no quicker way to get gold than as bettor in the dragon-pits. And there was nothing Jakkin wanted more than to be free. He had lived over half his life bonded to the nursery, from the time his parents had died when he was four. And most of that time he had worked as a stall boy, no better than a human pit cleaner, for Sarkkhan's Dragonry. What did it matter that he lived and slept and ate with his master's dragons? He was allowed to handle only their fewmets and spread fresh sawdust for their needs. If he could not raise a fighting dragon himself and buy his way out of bond, he would end up an *old* stall boy, like Likkarn, who smoked blisterweed, dreamed his days away, and cried red tears.

So Jakkin had watched and waited and learned as much as a junior stall boy could about dragon ways and dragon-lore for he knew the only way out of bond was to steal that first egg and raise it up for fighting or breeding or, if need was great, for the stews. But Jakkin did not know eggs, could sense nothing through the elastic shell, and so he had stolen a young dragon instead. It was a greater risk, for eggs were never counted but the new-hatched dragons were. At Sarkkhan's Dragonry old Likkarn kept the list of hatchlings. He was the only one of the bonders who could write, though Jakkin had taught himself to read a bit.

Jakkin had worried all through the first days that Likkarn

would know and, knowing, tell. He kept the hatchling in a wood crate turned upside-down way out in the sands. He swept away his footsteps to and from the crate and reckoned his way to it at night by the stars. And somehow he had not been found out. His reward had come as the young worm had grown.

First the hatchling had turned a dull brown and could trickle smoke through its nose slits. The wings on its back, crumpled and weak, had slowly stretched to a rubbery thickness. For days it had remained mud-colored. Another boy might have sold it then to the stews, keeping the small fee in his leather bond bag that swung from the metal bond chain around his neck. It would have been a laughable amount, a coin or two at the most, and the bag would have looked just as empty as before.

But Jakkin had waited and the dragon finally molted, patchworking into a red. The nails on its foreclaws, which had been as brittle as jingle shells, were now as hard as golden oak and the same color. Its hindclaws were dull and strong as steel. Its eyes were two black shrouds and it had not roared yet, but Jakkin knew that roar would come, loud and full and fierce, when it was first blooded in the ring. The quality of the roar would start the betting rippling again through the crowd who judged a fighter by the timbre of its voice.

Jakkin could hear the cleaners clanking out of the ring through the mecho-holes. He ran his fingers through his straight brown hair and tried to swallow, then touched a dimple on his cheek that was as deep as a blood score. His hand found the bond bag and kneaded it several times for luck.

"Soon now," he promised the red dragon in a hoarse whisper, his hand still on the bag. "Soon. We will show them a first fight. They will remember us."

The red was too busy munching on blisterwort to reply.

A disembodied voice announced the next fight. "Jakkin's Red, Mekkle's Bottle O' Rum."

Jakkin winced. He knew a little about Mekkle's dragon already. He had heard about it that morning as they had come into the pit stalls. Dragon masters and trainers did not chatter while they groomed their fighters, but bettors did, gathering around the favorites and trading stories of other fights. Mekkle's Rum was a light-colored male that favored its left side and had won three of its seven fights— the last three. It would never be great, the whispers had run, but it was good enough, and a hard draw for a new dragon, possibly disastrous for a would-be dragon master. Jakkin knew his red could be good with time, given the luck of the draw. It had all the things a dragon fighter was supposed to have: it had heart, it listened well, it did all he asked of it. But just as Jakkin had never run a fighter before, the red had never been in a ring. It had never been blooded or given roar. It did not even have its true name yet. Already, he knew, the betting was way against the young red and he could hear the murmur of new bets after the announcement. The odds would be so awful, he might never be able to get a sponsor for a second match. First fights were free, but seconds cost gold. And if he had no sponsor, that would leave only the stews for the dragon and a return to bond for himself.

Jakkin stroked the bond bag once more, then buttoned his shirt up over it to conceal it. He did not know yet what it felt like to be free, so he could stand more years as a bonder. And there might always be another chance to steal. But how could he ever give up the red to the stews? It was not any old dragon, it was his. They had already shared months of training, long nights together under the Austar moons. He knew its mind better than his own. It was a deep glowing cavern of colors and sights and sounds. He remembered the first time he had really felt his way into it, lying on his side, winded from running, the red beside him, a small mountain in the sand. The red calmed him when he was not calm, cheered him when he thought he could not be cheered. Linked as he was with it now, how could he bear to hear its last screams in the stews and stay sane? Perhaps that was why Likkarn was always yelling at the younger bonders, why he smoked blister-weed that turned the mind foggy and made a man cry red tears. And perhaps that was why dragons in the stews were always yearlings or the untrained. Not because they were softer, more succulent, but because no one would hear them when they screamed.

Jakkin's skin felt slimed with perspiration and the drag-on sniffed it on him, giving out a few straggles of smoke from its slits. Jakkin fought down his own fear. If he could not control it, his red would have no chance at all, for a dragon was only as good as its master. He took deep breaths and then moved over to the red's head. He looked into its black, unblinking eyes.

"Thou art a fine one, my Red," he whispered. "First fight for us both, but I trust thee." Jakkin always spoke *thou* to his dragon. He felt, somehow, it brought them closer. "Trust me?"

The dragon responded with slightly rounded smokes. Deep within its eyes Jakkin thought he detected small lights.

"Dragon's fire!" he breathed. "Thou *art* a fighter. I knew it!"

Jakkin slipped the ring from the red dragon's neck and rubbed its scales underneath. They were not yet as hard as a mature fighter's and for a moment he worried that the older Bottle O' Rum might tear the young dragon beyond repair. He pulled the red's head down and whispered into its ear. "Guard thyself here," he said, rubbing with his fingers under the tender neck links and thinking danger at it.

The dragon shook its head playfully and Jakkin slapped it lightly on the neck. With a surge, the red dragon moved out of the stall, over to the dragonlock, and flowed up into the ring.

"It's eager," the whisper ran around the crowd. They always liked that in young dragons. Time enough to grow cautious in the pit. Older dragons often were reluctant and had to be prodded with jumpsticks behind the wings or in the tender underparts of the tail. The bettors considered that a great fault. Jakkin heard the crowd's appreciation as he came up into the stands.

It would have been safer for Jakkin to remain below, guiding his red by mind. That way there would be no chance for Master Sarkkhan to find him here, though he doubted such a well-known breeder would enter a back-country pit fight. And many trainers, Mekkle being one of them, stayed in the stalls drinking and smoking and guiding their dragons where the crowd could not influence them. But Jakkin needed to see the red as well as feel it, to watch the fight through his own eyes as well as the red's. They had trained too long at night, alone, in the sands. He did not know how another dragon in a real fight would respond. He had to see to understand it all. And the red was used to him being close by. He did not want to change that now. Besides, unlike many of the other bonders, he had never been to a fight, only read about them in books and heard about them from his bond mates. This might be his only chance. And, he further rationalized, up in the stands he might find out more about Mekkle's orange that would help him help the red.

Jakkin looked around the stands cautiously from the stairwell. He saw no one he knew, neither fellow bonders nor masters who had traded with Sarkkhan. He edged quietly into the stands, just one more boy at the fights. Nothing called attention to him but the empty bond bag beneath his shirt. He checked his buttons carefully to make sure they were closed. Then he leaned forward and watched as his red circled the ring.

It held its head high and measured the size of the pit, the height of the walls. It looked over the bettors as if it were counting them, and an appreciative chuckle went through the crowd. Then the red scratched in the sawdust several times, testing its depth. And still Bottle O' Rum had not appeared.

Then with an explosion, Bottle O' Rum came through the dragonlock and landed with all four feet planted well beneath the level of the sawdust, his claws fastened immoveably to the boards.

"Good stance," shouted someone in the crowd and the betting began anew.

The red gave a little flutter with its wings, a flapping that might indicate nervousness and Jakkin thought at it: "He is a naught. A stander. But thy nails and wings are fresh. Do not be afraid. Remember thy training." At that the little red's head went high and its neck scales glittered in the artificial sun of the pit.

"Watch that neck," shouted a heckler. "There's one that'll be blooded soon."

"Too soon," shouted another from across the stands at him.

Bottle O' Rum charged the inviting neck.

It was just as Jakkin hoped, for charging from the fighting stance is a clumsy maneuver at best. The claws must be retracted simultaneously, and the younger the dragon the more brittle its claws. The orange, Rum, was seven fights older than the red, but it was not yet mature. As Rum charged, one of the nails on his front right claw caught in the floor-boards and splintered, causing him to falter for a second. The red shifted its position slightly. Instead of blooding the red on the vulnerable neck, Rum's charge brought him headlong onto the younger dragon's chest plates, the hardest and slipperiest part of a fighting dragon's armor. The screech of teeth on scale brought winces to the crowd. Only Jakkin was ready, for it was a maneuver he had taught his dragon out in the hidden sands.

"Now!" he cried out and thought at once.

The young red needed no urging. It bent its neck around in a fast, vicious slash, and blood spurted from behind the ears of Mekkle's Rum.

"First blood!" cried the crowd.

Now the betting would change, Jakkin thought with a certain pleasure, and touched the bond bag through the thin cloth of his shirt. Ear bites bleed profusely but were not important. It would hurt the orange dragon a little, like a pin-prick or a splinter does a man. It would make the dragon mad and—more important—a bit more cautious. But first blood! It looked good.

Bottle O' Rum roared with the bite, loud and piercing. It was too high up in the throat yet with surprising strength. Jakkin listened carefully, trying to judge. He had heard dragons roar at the nursery in mock battles or when the keepers blooded them for customers intent on hearing the timbre before buying. To him the roar sounded as if it had all its power in the top tones and none that resonated. Perhaps he was wrong, but if his red could *outlast* the orange, it might impress this crowd.

In his eagerness to help his dragon, Jakkin moved to the pit rail. He elbowed his way through some older men.

"Here youngster, what do you think you're doing?" A man in a grey leather coverall spoke. He was obviously familiar with the pits. Anyone in leather knew his way around. And his face, what could be seen behind the grey beard, was scored with dragonblood scars.

"Get back up in the stands. Leave ringside to the money men," said his companion, taking in Jakkin's leather-patched cloth shirt and trousers with a dismissing look. He ostentatiously jounced a full bag that hung from his wrist on a leather thong.

Jakkin ignored them, fingering his badge with the facs picture of the red on it. He leaned over the rail. "Away, away good Red," he thought at his dragon and smiled when the red immediately wheeled and winged up from its blooded foe. Only then did he turn and address the two scowling bettors. "Pit right, good Sirs," he said with deference, pointing at the same time to his badge.

They mumbled, but moved aside for him.

The orange dragon in the pit shook its head and the blood beaded its ears like a crown. A few drops spattered over the walls and into the stands. Each place a drop touched burned with that glow peculiar to the acidy drag-on's blood. One watcher in the third row of the stands was not quick enough and was seared on the cheek. He reached up a hand to the wound but did not move from his place.

The orange Rum stood up tall again and dug back into the dust.

"Another stand," said the grey leather man to Jakkin's right.

"Pah, that's all it knows," said the dark man beside him. "That's how it won its three fights. Good stance, but that's it. I wonder why I bet it at all. Let's go and get something to smoke. This fight's a bore."

Jakkin watched them leave from the corner of his eye, but he absorbed their information. If the orange was a stander, if the information were true, it would help him with the fight.

The red dragon's leap back had taken it to the north side of the pit. When it saw that Bottle O' Rum had chosen to stand, it circled closer warily.

Jakkin thought at it, "He's good in the stance. Do not force him there. Make him come to thee."

The dragon's thoughts, as always, came back clearly to Jakkin wordless but full of color and emotion. The red wanted to charge; the dragon it had blooded was waiting. The overwhelming urge was to carry the fight to the foe.

"No, my Red. Trust me. Be eager, but not foolish," cautioned Jakkin, looking for an opening.

But the crowd, as eager as the young dragon, was communicating with it, too. The yells of the men, their thoughts of charging, overpowered Jakkin's single line of calm. The red started to move.

When it saw the red bunching for a charge, Rum solidified his stance. His shoulders went rigid with the strain. Jakkin knew that if his red dived at that standing rock, it could quite easily break a small bone in its neck. And rarely did a dragon come back to the pit once its neck bones had been set. Then it was good only for the breeding nurseries—if it had a fine pit-record—or the stews.

"Steady, steady," Jakkin said, aloud. Then he shouted and waved a hand, "NO!"

The red had already started its dive, but the movement of Jakkin's hand was a signal too powerful for it to ignore and, at the last possible minute, it pulled to one side. As it passed, Rum slashed at it with a gaping mouth and shredded its wingtip.

"Blood," the crowd roared and waited for the red dragon to roar back.

Jakkin felt its confusion and his head swam with the red of dragon's blood as his dragon's thoughts came to him. He watched as it soared to the top of the building and scorched its wingtip on the artificial sun, cauterizing the wound. Then, still hovering, it opened its mouth for its first blooded roar.

There was no sound.

"A mute!" called a man from the stands. He spit angrily to one side. "Never heard one before."

A wit near him shouted back, "You won't hear this one, either."

The crowd laughed at this, and passed the quip around the stands.

But Jakkin only stared up at his red bitterly. "A mute," he thought at it. "You are as powerless as I."

His use of the distancing pronoun *you* further confused the young dragon, and it began to circle downward in a disconsolate spiral, closer and closer to the waiting Rum, its mind a maelstrom of blacks and greys.

Jakkin realized his mistake in time. "It does not matter," he cried out in his mind. "Even with no roar, thee wilt be great." He said it with more conviction that he really felt, but it was enough for the red. It broke out of its spiral and hovered, wings working evenly.

The maneuver, however, was so unexpected that the pit-wise Bottle O' Rum was bewildered. He came out of his stance with a splattering of dust and fewmets, stopped, then charged again. The red avoided him easily, landing on his back and raking the orange scales with its claws. That drew no blood, but it frightened the older dragon into a hindfoot rise. Balancing on his tail, Rum towered nearly eight feet high, his front claws scoring the air, a single shot of fire streaking from his slits.

The red backwinged away from the flames and waited.

"Steady, steady," thought Jakkin, in control again. He let his mind recall for them both the quiet sands and the cool nights when they had practiced with the wooden dragon-form on charges and clawing. Then Jakkin repeated outloud, "Steady, steady."

A hard hand on his shoulder broke through his thoughts and the sweet-strong smell of blisterweed assailed him. Jakkin turned.

"Not so steady yourself," came a familiar voice.

Jakkin stared up at the ravaged face, pocked with blood scores and stained with tear-lines.

"Likkarn," breathed Jakkin, suddenly and terribly afraid.

Jakkin tried to turn back to the pit where his red waited. The hand on his shoulder was too firm, the fingers like claws through his shirt.

"And how did you become a dragon trainer?" the man asked.

Jakkin thought to bluff. The old stall boy was often too sunk in his smokedreams to really listen. Bluff and run, for the wild anger that came after blister-dreams never gave a smoker time to reason. "I found . . . found an egg, Likkarn," he said. And it could be true. There were a few wild dragons, bred from escapes that had gone feral.

The man said nothing but shook his head.

Jakkin stared at him. This was a new Likkarn, harder, full of purpose. Then Jakkin noticed. Likkarn's eyes were clearer than he had ever seen them, no longer the furious pink of the weeder, but a softer rose. He had not smoked for several days at least. It was useless to bluff or run. "I took it from the nursery, Likkarn. I raised it in the sands. I trained it at night, by the moons."

"That's better. Much better. Liars are an abomination," the man said with a bitter laugh. "And you fed it what?

Goods stolen from the master, I wager. You born-bonders know nothing. Nothing."

Jakkin's cheeks were burning now. "I am no born-bonder. And I would never steal from the Master's stores. I planted in the sands last year and grew blisterweed and burnwort. I gathered the rest in the swamps. *On my own time.*" He added that fiercely.

"Bonders have no time of their own," Likkarn muttered savagely. "And supplements?"

"The Master says supplements are bad for a fighter. They make a fighter fast in the beginning, but they dilute the blood." Jakkin looked into Likkarn's eyes more boldly now. "I heard the Master say that. To a buyer."

Likkarn's smile was wry and twisted. "And you eavesdrop as well." He gave Jakkin's shoulder a particularly vicious wrench.

Jakkin gasped and closed his eyes with the pain. He wanted to cry out, and thought he had, when he realized it was not his own voice he heard but a scream from the pit. He pulled away from Likkarn and stared. The scream was Bottle O' Rum's, a triumphant roar as he stood over the red whose injured wing was pinioned beneath Rum's right front claw.

"*Jakkin . . .*" came Likkarn's voice behind him, full of warning. How often Jakkin had heard that tone right before old Likkarn had roused from a weed dream to the fury that always followed. Likkarn was old, but his fist was still solid.

Jakkin trembled, but he willed his focus onto the red whose thoughts came tumbling back into his head now in a tangle of muted colors and whines. He touched his hand to the small lump under his shirt where the bond bag hung. He could feel his own heart beating through the leather shield. "Never mind, my Red," soothed Jakkin. "Never mind the pain. Recall the time I stood upon thy wing and we played at the Great Upset. Recall it well, thou mighty fighter. Remember. Remember."

The red stirred only slightly and made a flutter with its free wing. The crowd saw this as a gesture of submission. So did Rum and, through him, his Master Mekkle. But Jakkin did not. He knew the red had listened well and understood. The game was not over yet. Pit-fighting was not all brawn; how often Master Sarkkhan had said that. The best fighters, the ones who lasted for years, were cunning gamesters and it was this he had guessed about his red from the first.

The fluttering of the unpinioned wing caught Bottle O' Rum's eye and the orange dragon turned towards it, relaxing his hold by a single nail.

The red fluttered its free wing again. Flutter and feint. Flutter and feint. It needed the orange's attention totally on that wing. Then its tail could do the silent stalking it had learned in the sands with Jakkin.

Bottle O' Rum followed the fluttering as though laughing for his own coming triumph. His dragon jaws opened slightly in a deadly grin. If Mekkle had been in the stands instead of below in the stalls, the trick might not have worked. But the orange dragon, intent on the fluttering wing, leaned his head way back and fully opened his jaws, readying for the kill. He was unaware of what was going on behind him.

"Now!" shouted Jakkin in his mind and only later realized that the entire stands had roared the words with him. Only the crowd had been roaring for the wrong dragon.

The red's tail came around with a snap, as vicious and as accurate as a driver's whip. It caught the orange on its injured ear and across an eye.

Rum screamed instead of roaring and let go of the red's
wing. The red was up in an instant and leaped for Bottle O'
Rum's throat.

One, two and the ritual slashes were made. The orange
throat was coruscated with blood and Rum instantly
dropped to the ground.

Jakkin's dragon backed at once, slightly akilter because
of the wound in its wing.

"Game to Jakkin's Red," said the disembodied voice
over the speaker.

The crowd was strangely silent. Then a loud whoop
sounded from one voice buried in the stands, a bettor who
had taken a chance on the First Fighter.

That single voice seemed to rouse Bottle O' Rum. He
raised his head from the ground groggily. Only his head
and half his neck cleared the dust. He strained to arch his
neck over, exposing the underside to the light. The two red
slashes glistened like thin hungry mouths. Then Rum
began a strange, horrible humming that changed to a
high-pitched whine. His body began to shake and the
shaking became part of the sound as the dust eddied
around him.

The red dragon swooped down and stood before the
fallen Rum, as still as stone. Then it, too, began to shake.

The sound changed from a whine to a high roar. Jakkin
had never heard anything like it before. He put his hands
to the bond bag, then to his ears.

"What is it? What is happening?" he cried out, but the
men on either side of him had moved away. Palms to ears,
they backed towards the exits. Many in the crowd had
already gone down the stairs, setting the thick wood walls
between themselves and the noise.

Jakkin tried to reach the red dragon's mind, but all he
felt were storms of orange winds, hot and blinding, and a

shaft of burning white light. As he watched, the red rose up on its hind legs and raked the air frantically with its claws as if getting ready for some last deadly blow.

"Fool's Pride," came Likkarn's defeated voice behind him, close enough to his ear to hear. "That damnable dragon wants death. He has been shamed and he'll scream your red into it. Then you'll know. All you'll have left is a killer on your hands. I lost three that way. *Three*. Fool's Pride." He shouted the last at Jakkin's back for at his first words, Jakkin had thrown himself over the railing into the pit. He landed on all fours, but was up and running at once.

He had heard of Fool's Pride, that part of the fighting dragon's bloody past that was not always bred out. Fool's Pride that led some defeated dragons to demand death. It had nearly caused dragons to become extinct. If men had not carefully watched the lines, trained the fighters to lose with grace, there would have been no dragons left on Austar IV. A good fighter should have a love of blooding, yes. But killing made dragons unmanageable, made them feral, made them wild.

Jakkin crashed into the red's side. "No, no," he screamed up at it, beating on its body with his fists. "Do not wet thy jaws in his death." He reached as high as he could and held on to the red's neck. The scales slashed one of his palms, but he did not let go.

It was his touch more than his voice or his thoughts that stopped the young red. It turned slowly, sluggishly, as if rousing from a dream. Jakkin fell from its neck to the ground.

The movement away shattered Bottle O' Rum's concentration. He slipped from screaming to unconsciousness in an instant.

The red nuzzled Jakkin, its eyes unfathomable, its mind

still clouded. The boy stood up. Without bothering to brush the dust from his clothes, he thought at it, *"Thou mighty First."*

The red suddenly crowded his mind with victorious sunbursts, turned, then streaked back through the hole to its stall and the waiting burnwort.

Mekkle and two friends came up the stairs, glowering, leaped into the pit and dragged the fainting orange out through a mecho-hole by his tail.

Only then did Jakkin walk back to ringside, holding his cut hand palm up. It had just begun to sting.

Likkarn, still standing by the railing, was already smoking a short strand of blisterweed. He stared blankly as the red smoke circled his head.

"I owe you," Jakkin said slowly up to him, hating to admit it. "I did not know Fool's Pride when I saw it. Another minute and the red would have been good for nothing but the stews. If I ever get a Second Fight, I will give you some of the gold. *Your bag is not yet full."*

Jakkin meant the last phrase simply as ritual, but Likkarn's eyes suddenly roused to weed fury. His hand went to his throat. "You owe me nothing," said the old man. He held his head high and the agelines on his neck crisscrossed like old fight scars. *"Nothing.* You owe the master everything. I need no reminder that I am a bonder. *I fill my bag myself."*

Jakkin bowed his head under the old man's assault. "Let me tend the red's wounds. Then do with me as you will." He turned and, without waiting for an answer, ducked through the mecho-hole and slid down the shaft.

Jakkin came to the stall where the red was already at work grooming itself, polishing its scales with a combination of fire and spit. He slipped the ring around its neck and

knelt down by its side. Briskly he put his hand out to touch
its wounded wing, in a hurry to finish the examination
before Likkarn came down. The red drew back at his
touch, sending a mauve landscape into his mind, dripping
with grey tears.

"Hush little flametongue," crooned Jakkin, slowing
himself down and using the lullaby sounds he had in-
vented to soothe the hatchling of the sands. "I won't hurt
thee. I want to help."

But the red continued to retreat from him, crouching
against the wall.

Puzzled, Jakkin pulled his hand back, yet still the red
huddled away, and a spurt of yellow-red fire flamed from
its slits. "Not here, furnace-lung," said Jakkin, annoyed.
"That will set the stall on fire."

A rough hand pushed him aside. It was Likkarn, no
longer in the weed dream but starting into the uncontrollable fury that capped a weed-sequence. The dragon, its
mind open with the pain of its wound and the finish of the
fight, had picked up Likkarn's growing anger and reacted
to it.

"You don't know wounds," growled Likkarn. "I'll show
you what a *real* trainer knows." He grabbed the dragon's
torn wing and held it firmly, then with a quick motion, and
before Jakkin could stop him, he set his mouth on the
jagged tear.

The dragon reared back in alarm and tried to whip its tail
around, but the stalls were purposely built small to curb
such motion. Its tail scraped along the wall and barely
tapped the man. But Jakkin grabbed at Likkarn's arm with
both hands and furiously tore him from the red's wing.

"I'll kill you, you weeder," he screamed. "Can't you
wait til a dragon is in the stews before you try to eat it. I'll kill
you." He slammed at Likkarn with his fist and feet, know-

ing as he did it that the man's weed-anger would be turned
on him and he might be killed by it, and not caring.
Suddenly Jakkin felt himself being lifted up from behind,
his legs dangling, kicking uselessly at the air. A strong arm
around his waist held him fast. Another pushed Likkarn
back against the wall.

"Hold off, boy. He was a good trainer—once. And he's
right about the best way to deal with a wing wound. An
open part, filled with dragon's blood, might burn the tongue surely. But a man's tongue heals quickly, and there is
something in human saliva that closes these small tears."

Jakkin twisted around as best he could and saw the man
he had most feared seeing. It was Master Sarkkhan himself, in a leather suit of the red-and-gold nursery colors. His
red beard was brushed out and he looked grim.

Sarkkhan put the boy down but held on to him with one
hand. With the other, he brushed his hair back from a
forehead that was pitted with blood scores as evenly
spaced as a bonder's chain. "Now promise me you will let
Likkarn look to the red's wing."

"I will not. He's a weeder and he's as likely to rip the red
as heal it and the red hates him—just as I do," shouted
Jakkin. There he stopped and put the back of his hand
over his mouth, shocked at his own bold words.

Likkarn raised his hand to the boy and aimed a blow at
his head, but before the slap landed, the dragon nosed
forward and pushed the man to the ground.

Master Sarkkhan let go of Jakkin's shoulder, and
considered the red for a moment. "I think the boy is right,
Likkarn. The dragon won't have you. It's too closely linked. I wouldn't have guessed that, but there it is. Best leave
this to the boy and me."

Likkarn got up clumsily and brushed off his clothes. His
bond bag had fallen over the top of his overall bib in the

scuffle and Jakkin was shocked to see that it was halfway plump, jangling with coins. Likkarn caught his look and angrily stuffed the bag back inside, then jabbed at the outline of Jakkin's bag under his shirt with a reddened finger. "And how much have *you* got there, boy?" He walked off with as much dignity as he could muster to slump by the stairwell and watch.

Sarkkhan ignored them both and crouched down by the dragon, letting it get the smell of him. He caressed its jaws and under its neck with his large, scarred hands. Slowly the big man worked his way back towards the wings, crooning at the dragon in low tones, smoothing its scales, all the while staring into its eyes. Slowly the membranes, top and bottom, shuttered the red's eyes and it relaxed. Only then did Sarkkhan let his hand close over the wounded wing. The dragon gave a small shudder but was otherwise quite still.

"Your red did a good job searing its wound on the light. Did you teach it that?"

"No," the boy admitted.

"Of course not, foolish of me. How could you. No light in the sands. Good breeding then," said Sarkkhan with a small chuckle of appreciation. "And I should know. After all, your dragon's mother is my best—Heart O' Mine."

"You . . . you knew all along, then." Jakkin felt as confused as a blooded First.

Sarkkhan stood up and stretched. In the confines of the stall he seemed enormous, a red-gold giant. Jakkin suddenly felt smaller than his years.

"*Fewmets,* boy, of course I knew," Sarkkhan answered. "I know *everything* that happens at my nursery."

Jakkin collapsed down next to his dragon and put his arm over its neck. When he finally spoke, it was in a very small voice. "Then why did you let me do it? Why did you let me steal the dragon? Were you trying to get me in trouble? Do you want me in gaol?"

The man threw back his head and roared, and the dragons in neighboring stalls stirred uneasily at the sound. Even Likkarn started at the laugh and a trainer six stalls down growled in disapproval. Then Sarkkhan looked down at the boy, crouched by the red dragon. "I'm sorry, boy, I forget how young you are. Never known anyone quite that young to successfully train a hatchling. But every man gets a chance to steal one egg. It's a kind of test, you might say. The only way to break out of bond. Some men are meant to be bonders, some masters. How else can you tell? Likkarn's tried it—endless times, eh old man?" The master glanced over at Likkarn with a look akin to affection, but Likkarn only glared back. "Steal an egg and try. The only things it is wrong to steal are a bad egg or your master's provisions." Sarkkhan stopped talking for a minute and mused, idly running a hand over the red dragon's back as it chewed contentedly now on its burnwort, little grey straggles of smoke easing from its slits. "Of course most *do* steal bad eggs or are too impatient to train what comes out and instead they make a quick sale to the stews just for a few coins to jangle in their bags. Then it's back to bond again before a month is out. It's only the ones who steal provisions that land in gaol, boy."

"Then you won't put me in gaol. Or the red in the stews? I couldn't let you do that, Master Sarkkhan. Not even you. I wouldn't let you. I . . ." Jakkin began to stutter as he often did in his master's presence.

"Send a First Fighter, a *winner* to the stews? *Fewmets,* boy, where's your brain. Been smoking blisterweed?" Sarkkhan hunkered down next to him.

Jakkin looked down at his sandals. His feet were soiled

from the dust of the stall. He ordered his stomach to calm down, and he felt an answering muted rainbow of calm from the dragon. Then a peculiar thought came to him. "Did *you* have to steal an egg, Master Sarkkhan?"

The big red-headed man laughed and thrust his hand right into Jakkin's face. Jakkin drew back but Sarkkhan was holding up two fingers and wiggling them before his eyes.

"Two! I stole two. A male and a female. And it was not mere chance. Even then I knew the difference. *In the egg* I knew. And that's why I'm the best breeder on Austar IV." He stood up abruptly and held out his hand to the boy. "But enough. The red is fine and you are due upstairs." He yanked Jakkin to his feet and seemed at once to lose his friendliness.

"Upstairs?" Jakkin could not think what that meant. "You said I was not to go to gaol. I want to stay with the red. I want . . ."

"*Worm-wort,* boy, have you been listening or not? You have to register that dragon, give her a name, record her as a First Fighter, a winner."

"*Her?*" Jakkin heard only the one word.

"Yes, a her. Do you challenge *me* on that? And I want to come with you and collect my gold. I bet a bagfull on that red of yours—on Likkarn's advice. He's been watching you train, my orders. He said she was looking good and sometimes I believe him." Sarkkhan moved towards the stairwell where Likkarn still waited. "I owe him you know. He taught me everything."

"Likkarn? Taught you?"

They stopped by the old man who was slumped again in another blisterweed dream. Sarkkhan reached out and took the stringy red weed ash from the old man's hand. He threw it on the floor and ground it savagely into the dust.

"He wasn't born a weeder, boy. And he hasn't forgotten all he once knew." Then shaking his head, Master Sarkkhan moved up the stairs, impatiently waving a hand at the boy to follow.

A stray strand of color-pearls passed through Jakkin's mind and he turned around to look at the dragon's stall. Then he gulped and said in a rush at Sarkkhan's back, "But she's a mute, Master. She may have won this fight by wiles, but she's a mute. No one will bet on a dragon that cannot roar."

The man reached down and grabbed Jakkin's hand, yanking him through the doorway and up the stairs. They mounted two at a time. "You really are lizard-waste," said Sarkkhan, punctuating his sentences with another step. "Why do you think I sent a half-blind weeder skulking around the sands at night watching you train a snatchling? Because I'd lost my mind? *Fewmets,* boy. I want to know what is happening to every damned dragon I have bred because I have had a hunch and a hope these past two years, breeding small-voiced dragons together. I've been *trying* to breed a mute. Think of it, a mute fighter—why, it would give nothing away, not to pit foes or to bettors. A mute fighter and its trainer . . ." and Sarkkhan stopped on the stairs, looking down at the boy. "Why they'd rule the pits, boy."

They finished the stairs and turned down the hallway. Sarkkhan strode ahead and Jakkin had to doubletime in order to keep up with the big man's strides.

"Master Sarkkhan," he began at the man's back.

Sarkkhan did not break stride but growled, "I am no longer your master, Jakkin. *You* are a master now. A master trainer. That dragon will speak only to you, go only on your command. Remember that and act accordingly."

Jakkin blinked twice and touched his chest. "But . . .

but my bag is empty. I have no gold to fill it. I have no sponsor for my next fight. I . . .''

Sarkkhan whirled, and his eyes were fierce. "*I* am sponsor for your next fight, I thought that much, at least, was clear. And when your bag is full, you will pay me no gold for your bond. Instead I want pick of the first hatching when the red is bred—to a mate of my choosing. If she is a complete mute, she may breed true, and *I* mean to have it."

"Oh, Master Sarkkhan," Jakkin cried, suddenly realizing that all his dreams were realities, "you may have the pick of the first *three* hatchings." He grabbed the man's hand and tried to shake his thanks into it.

"*Fewmets!*" the man yelled, startling some of the passers-by. He shook the boy's hand loose. "How can you ever become a bettor if you offer it all up front. You have to disguise your feelings better than that. Offer me the pick of the *third* hatching. Counter me. Make me work for whatever I get."

Jakkin said softly, testing, "The pick of the third."

"First two," said Sarkkhan, softly back and his smile came slowly. Then he roared, "Or I'll have you in gaol and the red in the stews."

A crowd began to gather around them, betting on the outcome of the uneven match. Sarkkhan was a popular figure at pit-fights and the boy was leather-patched, obviously a bonder, an unknown, worm-waste.

All at once Jakkin felt as if he were at pitside. He felt the red's mind flooding into his, a rainbow effect that gave him a rush of courage. It was a game, then, all a game. And he knew how to play. "The second," said Jakkin, smiling back. "After all, Heart's Blood is a First Fighter, and a winner. And," he hissed at Sarkkhan so that only the two of them could hear, "she's a mute." Then he stood straight and said loudly so that it carried to the crowd. "You'll be lucky to have pick of the second."

Sarkkhan stood silently as if considering both the boy and the crowd. He brushed his hair back from his forehead, then nodded. "Done," he said. "A hard bargain." Then he reached over and ruffled Jakkin's hair and they walked off together.

The crowd, settling their bets, let them through.

"I *thought* you were a good learner," Sarkkhan said to the boy. "Second it is. Though," and he chuckled and said quietly, "you should remember this. There is never anything good in a first hatching. Second is the best by far."

"I didn't know," said Jakkin.

"Why should you?" countered Sarkkhan. "*You* are not the best breeder on Austar IV. I am. But I like the name you picked. Heart's Blood out of Heart O' Mine. It suits."

They went through the doorway together to register the red and to stuff Jakkin's bag with hard-earned dragon's gold.

FROM BACH TO BROCCOLI

RICHARD KEARNS

ILLUSTRATIONS BY
GEOFREY DARROW

So they think they can get away with it here.

In *my* forest.

The breeze lightly fingers the branches in front of me, making the sunny leaves flutter, and I catch momentary jigsaw puzzle glimpses of the thing. It's not the usual manifestation of the Building. Instead of the typical red brick and white mortared box, this one is glass enclosed, with fluorescent lights marking the longitude in a sea of ceiling tiles. The word "GROCERIES" is poised, diverlike, on the edge of the roof.

I should have suspected it weeks ago, when those green gravel paths began to appear, when I found the bushes and smaller trees trimmed and sculpted into spheres, cubes, and pyramids, when I began to run into well-organized compost heaps. At the time, I figured it was the work of an escaped park keeper. Or maybe a retired gardner. Minor irritations at the most.

It wasn't until the last few days, when I started finding dozens of neatly painted nature trail signs placed conspicuously in the underbrush that I knew for sure. At first they were of a helpful nature, planted carefully in various patches of poison ivy, informing me that *"Rhus To-xicodendron,* a climbing plant related to Sumac *(Rhus Aromatica),* can be recognized by its shiny 3-parted leaves, and may irritate the skin of one who touches it." Not that I didn't know that already, of course.

The signs quickly became more sinister: "Keep Off The Grass;" "No Swimming;" "No Fishing;" "No Strolling After Dark;" and finally, "Absolutely No Whistling Or Humming Permitted."

Clear unmistakable indications.

I knew there had to be a Building in the area. And that the Administration was on the move again.

They got Louie with a library last spring. And Angelina with a hotel before that. And I'm sure Dirk was polished off by the grinding mill too, although no one else is quite so convinced about that.

We dealt with those Building incursions—firmly, decisively, holding our ground, stopping the westward expansion of the Administration into Midworld territory. They've never been able to stand up to the combined strength of the Midworld lords. But it was costly: acres of first class wilderness were destroyed, wilderness that will take centuries to rebuild.

I peer down at the grocery store again. Already I can spot signs of a parking lot beginning to form around the Building periphery, and that's all it'll take to destroy what is left of the clearing.

It intrigues me, though. I've never seen the Building in grocery store form before. Never heard of it that way, either. So it constitutes new game afoot, a new challenge. I like that.

I made this forest what it is today. I planted most of the saplings, tended the undergrowth, supervised the annual rate of decay in compliance with the current Midworld regulations. I'll be damned if I'm just going to sit back and let the Building eat my work away. I'll have to go inside.

I kneel and fill my coat pockets with stones, dead leaves, and dirt—just in case. Then I move forward, cautiously.

Close up, the grocery store is not as impressive as it was from a distance. Sections of it, like the edges of the parking lot, are still newly grown and very spongy. It's obvious the thing hasn't put down roots yet.

Inside, the predominant color is white faded into beige, flecks of color here and there adding a stale kind of life to the scene. The checkout counters stand in a solemn line, unattended, dark, mostly brown. Beyond lies an infinity of shelves. The air hums a dead nothing, a buzz that isn't there.

I hear a soft sound behind me, and turn quickly, only to find that my escape has been cut off. I should have expected it—not that it makes any difference now.

Outside, my beautifully forested morning has receded to a mural, a nine by twelve foot black and white glossy print complete with frame. This isn't good.

I look around for signs of activity. Usually when you enter the Building, there's a department manager standing nearby, armed to the teeth with the local variety of thunderbolt, ready to dispute your passage in or out. This is because even singly, we Midworlders are not without our own resources.

No one seems to be stirring, so, resources present and accounted for, I turn my attention to the mural. Black and white and grey frown back at me.

I concentrate. The image wavers, and then turns brown, sepia-toned, warm feelings flooding the scene. Red appears, marking a few flower patches. Then orange. Then yellow. Green blotches show up where there should be underbrush and tree leaves. The sky blue sky winks in, along with a couple of fresh-scrubbed clouds.

Then nothing.

I can't get it to budge.

The mural just sits there, looking like a postcard with a thyroid condition.

I study the thing, accepting the fact that I am stuck. For a while, at least. I wonder if there's a way to get any messages out.

"Oh! I'm glad to see you're here on time! It's such a good way to start out!"

Whirling, I discover a checker, dressed in a pink gingham jacket, jeans, and blue tennis shoes. Her hair is cut short, and is brown, like the counters. Her eyes are blue, like the sky through the spokes of a bicycle wheel, turning. Her smile comes out warm, like the summer day that goes 'round in her eyes. Her badge says "Helen."

I smile back. "Hi!" Positive approaches are often well received in difficult situations.

"Hmph." The smile fades as she glances at the mural, her eyeblue changing from summer to metallic, ice cold, calculating. Eyes cold, even "Well, you'd better start. The Maestro will be here later to check your work."

"The Maestro?" That would probably be the missing department manager—but a Maestro in a grocery store?

"Yeah. He'll be back soon, so you'd better get a move on. If you start now, you can finish the broccoli and start scoring the peas and carrots before lunch."

"Peas and carrots? Broccoli?"

"What'd you think? You were going to start out on steak and seafood?"

"Well, that's not—"

"You better believe it's not. So get going! You know what they do to lazy people around here, don't you?"

"I can guess."

"Keep guessing then. But get the lead out. Paper is over there on the counter, along with pencils and stuff."

"See you at lunch?"

She lets loose a brief fragment of a smile. "Sure." Then she flounces off around a corner and down one of the aisles.

Good. I'm unrecognized. That ups my chances of survival several thousand percent. If I can avoid blowing my ready-made cover, I can probably manage to pull this whole thing off, given enough time. I would have had to wait for the manager to show up anyway.

I trudge over to the indicated register and put on the apron I find draped over the counter. Might as well be dressed for the part. Grabbing a notebook and a handful of pens and pencils, their colors oddly recalling an arrogant patch of wildflowers I had to work with once, I set off in search of the broccoli.

Broccoli, I find, resides halfway down aisle 16. Beneath the white on red placard that makes the pronouncement, I find shelves and shelves of silvery cans, their contents indicated in black stamped letters.

I seat myself on the floor and open the notebook. Inside, I find musical scores, filling, perhaps, half the pages. The other half of the book is filled with empty staff lines: bases and trebles cleffed, times timed, keys keyed, and the measures measured—but no notes.

Hm.

On the shelves behind me a riot of brussel sprouts shouts itself hoarse in a flurry of labels and prices, so I check the last completed composition in my notebook. Several pages of music have been sketched in under the dubious title of "Overture to Beets and Brussel Sprouts."

Everything is beginning to make sense, if that's what you call it.

The time has come for an experiment. I pick up a black pen from my pile and tentatively sketch a quarter note in the empty treble cleff. Softly, a click snicks itself out from the top shelf, revealing a labeled (green, yellow, brown, black, white, and 37¢) can of broccoli.

Double hm.

I change the quarter note into an eighth, adding a twin beside it. Now there are two labeled cans, this time 2 for 75¢. Presto! Instant cover!

Filling in the measure's melody to an accompanying chorus of click snicking, I sketch out the harmony, which finishes the shelf. Different colored notes, I discover, flavor the broccoli, even adding ingredients on occasion (like cheese or butter). Chords tend to change the labeling or packaging (I managed to change some cans into glass jars once, using the chord progression from an old Harrison tune).

Time passes, and so does the broccoli. Midway through the peas and carrots (if you handle them the right way, you can usually add pearl onions and a butter sauce), I notice I'm being followed.

At first glance, he looks like a penguin. His skin is a pale frost white, his head balding over his glasses, which makes saucers out of his two too blue eyes. He smiles when he sees the glass broccoli, and his smile is like cold whitecaps breaking on a bitter shore. Three feet tall, he wears a tuxedo buttonholed with a red carnation. He bumps into me as he begins to assess the peas and carrots.

I apologize.

"No, no, that's quite all right," he counters, in what must be his best professional manner. He pulls out one of the finished cans and examines it with a magnifying glass. "This could really be quite good, you know. Quite good."

"Oh." No one has ever complemented my vegetables before. Still, we have to please ourselves first. I turn to regard my work.

"Maestro, just call me Maestro. You know, we weren't expecting you until tomorrow afternoon. Remarkable, the things they're doing in the Placement Division these days, just remarkable. Pity what happened to those last three clerks—quite sad."

"Sad?"

"Yes. Pity. But never mind—please continue—so much to do and all that, you know."

"Right—sir. Um—will you be observing me, then?"

"Hm? Oh, yes, quite, quite. Shy in the face of true greatness and all of that. I keep forgetting. Here, hand that over. I'll show you how to do this the right way."

He snatches the notebook and faces the unfinished peas and carrots. Holding the staff paper stiffly in his left hand, he slowly raises his right fingers to his forehead and half-closes his eyes.

I exhale slowly, seat myself, and commence waiting. Maybe the right opportunity will present itself, and I'll be out of here before lunch—although it would be a shame to have to skip lunch with Helen. Duty is duty, though.

Five minutes.

Ten minutes. I marvel at my fortitude.

Fifteen minutes. I wonder what the Maestro would look like wrapped in a broccoli label.

"Is anything supposed to happen?"

"Hush! I'm being inspired!"

"Oh."

Twenty minutes. Inspiration must be an elusive thing when it comes to peas and carrots.

Twenty-five minutes. The Maestro bends down and picks up my yellow felt-tip marker, uncapping it with a dramatic flair.

"Anarchist!" he cries, and starts throwing cans at me."

Poising the pen, he looks back and forth between the shelf and the music several times, evidently checking his inspiration. Suddenly, with a quick, furious scribbling motion, he colors in about five measures worth of work, bass and treble cleffs. He takes a deep breath and lets it out again, evidently relieved, as he dabs his forehead with a white silk handkerchief.

I am mystified. I walk over and look at the unchanged cans, which grin back at me like bad teeth. I walk back to the sheet and look at the five yellow measures. I look at the Maestro.

"Well?"

"Watch," he says, finger astride his nose.

"Watch what—"

"Hush, hush! You can't have good art or good music or good food without mood."

And here am I, worried about packaging.

He produces a fountain pen from inside his coat. Daintily, he sketches four whole notes in four measures, and completes the chords underneath them. He frowns at the page. Then he throws in a final whole note chord to complete the sequence. Still not satisfied, he adds a slow crescendo from beginning to end, with a fermata holding the last resolve until cut off by the director.

A miniature machine gun crackling can be heard from the top of the shelves in front of us, producing tiny one ounce cans of peas and carrots. I pick one up, and find that the can is now made of solid gold. Instead of a paper label, letters have been skillfully painted on the can, a miniature of The Blue Boy flanking the nutritional breakdown. On the second set of shelves, I find two ounce cans, still gold and still hand painted.

A slow smirk creeps across my face, but I try to hide it anyway. The weight of the cans is increasing geometrically! Ounces are rapidly approaching the pound barrier, and once that goes just a little further—

"What did you do that for?" I scream above the racket, wide-eyed with all the fear I can muster.

He beams. "It's beautiful," he says, picking an eight ounce can off the shelf, admiringly. "It's art. It's wonderful. You should learn to appreciate it. Every time I see one of our new creations, I can't help but—"

I grab him by his shiny tiny lapels, shaking vigorously. "You're going to get us all killed!" Shake. Shake. "Those cans aren't stopping—they're just getting bigger!" Rattle. Rattle. "You've got to do something!" Shake, shake, shake, and he can't do anything but sputter.

His glasses go flying down the aisle as two and four pound cans cascade off the shelves ten feet away.

I find myself thrown against a wall of broccoli—didn't know he was that strong. "Really. You must control yourself, sir!" he fumbles. "Now where have my glasses gotten to?"

I watch, entranced, as 8, 16, and 32 pound gold barrels put in their appearance—a brief wink and then a quick exodus to the aisle floor. The Maestro locates his glasses and fits them on his face as he sits up.

"Really," he fumes, "this will never do!"

64 pound depth charges begin to thud in the distance. He stands as tall as three feet will permit and pulls a baton out of his sleeve. This is what I've been waiting for—the master control element. I move in closer.

Raising his hands over his head, he makes a decisive, angled cutting motion.

Silence reigns.

A dripping begins in the distance, and a pool of pea and carrot juice begins to ooze in our direction.

I switch to a crouching position as he fiddles with the

bulb at the bottom of his baton. "Let's see here," he mumbles, "fifteen hundred volts should be enough to clean it up." He pauses. "Such a shame to waste all that gold, though. Still—"

Hands raised again!

I kick and turn at the same time, sending the baton flying in among the wreckage. The Maestro screeches.

I continue to pivot, and catch him by the coat tails the second time around. I heave, and his screech turns into a howl as he goes careening up the aisle in the other direction. I scramble after the baton.

"Anarchist!" he cries, and starts throwing cans at me. He's got lousy aim. I continue, unhit.

"You filthy outdoorist traitor! You're a miserable Midworlder or I'm a turnip!" His aim improves, and a can grazes my shoulder. I've found the baton, though.

"I'll fry your liver," he snarls, moving toward me, "and sell it for lunchmeat in the deli!"

I laugh. Struggling to a kneeling position in the muck, I break the baton over my knee, once, twice, and the lights fade and flare in accompaniment. The pieces sizzle and spark at the broken ends, and I toss them behind me. The cans clatter hollowly as I stand.

The Maestro is still foaming at the mouth. "I'll cut you up and sell you for dogfood! I'll make soap with your bones! I'll drink coffee in your—"

"Now, now, is that any way to talk? There's no need to take this personally—"

There is a minor explosion behind me, and I am thrown off my feet. Cans go flying everywhere, and I look up to see the Maestro beating a hasty retreat down the aisle. I add more cans to the airborn division, hitting him maybe four times. But not stopping him.

Rats.

"What are you going to do now?"

"Do?" I study Helen's face for a moment, considering her question as well as her ulterior motives.

The mural looms behind us, and I am still irritated that it didn't switch back to a window when I destroyed the Maestro's baton. While he may still be able to exercise rudimentary control over the Building functions, I expect that, without the baton, the grocery should start reverting to forest fairly soon—a process that tends to be unhealthy to watch from the inside. I had hoped the window would revert first, providing an easy way out.

There are lots of ways to escape into the world, though. I'm not worried.

Helen is another matter. She's not good at hiding her emotions, and it's plain she is curious, a little envious, even hankering after some adventure.

I shrug, maintaining an air of neutrality. "I don't know. Plot. Cultivate patience. Grow older, I suppose. What did you have in mind?"

She sighs, betraying massive amounts of frustration. "It won't do you any good, you know. He's run up against people like you before."

I rise to the bait. "Oh yeah? Well, I've run into people like him who have run into people like me before. It didn't help them, either."

"Really?"

"Sure." I lean back against the register in an effort to get more comfortable. My feet are bare; my pants are almost dry. My shoes and socks are getting the heat lamp treatment over by the fresh-baked pie display.

I feel a lot better with food inside me. Lunch was a fourteen-course scavenged delight: nuts, cold cuts, fresh bread, cheese, potato chips, and cold pop.

Things have been going smoothly with Helen. We're just about friends now.

"You realize, of course," she says very solemnly, "that it's entirely possible he may have run into people like you who have run into people like him who have run into people like you before."

"I had thought about that. But I'll have you know that I have often run into people—"

"No, no! Stop!" She raises her hands in mock protest. "I promise I won't do it again!"

"You're sure."

"Yes—honest."

"Well, I would have gotten it right, you know."

We stare at each other for a moment, and then break into a chorus of giggles.

"What is he really like?"

"The Maestro?"

"Yeah."

She turns around on the counter and sits crosslegged. Thoughtfully, she tears open a bag of chocolate chip cookies.

"I think he's a very spiritual person."

"No!"

"Yeah, it's true! I can remember," she says, munching happily, "how he used to talk about Art, and Music, and the Rhythms of life, and the Architecture of Creation. He said that the grocery is one of the Great Storerooms from which all things originate in all their forms. That's why our work here is so important."

"Gee, I never had him pegged as the guru type. Do you really believe all that?"

"It's true! I know it's true! I myself came from the illustration wrapper for an aluminium roasting pan. The checker before me came from the front of a box of laundry detergent—she left though. She married an ex-coin changer who made it big in Accounting."

"How about the Maestro?"

"He came from the front of a bag of ice. He's probably over in the freezer section right now. That's where he tends to sulk whenever anything goes wrong around here."

"Did I ever tell you how fond I am of women who look like aluminium cookware?"

A smile draws itself across her lips—reflex action. "Well, if I really take the time to think about it, I don't b'lieve I can recall ever hearing your views on the subject prior to right now."

"Gad! It's hard to believe I could have overlooked something so basic."

"Yeah."

I lean toward her. "Come away with me and I'll make you forget you ever punched out a cash register."

"Or overstuffed a paper bag?"

"That too."

She frowns, looking at me suspiciously. "Where?"

I point at the mural. "There."

She stares in disbelief at it, and then at me. "You live in a picture?"

"No. I live outside."

"Oh." She puts the cookies down, laces her fingers together and inspects her upturned palms. "I thought you were serious for a moment," she says, without looking at me.

"I am."

She turns her head quickly and meets my gaze. "But that's a fairy tale. There is no outside."

"Of course there is."

"No!"

"Yes."

"There can't be."

"Why not?"

"Well—"

"Yes?"

"Well, if there's an outside," she says, looking around to make sure she's not overheard, "then how do we get there?"

I try to spot the eavesdroppers. Then I lean closer. "We escape."

"Escape?"

"In as graceful and dignified a manner as possible."

"You're crazy!"

"No—I'm not! Really!" I jump down off the counter and grab my coat, digging some of the dirt out of the pocket. "Look, I'll prove it to you."

"What's that?"

"Dirt. Get behind me and watch."

I make a neat pile on the counter, wipe my hands off on my pants, step back, and concentrate.

It stirs. Or at least something within it stirs. Twice. A wrinkled green blotch tosses a minute fistful of soil aside and stretches in the overhead light. The pile grows, eating up sections of the counter.

A plant occurs, spreading its leaves, growing, thickening, almost breathing. Atop, a cluster of buds appears, and we are now standing at the foot of a black dirt mound in front of the window mural. Helen claps her hands and laughs.

More shoots spring up out of the soil as flowers blossom at the peak of an eight foot hill, flowers that are pink, yellow, blue, and fragrant—peonies, because those are easier. I turn and take a bow as color sweeps the rest of the hill.

"That was very good. Is it real?"

"Of course it is. I only deal in quality stuff. I am pleased, though. This is a good beginning, and I feel my power growing. Come."

"Now where?"

"Two counters down. I need elbow room."

I scoop up a handful of the new dirt and mix it with a couple of dead leaves from my coat pocket. Stones are for last resorts only.

Six feet away, I toss the mixture at the counter. Branches, like arms, unfold themselves, and the register, now the crest, rears itself in a gigantic untimber. Sunlight seems to flash through the silver-green leaves, only for a moment.

Roots churn up the floor in chunks of tile and cement, like a bizarre mixmaster. Overhead, there is a cracking and rending, as blossom- and moss-covered boughs break through the roof revealing—

Nothing.

Blackness.

Dark, dark, and dark.

Ouch and damn.

Another room, perhaps. I didn't remember any on the way in. The Maestro is stronger than I thought. And in the freezer section.

"That's too bad," she says, watching the darkness with me. "For a moment I thought we might actually get out of here."

"Yeah. I had hoped we could climb the tree to freedom. Unfortunately, this is going to be much more difficult now. The Maestro has managed to maintain enough control to block our exit. I'll have to go see him."

"You're not giving up!"

"Me? Of course not." I smile at her. "I always save my best tricks for last."

"Good. I'm ready. What do we do?"

"You wait here. I don't think you'd be too thrilled about being caught in the crossfire.

"Oh."

"I shouldn't be too long."

"Yeah. Well, look, uh, don't do anything stupid—OK? It'd be kind of dull around here without you."

"Sure."

I head toward the freezer section trying to look confident. No furrowed brows or frowns. Not a hint that I'm worried. If we don't get out of here soon, though, we could end up being bushes. Or maybe clumps of ragweed. Or quite possibly oak trees, but that's only if we're lucky.

Coldness descends, like a wave on an invisible shore, and I recognize the Maestro's smile. This time it comes from ten feet up, and he is huge. He sits straddling the freezer case down by the orange juice, some thirty feet down the aisle from me.

I shrug on my jacket, sticking my hands in the pockets as I get it on.

"Well, well, well, look who showed up," he rumbles.

"Hello!" I call back, waving, using the motion to cover up the fact I am sprinkling my end of the freezer with dirt. "You seem to have grown."

"Oh my yes. Rather impressive—isn't it?"

"It'll do."

He chuckles, a sound basically akin to that of a diesel engine with lung cancer. "That was clever with the tree. You actually managed to inflict some structural damage before I stopped you." He gestures vaguely. "It's the vantage point, you know. I never would have spotted you otherwise."

"It was a good tree. Listen—why don't you give up before we all get hurt?"

"Give up?" He chuckles again. "You are the one that had better give up!"

"Me?"

He folds his arms. "You can't stand in the way of Progress, shorty. Admit it. Besides," he says, leaning forward, "I've already called for Security. They should be here in another half hour."

"I doubt there will be anything for them to find."

"Really?"

"Really. I don't know how you're holding it back, but it won't be too long before this whole place will revert to a forest."

"A forest?"

"You got it. And I, for one, don't want to revert with it. But I'm a reasonable individual. I'm willing to let you clear out too—before it's too late."

"Clear out?" he giggles. "Give up on a new venture, all on the word of a two bit moth-eaten anarchist?" and the laughter eeks out, raucously, as he leans back to accommodate his mirth. All show.

I kick my end of the freezer, starting a chain-reaction slushbank, depositing the Maestro on his back on the floor. The laughter ceases.

"That wasn't very funny," he says, first sitting up and then struggling to stand in the wet snow. I'm good at slush.

Depends on your point of view," I point out, and I toss a couple of pebbles into the scum at my end. They turn yellow, then green, now oily, now bubbling. Ooze pools on the melted water.

"What are you doing?" he roars, and screams, kicking furiously.

"What's the matter—can't stand a little competition? I'm heading home—you do what you want to."

Inarticulate, he roars again, and changes/flickers, man / penguin / man / penquin / panda / penquin / panda / man / panda / polar / panda / panda / polar / polar / polar, and lunges after me, just exactly too late.

My poor little oil slick, my green green pool, has bubbled, boiled, risen up, now slime, now scaled, now headed and snake necked, claws scraping at the edges of the pool, still growing. Amber is the color of his slitted eyes, matching the flame he belches ceilingward, his tail massacring the remaining freezer bank, while his amber breast flashes, bejeweled, in the dancing flames, and he roars in his own right as he grows bigger still.

The Maestro / polar / panda / Maestro stops in his tracks, which would seem to be a wise thing to do at this point. Deciding on sheer size and weight as his best defense, he telescopes his height, soaring past the flame-scorched ceiling tiles, standing tall in the midnight velvet void that shimmers overhead.

My dragon rears upward too, breathing bouquets of flame, tangerine, sapphire, and rose, like the shimmering in his unfurled wings, as he spurts two new necks with heads that quickly add their own pyrotechnic comments to the situation.

The Maestro, who now looks something like a cross between King Kong and an English sheepdog, has not taken kindly to his newly-singed hair, and takes a swipe at Rover.

I back into Helen, who left her tree to watch the spectacle.

"What are you doing here?" I shout over the din. "I told you to wait by the tree!"

"Are you kidding? I wouldn't miss this for the world!"

"Look—we've got to clear out of here! The fight isn't going to last that long anyway, and once it's over, we're going to have to move quickly—"

The floor and the shelves shake as Rover roars in pain from a left jab that connects with one of his noses; he retaliates by torching the Maestro with all three heads at once.

The Maestro melts.

His features flow down his chest, doing Picasso one better, and he becomes a study in rounded wet crystal—a lump of ice in motion. His coloring evaporates in clouds of angry steam, his claws drip away, the details from his furry grey coat crumble, leaving behind wrinkled rivulets clogged with carbon film.

The dragon pauses to take a deep breath while the Maestro / iceberg backs away. He then lets loose another triple sheet of flame.

The second dose does the Maestro in. He cracks, thunderously, falling in a hundred splintered see-through pieces, all melting rapidly.

Helen and I are thrown off our feet as the entire grocery shudders like an earthquake, shelves falling, glass breaking, cans clattering all around us. Close by, the salad dressing section shimmers, goes out of focus, and is replaced by half a dozen hawthorns, large starched white blossoms covering their branches instead of leaves.

We manage to regain our feet in time to see a fast-rising pine tree puncture the dragon. He begins to deflate, sending a warm breeze in our direction.

As he billows away, the grocery goes through convulsions again, and faunaless flora begin to appear all around us. I grab Helen's hand, and we head for the window, threading our way through the new growth. The roof still looms over our heads.

We find a stand of poplar trees where the checkout counters used to be, their pallette-shaped leaves flapping while their trunks grow thicker, exploratory branches appearing up and down their length. Beyond we find the picture postcard mural, still not a window.

I swear, and start digging through my pockets.

Helen lets out a little screech as a clump of wild grasses

begins to fondle her ankles, and the only way we can free her is to take off her shoes. Or at least untie them so she can step out—they've taken root.

I find what I'm looking for—a black magic marker—as the poplar tree branches reach for us with long, knobby, budding green fingers. Pieces of the roof fall in large chunks, turning into boulders on the way down, cutting off our predators instead of eliminating us.

I draw a jagged line on the mural, a poorly done star. There is a crackling, not of cans, but of glass, and the interior of the star falls away, making room for the streaming sunlight. Quickly, I enlarge the hole.

I take Helen's hand once again, and we step through, just as the major portion of the roof caves in, its rumble changing into chirps and chitters as it changes into a rainbow assortment of birds, butterflies, and confused moths, all trying to get away from one another and from the ominous roars further back in what is left of the store.

Helen and I run up the surveillance hill, preceded by a batallion of sable-colored squirrels. A hot wind escorts us, and we make it to the top, safe.

We turn around and watch a green mist surround what is left of the Building. Helen sniffles.

"Well, that's that," she says.

"Yeah. Not with a scream or whimper, but with a big bang." I look at her. "Welcome to the world. You've never seen any of this before—have you?"

She looks around, dubiously. "Not really. Heard lots of rumors, but never ran into the actual items themselves."

"I'm sure there's lots of things you'll want to see and experience for yourself."

"I'm sure."

"But first—"

"But first?"

"I know a place."

"Yes?"

"Moss covered stones. Lots of tall eucalyptus trees. African violets tastefully scattered here and there. Close to a discreetly babbling brook."

"Sounds interesting."

"I often go there, to relax, to retreat from the din and clamor of an ungrateful world."

"I see."

I offer her my arm. "Shall we, then?"

She takes it. "Undoubtedly."

I am an expert woodsman. We leave no tracks.

DRAGON TOUCHED

DAVE SMEDS

ILLUSTRATIONS BY
MICHAEL HAGUE

> Arrogant dragon will have cause to repent. For
> what is at the full cannot last.
> —I Ching, First Hexagram, Sixth Line

The shack stood at the very edge of the Dragon Sea,
along a beach where only hardy tufts of salt grass could
grow. To the north, the city of T'jet was strewn across the
hills hugging the rivermouth and bay, scented with rotting
fish and crowded humanity. Two men and a woman
approached the hut from the city, glad to be free of the port
and out among the sea wind and stark sand.

A gnarly, tall, wizened man was mending a net on the
stoop of the shack, casting weatherwise glances at the
clouds over the ocean to the east. He looked like an odd
sea creature with arms and legs, cured and seasoned over
the years by the wind and water and salt. He spared the
approaching strangers one long stare before returning his
eyes to the work, never pausing in his weaving. The
foremost of the newcomers stepped ahead of his companions and spoke.

"Are you Darel?" he asked.

The shack's owner cinched off one more knot. He examined his visitor with precise, calculated glances, noting the leather tunic reminiscent of a warrior, the silver inlay of the quality and workmanship as that worn by royalty, and the impression of age behind the man's apparent youth and strength. "Who wants to know?"

"My name is Alemar," the man said.

Darel shrugged. "Never heard it."

The man seemed irritated, and turned to gesture at the woman with him. She was nearly his twin—short, dark-haired, with a few fine wrinkles to hint at the departure of youth. "Perhaps you know the Lady Miranda, my sister?" Alemar asked.

Darel raised his eyebrow. "Aye," he murmured. "I know the lady of magic. What brings you to me?"

"I need a man familiar with the Dragon Sea, to sail with me, to be my pilot. We thought you might be interested."

Darel spat something brown and thick into a spittoon at his feet. "These things cost money."

"Name your price."

Darel blinked, swallowed abruptly, and a change came over his attitude. "Well, now," he said, getting to his feet, "this is no place to conduct business." He stretched, popping several vertebrae, and lifted the drape that covered the doorway. "Come in, come in."

Alemar strode slowly into the dim, single room. At one side of the squalor, a middle-aged, cow-breasted woman stirred a suspicious looking stew over a fire pit, and to the other side a thin, pale man drooled and stared blankly at a wall. The crone received one glance, the idiot three. Alemar waited standing for the others to come in. Darel was last, ducking his head to fit through the opening.

"Sit down," Darel said, with a crusty sort of grace, and headed toward a cabinet from which he pulled an earthenware jug and four somewhat dingy winecups.

The only place to sit was hardpacked dirt. The three visitors remained standing. Darel shrugged, and poured the cups full of a thick, deep red wine. He began handing them out.

"To the famous lady and her brother," he said, "And to . . . ?"

"Polk," said the third person, a tall, brown-haired, healthy-looking teenager.

"Ah," Darel said. "Take care this doesn't rot out that young gut, m'boy." The sailor smiled as Polk blushed.

Darel downed a stout swallow, smacked his lips, and said, "Pardon my bluntness, but before we go any farther, I'd like a look at the color of your silver."

Alemar calmly unfastened a pouch from his belt and tossed it to Darel, who poured out several coins into his palm. He held one up to the light gleaming through a crack in the wall. "The tender of Moin. You've come a long way overland."

"We are emissaries of the council of elders of that country," Alemar said. "I am one of those elders."

Darel glanced again at Alemar's relatively young features and returned a skeptical look, but nodded obligingly.

"Will twelve leits per week, with five week's worth in advance, be sufficient?" Alemar asked.

Darel stopped in mid-swallow. "It . . ." he coughed, "will do, my lord . . ." His tone made it obvious that he would have accepted considerably less, and he added cautiously, "Perhaps I should know just what sort of thing I'm getting into . . .?"

"We are sailing to the Lost Isles."

"What?" Darel snapped, quickly making the sign against the evil eye between himself and Alemar. In the corner, the idiot abruptly stopped drooling and screamed—a short, strangled outburst—after which he began to shudder until it threatened to splinter his frail bones.

"What's wrong with him?" Polk asked.

"You leave Yonni alone!" Darel shouted. "You shouldn't have mentioned that place in this house. It's dragon country. No man goes there."

"Unless," Alemar said, "one goes to kill dragons."

Darel stepped back, and seemed caught between charging forward or bolting for the door. He relaxed with a loud sigh, dropped his eyes, and jabbed a finger in the direction of the idiot.

"Yonni has seen a dragon."

Yonni had his face buried in his palms, emitting small mewling cries and continuing to shudder. As Darel glared anxiously, Alemar walked calmly forward, lifted the man's head gently by the chin, and whispered a few words too low for the others to hear.

"Stay away from him!" Darel warned, tightening his fists but not moving. Increasingly, however, the sailor's attention was pulled toward Yonni's eyes, that stared back at Alemar and stage by stage lost the glaze of feeble-mindedness. Those eyes ran a gamut of emotions—blankness to curiosity to fear to calm—a communication denied to the others in the room, shared only by Alemar. After an age, the idiot sagged down on his thatch mat, breaking the gaze. He turned to Darel and whispered three clear words.

"Go with him."

Darel's eyes widened. On the far side of the room, the crone was hugging her ladle across her chest, whimpering softly. Darel was no longer rigid; rather, his attitude toward Alemar was one of sincere deference, and more than a taste of awe. "Sorcerer!" he said.

Alemar nodded, adding simply, "We leave in three

days. Meet us at the long wharf before the morning tide turns." He gestured at Yonni. "I want him to come, too."

Polk was exploring a world new and fascinating to him. He looked up to see a school of small fish swarm around the scraps someone had just thrown overboard, their silvery bottoms tiny streaks of light completely unlike the dark little figures seen when observed from above the surface. The protective camouflaging, like so many things in this new place, spoke of rules and laws of life of a completely different order. The water was warm and caressing, and reminded him of being in a woman. The security combined with excitement was the same. He stroked, pitting developing muscles against ocean, pleased at the challenge.

Over his face he wore a transparent membrane stretched around a framework of gold wire. As he breathed, only the slight flutter of the membrane toward and away from his nostrils showed that he was not breathing water.

The water was clear. He could see the profuse growth of coral along the bottom. Even here, well beyond sight of the coast, the sea was shallow. He continued on toward the ship, a large, quick schooner, and tugged at barnacles fastened to the lower hull. They were back already, after he and others of the crew had worked to thoroughly remove them during the past month in T'jet.

As he gripped the hull, he felt the tug of its movement. So the wind had returned. He realized regretably that he had to surface or be left behind when the sails filled. He grabbed the rope ladder that hung over the side and climbed it. As he broke surface, the water beaded and dripped across his mask, obscuring his vision. He removed it and continued upward. A hand reached for him. Automatically he took it and accepted the assistance in climbing over the rail.

"I still don't believe it," Darel said, letting go of Polk's hand and tapping the breathing mask.

"You should try it yourself," Polk said amiably. "Alemar insisted that all of us learn to use the lung." He liked the old sailor, in spite of the man's perpetually somber mood since boarding the day before. Already Darel had impressed him with his feel for sailcraft. Within the day, the new pilot had established his authority over the entire crew, with the logical exception of the sorceror and his sister, and not with domineerance, but with a straightforward exhibition of competence.

"No," Darel said. "If man were meant to swim like a fish, he would have been given gills."

"But we have," Polk said, holding up the mask. Out of the water, it was a delicate frame of thin metal. The youth carefully stored the device in a trough of salt water, so as not to dry and crack the membranes. "Thanks to Miranda's inventiveness."

Darel swished his fingers in the trough, where more masks were lightly fastened, one for each member of the crew. "It's sorcery. Best leave that to dragons. It leads to no good."

"But aren't you amazed? To be able to breathe indefinitely underwater?"

"Man's not meant to live down there. It's not his world."

"On the contrary, it's the goal of this expedition," Polk said. "You're from T'jet. You must have seen the house Miranda lives in, under the water of the bay."

Darel shrugged. "I have heard of it. A house of glass blown from var sand. She built it years ago." It was obvious that he had deliberately avoided visiting it. Polk wondered about this. Though it was common for ordinary men to be suspicious of magic, most were drawn to witness the spectacle as often as possible.

"It's Alemar's belief that whole cities can be built like that, entirely beneath the sea, given shallow water for sunlight and enough var for the construction. Both are available in the Lost Isles."

"I know," Darel said. "And so are the dragons. I would be wary of that man's schemes. He is a bit too sure of himself."

"That's what my grandfather thinks," Polk answered. Darel could tell by the pause that Polk wished this were not so. Underneath that young enthusiasm lurked some doubts as well. Darel relaxed his tone and for the first time in the journey, became ready to listen.

"Who is your grandfather?"

"Batel, the Eldest of Moin. He and others on the council do not trust the lord Alemar. The vote to support this expedition was close. The council felt it had no choice. The barbarians have virtually circled our country since the fall of Numaron. With no port, we could easily be besieged. We need a sanctuary, and Alemar proposed to take the Lost Isles and build cities there, both above and below the sea."

Darel shook his head back and forth, incredulous. "It's foolishness. I've heard of Moin's situation . . . but . . . it makes me wonder that your elders could have adopted the plan."

Polk shrugged. "The Lost Isles were one of the most beautiful places to live before the dragons came . . . and rich. And Alemar can be persuasive."

Darel was scanning over the waves, watching the antics of sea birds. He said pensively, "So I have seen." He looked up, staring Polk straight in the eye. "Tell me, what do you think of Lord Alemar?"

Polk lowered his glance, and began walking, still treading a bit warily from having been at sea his first time. "I . . ." he began, and licked his lips. "I do not agree with my grandfather. Alemar is a great man, and . . . I would follow him wherever he asks. He's been good to me. But there are times when he is . . . distant."

Darel saw that he was making Polk uncomfortable. He sighed loudly, tightened a knot, and said, "I'm curious. What did your council have to say about Faroc and Triss?"

"The dragons are the only thing in the way. Alemar vowed that he could kill both of them. If he succeeds, the council will support his plan."

"Aye," Darel muttered. "I'd venture any man would follow a dragonslayer, assuming it's possible to kill the beasts."

"It's happened before."

"In ancient times, in legend."

"But it happened," Polk insisted.

"Perhaps . . . but I will believe that when I see it, if I live to."

Polk considered what Darel hinted at—that this expedition would fail, and the dragons would destroy them. He answered optimistically, "Dragonbane kills them."

"To use poison, you have to reach your target."

"If you're so skeptical, why are you coming with us?"

Darel stroked his hand against a halyard, letting his eyes wander toward the cabin, where Alemar and Miranda hid from view. "Because," he said slowly, "a dragon owes me a debt, and I have a feeling that man can help me collect it."

Miranda awoke in the berth. The cabin was dimly lit— what time? Immediately she thought in nautical measures: watches, spells, and waves. She guessed dawn was still far off.

She sat up. Across the chamber, Alemar sat on a stool, opposite a small wooden table from the idiot. Both men were staring straight at one another, fingertips touching as their hands rested on the table. Yonni was slumped, and periodically drops of drool slipped off his lips onto the lap of his soiled clothing. Alemar was upright and close-mouthed, but shared the same bird-bright cast to his eyes that the other man had. They were in the position they had been in when Miranda had gone to sleep.

She did not disturb her brother, but slipped quietly into the galley, and obtained a haunch of meat and some of the dwindling supply of fresh fruit. Alemar would be ravenous when he came out of the meld with the dragon-touched.

She returned to the cabin and waited, watching. Tears were now streaming down Yonni's face, and he whimpered, but neither man looked away. Alemar too was trembling, and Miranda realized how seldom she had seen her brother this way. He was not the sort to be easily shaken. She brooded. Their hopes were rapidly approaching either fulfillment or ruin. The next weeks would tell, and the closer they came to the Lost Isles, the more acute was the need to know. But even her considerable power provided no precognition.

Yonni began to sob, and abruptly fell off of his stool, where he remained in a quivering heap, breathing heavily. Alemar sighed deeply, and closed his eyes, leaning heavily on the table. Miranda sat down at the table but did not speak.

After some time, Alemar opened his eyes. They were bloodshot but alert. Miranda handed him a piece of fruit, which he stared at as if he didn't recognize it. He took it tentatively, bit slowly and let the juice dribble into his beard. Eventually his mouth began working, and gradually he began eating normally. Soon he was gorging, and did not stop until most of the food was gone. Only then did he speak.

"Awesome," he said.

"What did you see?" she asked.

He shrugged. "Shattered thoughts, random memories, and above all, his fear coupled with the mirth of a dragon. The beast enjoyed doing this to him. She took her time. I didn't think I would find anything coherent within him."

"Did you?"

"He is not a man anymore. Nothing is in any sort of order, but the emotions are woven with repeated images, some of them so bizarre that they must be non-human in origin."

"Eh?"

"I mean that the dragon reached so far into him that she left traces of her own mind behind, and it is beyond the man's capacity to drive them out and become himself. That is the nature of their magic—while men wrap sorcery in things, in talismans and magic tools, dragons work with the mind."

"We already knew this."

"Yes," he said quietly. "But I didn't guess just how strong they might be. These dragons are masters. Their powers grow stronger as they age, and both Faroc and Triss are millenia into their power. I should not care to let them get the upper hand . . ."

Miranda did not comment. She glanced at Yonni, who moaned on the floor. "What do we do with him?"

"Send him back to his brother, though as far as Yonni is concerned, he would just as soon go over the side."

As Polk stood next to Darel, who was manning the helm, he could feel the tension among the crew. Gone was the camaraderie of the first few days, when the inexperienced sailors exchanged seasickness jokes, and the giddiness of being on an adventure was greater than its distant danger. Now, after many days at sea, they cast frightened looks at the northern sky, and held their breath every time a large sea bird appeared in the distance.

"Yellow kelp," Darel muttered, pointing at the segments of seaweed boiling up beyond the rudder.

"What's it mean?" Polk asked.

"It only grows near the Lost Isles—it's that color because of the var, you know. When sailors on these waters see that, they tack the other way."

Polk nodded gravely.

Darel spat over the side. "I swear, boy, it was a good deal easier to put myself aboard this ship back in T'jet than be here now. I could have always jumped off in the harbor and swimmed back to shore." He waved at the bird watchers. "Those boys don't understand what they're going into. Won't, till they see Faroc or Triss."

As Darel hailed forward to tell a man to tighten the jib, Polk watched him. The pilot had spoken as if from personal experience, reawakening a curiosity Polk had felt throughout the journey. "Have *you* seen them?" he asked.

Darel jumped momentarily, but hid it well. His gaze was distant, his voice silent. Polk wondered if he had intruded upon their friendship, which had grown in the past days. Cautiously the young man added, "You said back in the shack that your brother had seen a dragon. I wondered, then, if you had."

"Aye," Darel said softly. "I have seen Triss—so close that my clothes were rippled by the force of her breath. She landed at my doorstep, when she returned Yonni to me."

"She *returned* him? I don't understand."

Darel spat again. "It has to do . . . with the way dragons are."

Polk closed his mouth, not wishing to press an issue that bothered his friend, but Darel finally seemed willing to talk.

"Two things are true about every dragon in the world: they like to brag, and they're jealous as can be over their territory. If a ship sails into their waters, they burn it. And often as not, they'll save one man, fly him back to land, and leave him to tell the story. But they don't always leave him whole . . ."

Both men involuntarily glanced down, where they knew Yonni lay in a hammock staring at the hull or murmuring incoherent phrases to himself. Polk looked up, guilty at expressing his pity.

"He never spoke a sane word from the day that she-dragon brought him back, until that sorceror came." Darel gripped the wheel until it threatened to dent the wood.

"Then . . . that's the debt the dragon owes you."

Darel pursed his lips, and stared at Polk. "You think I came for revenge, no?"

Polk shrugged. "I . . ."

"I did." His etched features flushed. "But I want you to know that I came for Yonni, too. *He* wanted to come. I think that sorceror knew that; I think that's why he came to me, when another pilot would do. It's the only want my brother has communicated in six years. I couldn't very well ignore it, and I couldn't very well leave him alone, could I? It's for Yonni that I follow Alemar and the witch of T'jet."

"The witch?" Polk asked strangely.

"As she's known in the city," Darel said. "The woman who never ages." He caught the bereft expression on his companion's face, and suddenly Darel's tone became sharp, the same one he used to command the crew. "You keep your mind off that woman. She's not meant for mortal man."

Polk backed up a step. He could tell Darel was quite serious—and concerned for him. "But . . ." he began, and could not finish. *But she's so beautiful.* As the silence became increasingly uncomfortable, Polk changed the subject. "I used to wonder, when I was a child, why dragons, if they were so powerful and greedy for space, didn't kill every man in the world and take all lands for themselves. What's to stop them?"

Darel seemed to accept the new topic. He shrugged. "Ain't enough of them, I guess. They don't get along. They keep killing each other off. Plus they like to stay near water, because that's where they grow up. Faroc and Triss, they're rare. They actually share their territory—Faroc in the southern half, Triss in the north. They're the only dragonmates anybody knows about nowadays. Even the males and females can't stop fighting each other."

"As far as I know, they're the only dragons alive at all."

"Hmmm, there're other ones, somewhere. North, or west. Lots of places no man's ever seen, except the barbarians. Have to admit, though, none have been seen inside the old Calinin Empire for centuries."

Abruptly the cabin door popped open, and Alemar stepped out. He stared straight at Darel. "You're off course," he said flatly.

Polk heard the pilot utter a low curse. "Aye, sir, but there's a reef over there, where you said to go." He pointed to starboard.

"Didn't I make myself clear yesterday? From here out, you are to keep my course *exactly.*"

"But . . ."

"The reef is passable, if you're careful. Stray from the course and we'll die for certain." Alemar raised to his full height, which was considerably shorter than Darel. "Do you understand?"

Darel swallowed hard. "Beg your pardon, m'lord." He shouted to the crew, "Prepare to come about." Alemar watched as the tack was changed, satisfied himself that the heading was true, and disappeared below.

"When he gives me that look," Darel told Polk, "it's all I can do to hold my shit. Damn wizard! Now he wants to be the pilot, too. Rand! Coller! Get up to the bow! Keep a sharp eye out for rocks! The bastard's going to get us killed before we ever get to the isles."

"How did he know you were off course?" Polk asked. "He didn't even look at the heading."

"He's a sorcerer," Darel said. "Who can tell how their minds work? I could understand it if I'd changed the tack, but all I did was hold the old one a bit longer than he'd said to. We couldn't have been more than a hundred paces off."

"It must be something crucial, or he wouldn't have plotted such an exact course. Why do you think he did it?"

Darel flicked his fingers. "Hmmmph, by the hair on my hole, it makes no sense to me. The chart has me tacking at the strangest times. We'll hold one mark for a whole watch, then make ten tacks in as many waves. It's got nothing to do with wind and currents, I'll tell you that. I understand it as much as these things."

Darel pointed to some of the many bizarre accoutrements Alemar had made the men add to the ship, back in port. In this case, it was the series of metal torch stands that ringed the entire deck. Every five paces one had been bolted to the hull, the plain metal rods rising up to shoulder level, where the oil-filled reservoirs still awaited their first lighting. They were too simple to be ornaments, and the vessel had already possessed harbor lamps.

"Well, sooner or later we'll learn what they're for," Polk said.

Coller hailed from the front. "Coral off the port bow!"

"Sorcerers!" Darel grumbled. "The death of me some-day." And he concentrated on bringing them through the reef in one piece.

Faroc watched the ship sail into his domain. The dragon remained as still as the weathered crag he perched on, seeming to be an extension of the rugged stone and sea-bird droppings. Only his whiteless eyes moved, watching, and watching more. It had been years since any men had dared to come close enough to his world that Faroc had been inclined to roast them. This ship was far from ordinary. It sailed straight for the isles, which men never did.

In four thousand years of life, Faroc had thought he had worn out his capacity to be surprised.

How incredibly audacious. The dragon permitted himself not to be irritated by the intrusion—it could prove entertaining. Of course, he couldn't brook this assault upon his territory, but at least killing these men might be more interesting than the usual lot. Already he could smell the sorcerer.

The scent of human magic was faint, by comparison with that of his kind, but it was distinctive. Languidly he remembered the last sorcerer who had tried to match powers with him, a few centuries back. Sadly Faroc had found him to be just as combustible as any other man. Sadder still to think that such beings could actually hope to develop enough power in their ephemeral lifetimes to challenge him, though occasionally their accomplishments impressed him.

There was definitely an adept aboard. It was plain in the way that the craft had tacked erratically toward the crags where Faroc waited. That course, meaningless to an ordi-nary human, kept the boat over thrijish coral. Thrijish sapped a dragon's magic, if coaxed by spells. Clever, that. However, the coral did not affect physical prowess. Faroc wondered how the sorcerer would deal with that.

Early in the afternoon, the ship reached the crags, several jagged spires jutting up from the sea, the first portion of the Lost Isles. While the craft was still several bowshots from the islets, Alemar suddenly ordered the sails lowered, and the anchor dropped.

The men stared at the wizard, but nevertheless hurried to obey. "Here?" Polk asked, as soon as it was done. "But I see nothing. Are we to wait for the dragon to come to us?"

"There is a dragon on the highest crag," Miranda explained.

Pandemonium reigned. Men dived for the bows and arrows they had prepared days earlier. Alemar kept his eyes on the rock and said, "Get out the pots of fellit and dip the arrows. The poison needs to be fresh to do its job quickly."

The man clambered below and reappeared with pots of ungent goo, which they treated with respect. Dragonbane could be years old and still kill a man with the slightest scratch. After Polk prepared his quiver, he did the same to the sorcerer's, and returned to Alemar's side.

"Light the torches," Alemar ordered. Moments later a ring of small flames decorated the ship.

"What will we do? Is there only one?" Polk asked.

Miranda gripped him on the shoulder. "He won't listen. He'll concentrate only on the beast now. Just be still, watch, and have your bow ready."

Alemar stepped to the very center of the deck. Polk had never seen a more imposing short man, and at that moment, the effect was more pronounced than ever. Then the sorcerer said, "Dragon! I am Alemar of Moin!"

"How can the creature hear that?" Polk asked. "He spoke in normal tones."

Then Polk's head seemed to burst, and in his pain, he saw the others, with the exception of Alemar and Miranda, clutching their scalps. Polk heard words—*between* his ears, a roaring that left him so dazed that the meaning of the message came through many moments later.

"I am Faroc. You are trespassing."

"I came in search of you," Alemar replied.

"No man seeks Faroc. Why have you come?"

"To destroy you."

Polk had the uncanny feeling that it was he who was laughing, because the mirth burst full blown into his mind. Even after he managed to mute the dragonspeech, he could not control the quivering in his muscles. Suddenly the top of the crag sprouted wings, and Faroc launched into the air.

Men gasped. The dragon's broad, batlike wings were five times the length of a man. A long, serpentine tail trailed behind, while a narrow, pointed head loaded with teeth and a pair of phosphorescent, bulging eyes led the way. Two pairs of legs hung slack in flight, boasting tremendous talons. And for its size, it was hideously fast. In one brief swoop, it was over the ship, belching a narrow stream of flame from its throat.

Several men hit the deck, and did not see the flame abruptly splatter into thousands of fiery fingers. For an instant, the ship was surrounded by a shell of fire; then the fire was gone and the torches flared into miniature orange suns. Crew men instinctively shrank back, only realizing afterward that no heat radiated from the torches.

"Stand your ground and keep your weapons ready!" Miranda shouted. "My brother can divert the flame, but not the dragon himself! Stand fast!"

Faroc was circling far above, apparently as amazed as the crew that his attack had failed. Polk traded glances between the monster and Alemar, who stood rigid, hanging onto the mast, sweat pouring off his body.

Uttering a trumpet that almost made knees collapse aboard the boat, Faroc dived again, straight down, sending ahead a bolt of flame far thicker than the first, and lasting three times as long. When it struck the wizard's barrier, the torches blazed higher than the windfeather, and the entire ship was pressed into the sea. As they popped up again, Polk regained enough presence of mind to shoot an arrow after Faroc, but the dragon's horrendous speed made a mockery of the attempt.

"Good," Miranda said. He turned to her and realized she too had shot. "Keep trying."

Polk noticed Alemar was shuddering.

"Can't you help him? You're a sorcerer, too."

"I dare not."

"But—"

"The dragon has no more than five or six bursts in him. If Alemar cannot hold them on his own, we are doomed." Her voice was steady, but Polk noted that her complexion was chalk-white.

Faroc wasted no time. He zoomed toward his prey from the starboard side. The bolt was nearly as strong as the one before. The barrier took it, rocking the ship to port. The dragon's roar froze most of the archers in their stances. As soon as he could circle, Faroc dived again, and again, and again. Each time the flame was weaker. After the final pass, Alemar slumped to a kneel, but he still watched Faroc intently.

The dragon screeched, and dived again. But this time he belched no flame.

"Archers!" Miranda cried.

Arrows flew. Polk waited until the final moment, and
saw his shaft fly true at the beast's throat. But the steel tip
stopped a few inches away from the hide, hung in midair
for an instant, then fell. Faroc, however, veered off, blowing a foul wind over the deck.

Alemar stood up, swayed, and took up his own bow.

Faroc did not take the bait. He returned to his crag and
rumbled.

Alemar gasped for air, great racking sobs that heaved his
chest, and spoke as soon as he could control his voice.
"Dragon! What's wrong?"

*"I salute you, man. Another wingspan closer to the
thrijish and I could not have warded the arrows. I smell the
fellit. You are a clever one, and a strong one."*

"Strong enough to destroy you."

"I think not."

"Then prove it."

*"I am proud, O man, but I am not so proud as to let
mockery dull my wits. No, fellit poison is not for me. I will
stay here. Though I cannot touch you, neither can you
touch me. Sooner or later, you must leave or starve. And if
you leave, sooner or later you will sail away from the
thrijish. Then I will have you, if not before."*

Alemar did not answer. After several moments, Faroc
sprang from his perch. The men saw a huge chunk of
rock held between his forelegs. When the dragon was
directly overhead, well above arrow range, he let it go.

Alemar raised his arms in a fending motion, and two
crewmen leaped overboard. Around the ship, a bubble of
green radiance outlined the ward that had been used to
fend off the fire. More radiance flowed from Alemar's
hands, bolstering the ward at the point the rock struck. The
chunk bounced, shattering into several large pieces that
rained into the ocean beyond the ship, as all those aboard

were knocked flat by the reaction. The splashes of the rocks soaked everyone.

Faroc trumpeted gleefully. *"And just to keep you from relaxing your ward, I'll do that every so often."* He scribed a lazy summersault in the air before returning to his perch.

"Damn him," Alemar whispered, staggering to his feet.

"Are you well?" Polk asked, lending support.

"Leave me be!" the wizard said, sluffing off the arm. He stood shakily. "I will not be coddled."

Polk let him be. Other crew members hauled aboard the two who had jumped. They hung their heads like wet cats, casting apprehensive glances alternately toward the wizard and the dragon. When Alemar roused from his daze, he strode to them.

"Idiots! I should have made that rock fall on you!" He passed his hand in front of them. Steam burst from their shirts. One man yelped, his face flushed red from the heat. "Desert your posts again, and it won't be the dragon you have to fear."

Polk noticed the frown on Miranda's lips, and the overly bright cast in Alemar's pupils, and felt his guts turn. The two chastised men cowered and mumbled weak apologies, then quickly bowed away from Alemar's anger. The sorcerer relaxed his stance very slowly, eventually walking back to the mast and sitting with his back to the timber, sight fixed upward at his opponent.

Miranda, after a moment, walked over to her brother, and stood beside him, waiting. Although she did not speak, Polk could see the question in her mind, and although Alemar never changed his stance, he could see also the acknowledgement in the wizard's expression.

Finally Alemar said, "I am well."

Polk saw the muscles in Miranda's back relax.

"He was stronger than I thought he would be, but I have the strength to do . . . what I need to do."

Miranda touched him gently once, and eventually strolled off toward the stern, leaving Alemar to stare at Faroc. Polk followed the lady, and when he was sure they were out of the sorcerer's hearing, said, "What now?"

"We wait for nightfall."

Her tone had a fatalistic ring that worried Polk. He leaned closer. "I don't understand why you couldn't help him during the attack."

She reached out and touched him, one of the first times she had ever done so. He felt tingles. "Because," she said, "dragons fight their own battles."

Faroc wondered if he should drop more rocks. He had dropped two more since the original. Both had shattered on the ward, rocking the ship and obviously costing the human energy, but doing no permanent damage. Faroc thought perhaps the sorcerer was nearing the limit of his endurance, but this was a difficult thing to determine from a distance. Certainly, if enough stone was dumped upon him, eventually it would overcome him, but that would be such a dull way to eliminate an exceptionally interesting opponent. There must be a more entertaining way to accomplish his end.

So the dragon waited. He expected other tricks, something beyond mere thrijish and wards and dragonbane. There would have to be more, for in a waiting game, Faroc was bound to win. He decided to let the man make the next move. All that was needed was to watch the ship very, very carefully, and sit safely inside his own ward. If the man were to make a move, he would have to drop the ward around the ship, and that would be instantly apparent. If he did drop it, long moments would be required to reestablish it, to say nothing of the extra power it would require. The move would have to be made then, because Faroc would have more than enough time to complete an attack.

And, of course, if the ward were not dropped, the man would collapse in a day or two. Fragile creatures, these humans.

The sea was calm as the last of twilight vanished. Stars appeared, dominated by the light of Motherworld and two of the moons. The ship remained easily visible, though the men aboard were reduced to vague shadows.

An hour after nightfall, Faroc felt a change in the ward, and keened his senses. The feeling grew, remained. The ward was still present, but the flavor of it was different. Suspicious, he watched the ship all the more closely, and the waters between it and the rocks.

Standing precariously on a rugged ledge, Alemar focused his concentration upon the rope that slid between his fingers. He spoke words to it long forgotten to any but sorcerers of Acalon, causing it to climb tenuously upward of its own accord, rising toward a protrusion of rock above. If he could get the rope to tie itself around the teat of stone, he would be able to reach the top at last. But before the knot was fast, Alemar was distracted and the rope fell into a limp coil at his feet.

He cursed to himself, pausing before he tried again. His head still swirled from the amount of power he'd been forced to expend this day. Scalding those two fools had been a mistake. He needed every last bit of his strength. He flexed his arms; they were sore. A sorcerer could climb a crag like this in a quarter of the time it would take a normal rockclimber, but that did not mean it was easy. Alemar was not as young as he had been once.

Some time before, he had heard the sound of a boulder crashing upon the ward, and, reassuringly, the hum of the ward destroying it. Soon after, the thud upon the crag told him Faroc had landed again. Luck held. Miranda was maintaining the ship's defenses adequately, and the dragon had not attempted a significant attack, nor had he flown around the back of the crag closely enough to notice a small, camouflaged figure clinging to the rock face.

Surprise was essential. It was the crux of Alemar's plan, the result of years of preparation. One does not kill a dragon with courage and purity of heart. Nevertheless, the sorcerer feared that when he reached the top, now so close, all he would find would be a dragon smiling down at him.

Below, in a tide pool at the bottom of the crag, he had left the artificial lung that had enabled him to swim to the rock undetected by Faroc, who knew that men could not swim that entire distance without coming up for air. He had left Miranda dressed in his cloak, her long hair concealed, and he had descended the far side of the hull, coming up on the side of the islet opposite the ship.

So far, things were going according to plan. The only miscalculation had been the strength of the dragonflame. If it had been any stronger, Miranda would have had to bolster him, and all would have been lost. The key to the plan, of course, was that the dragon assume only one magician was aboard. Such an assumption would be typical of dragon character. Dragons fought their own battles. It would never occur to Faroc to enlist the aid of Triss now that the conflict was under way—his arrogance would not have allowed it. Alemar had counted on this. The only risk had been the slight chance that Faroc and Triss might have been together when the men arrived.

This time he succeeded swiftly in taming the rope around the rock. He wiped the sweat off his palms, sucked a deep breath, and scaled the final distance to the top. Quiet was his watchword now. The top of the crag was several dragonlengths in diameter, and relatively flat.

Alemar cautiously raised his head above the ledge. Faroc was still at the far side, staring at the ship.

Alemar squirmed onto the flat and silently unhooked himself from his rope harness, pulse pounding. Still a chance, still a chance. He freed his bow and strung it, calculating. He would need to move closer, not a pleasant prospect. He smelled the sweet stench of dragon, overwhelming in its proximity. Should Faroc hear him now, one swipe of that tremendous tail could send him flying off the pinnacle.

There wasn't time to be awed. He strode forward as swiftly as stealth would allow, stopping at the center of the rock table. He withdrew a special arrow from his quiver. The point was a tremendous barb, the shaft extremely true, made especially for Alemar by the master archer of Lealin. Etched along the shaft were delicate runes, each of which had taken hours to carve just so. This single arrow was the most vital single piece of Alemar's plan.

Despite the barb's sharpness, it would never penetrate the dragon's hide by itself. At the moment, no ordinary weapon could touch Faroc, safe as he was inside his ward. In flight, in attack, the dragon could not always maintain his defense because of the intense concentration it required, but here, on the crag, there were no such distractions. And to create a diversion might bring attention to Alemar. To pass through Faroc's barrier, Alemar had spent days in the creation of and magical treatment of his arrows. If he was enough of a mage, if he had used the correct spells, if Faroc did not become aware of him and muster his ward to guard a specific area, then the shaft should penetrate. It was an uncompromising test of Alemar's power.

He fired.

Faroc screamed. His head swung around and bit at the

shaft jutting from his haunch. The arrow had barely
lodged, but it was enough. Glowing eyes searched for the
attacker, but Alemar was hidden behind a boulder, and in
the next moment, the dragon began to writhe. *"Deceit!"*
screamed his mind, a tsunami of telepathic outrage, even
as his tail jerked spasmodically, jarring loose chunks of
stone. Flame exploded out of his mouth, skyward.

*"Alemar! Your name is cursed! Down to the last genera-
tion! Beware of my spawn!"*

Alemar began to physically reel, and it was through
blurred vision that he saw the dragon's convulsions carry
him off the crag, toward a killing impact on the rocks of the
tide pools below. As the beast fell, he produced one last
mental scream.

"TRIIIIIISSSSSSSSSS!!!!!!"

Alemar sprawled on the stone, unable to rise from the
vertigo the dragonspeech had left. His ears rang, denying
him the satisfaction of hearing Faroc crash. He threw up.
Pain, pain, pain repeated in his mind, the remnants of
Faroc's last conscious sensation, and it traveled down into
the spine and arms and knees. He fought it back, had to
try, an urgent fear rising:

He had called Triss.

Alemar had never heard of dragons being able to
broadcast across the leagues that must be traversed to
reach Triss's part of the isles, but as he ached with the
savagery of Faroc's deaththought, he *knew* that such
power not only existed, but had just been used. Triss
would come.

He staggered to his feet, cautiously making his legs take
him to the edge. Faroc's final death throes were sending
dark, swamping waves toward the ship. Miranda's ward
took the brunt of the force, but the crew men riding out the
pitch and yaw, who should have been cheering the vic-

"As the beast fell, he produced one last mental scream."

tory, were sprawled over the decks, as stunned as Alemar. Abruptly, Miranda toppled, and the ward burst.

The ship swayed alarmingly, but retained its equilibrium. Faroc was now still. Fellit was a quick, thorough poison. Alemar's disorientation faded. He had to get back to the ship. He began running toward his rope. A shadow passed in front of Motherworld.

Nothing living could move so fast.

But Triss did. Alemar's breath caught in his throat. The dragon in the sky loomed larger each moment. She *couldn't* have come so far so fast; she must have been on her way anyway when she heard the deathknell. Pure bad luck.

The she-dragon circled the crag widely, noting the ship and its crew, Faroc's body on the rocks, and Alemar on the pinnacle. When she roared, she spat flame. Even at a distance, it was obvious she was larger than Faroc. With dragons, size was relative to age. And age was relative to power. Alemar realized he had chosen the wrong dragon to attack first.

After two circles, Triss seemed to make a decision, and swooped directly to the crag top, landing her great, bellowing, smoking mass in front of Alemar. As she lowered her head to examine him more closely, Alemar involuntarily shrank back.

"I am Triss."

The dragonspeech violated him, so painful he nearly fainted. She said nothing more; the implications within those three words were more than enough of an introduction. Alemar summoned his defiance, and said boldly, "I am Alemar, slayer of Faroc!"

"*Indeed?*"

Alemar could not get his muscles to work as Triss reached forward and took him up, surprisingly gently, in her talons. She brought him within a breath of her eyes.

"A mighty deed for one so small. How was it done?"

Alemar did not answer. Not out of obstinacy, but because fear had frozen his vocal cords.

"I smell magic upon you. And deceit. You will render your story before I am done with you." Triss flexed her wings, and set Alemar lightly down. *"But first, I will deal with the pawns."*

He fell to his knees when she let him go, then to his belly under the force of the wind from her wings. Stunned, bleeding from a cut on his jaw, he rose in time to see Triss make her dive upon the ship. His throat constricted, seeing the bolt of purple flame strike amidships. The craft exploded, sending flaming shards in every direction, while the bulk of the wood withered in mere moments. The hull disintegrated into the sea.

Triss scribed a wide arc, and returned to hover just over the ocean. She belched a wide, leisurely band of flame, which covered the surface of the water, transforming the area around the ship into instant death for any man who surfaced. Steam began to rise. She continued to sear the surface as long as her flame lasted, altogether many minutes duration.

For the first minute, Alemar was in shock. In the next, he became more himself, and knew that he could not give up. He saw one last desperate chance.

Swiftly he removed his quiver, and set it on the stone next to the point where he had ascended. He took out two arrows, both of them rune-scribed. He had made five in all. One was in Faroc's hide, two more had been on the ship. It would have been taxing to have made more, and he had never expected to have more than one shot for each dragon, anyway. One of these he tied to the rope, which he flung over the edge. It landed in the shallows at the base. The second he kept, as well as a few ordinary arrows, and notched it into his bow. Then he strode back to the place where Faroc had perched, and waited for Triss.

She finished her grisly task by diving to pluck one of the corpses from the ocean. She began carrying it in her talons toward the top of the crag. As she approached, Alemar loosed his arrow. As he had expected, she reinforced her ward, and his precious shaft simply splintered into shards. He notched one of the other arrows, which at least were coated in dragonbane, and tried to aim. Before he could succeed, she was upon him, and a single flap of her wings blew him down, sending the bow sailing off the crag.

She landed gracefully on three legs, balancing the corpse in the right foreclaw. It was Darel, whom she proceeded to rip into handy-sized pieces and chew directly in front of Alemar. The man had seen many deaths in his day, but this was the worst. He closed his eyes, only to hear the revolting crunching of bones and feel the blood splashing him. When he opened his lids, it was to see Darel's face, pallid in Motherworld's glow, disappearing down Triss' gullet.

One does not take vengeance on dragons, thought Alemar.

Triss finished her snack and announced, with what must have been a dragon grin, *"Now—we will begin."*

He rose and tried to back away, but it was a silly gesture. Triss calmly wrapped the talons of her free leg around him, not bothering to lift him off his feet. The gore remaining on her claw from her meal began to soak into Alemar's clothing, but the worst part was the utterly gentle grip she used. Alemar began to feel a thing he'd never felt before: dry mouth, heavy sweat, genitals knotted up against his crotch, and a smell—stronger than that of Triss, coming from his own perspiration—that made him know how a soldier feels to look down and see an arrow protruding from his chest.

All he could really do was shudder, so he did.

When it seemed that Triss was doing nothing, he thought she was deliberately waiting, to make him endure the anticipation. But gradually he realized that she had already started; he took note of his own drowsiness, which he knew to be false. Bit by bit, his awareness dimmed. Vision and hearing were increasingly difficult to attend to. Attention as a whole wavered, as in a dream, and it was difficult to hold any thought for more than a few moments. The only constant was a great, gnawing background presence, a sense of alienness, an Other. What Alemar thought, it would think; what he felt, it would feel. And soon, it had control, taking his mind where it willed . . .

The blood flowing from his forehead nearly blinded little Alemar, but his ears were fine, and they heard what they had heard so many times: laughter. Underneath the pain he throbbed with five-year-old outrage. He peeked out with his least afflicted eye—there was Occar, the bully, and the other boys who had thrown the rocks at him, the convenient foreigner. They continued to laugh, and repeatedly call him that name: Shortie, Shortie, Shortie . . . Occar laughed the hardest.

Someday, said Alemar's young heart, *I will get them for this.*

The Other took interest. Not to the incident itself, but to the emotional response: *I will get them.* The Other approved. More memories appeared . . .

She was vixenish in the dark, a slender, blonde, and worldly eleven to Alemar's eight. "I know a trick to show you," she said mischievously. She took her hand out of her pocket, and slowly opened her palm. Inside was a stone, quite ordinary looking except for the fact that it glowed, lighting Alemar's open-mouthed face.

"What is it?" he asked.

"Magic. And I can teach you."

And more memories, unbidden by him, raped from their keep. No distinction made between those that were sacred and those that he would have readily shared. Triss would have them all for her own. She guided their course, skipping from early youth to mastery and back, according to an unfathomable dragon logic. Certain ones were repeated; only that fact told Alemar that his resistance was accomplishing anything at all.

His father, always a socially minded man, was angry. His son had never been able to blend into the background as the old man wanted in order to bury the stigma of their foreign origins. This was Serthe, in the midst of the great Calinin Empire, and the inhabitants had little use for anyone from Neith. He slapped his son squarely in the face, saying, "Damn you! You'll never amount to anything!"

And thirteen-year-old Alemar, who had heard this from the same source so many times that his older self would be unable to remember the exact cause of the incident, then performed an act that, by contrast, would etch itself vividly in his mind: he pointed his finger, uttered a single word, and burned his father's nose off. The man clutched his face, screaming, and tumbled backwards across the furniture. For an awed moment, Alemar stood still, barely able to realize that he had found a way to exercise power over the one man he had ever feared. It was a lesson he would never forget. Then he ran.

Bubbling dragon laughter weaved in and out . . .

Lorathura the Old was playing with his favorite bauble, a crystal sphere that could show him happenings in distant lands, when Alemar slipped into the dim treasury keep. Lorathura glanced up, but was not disturbed. Alemar had been his student for forty years, diligently and faithfully applying himself to the art that had made Lorathura one of the greatest mages of the age. By now, Lorathura trusted

*Alemar so completely that he had shared with him and his
sister the art that had named him the Old, and the younger
sorcerer was welcome and familiar to this, Lorathura's
inner sanctum.*

*Alemar stepped close, smiling and greeting his teacher,
and furtively produced a wooden knife, a weapon so
ordinary that few wizards bothered to magically protect
themselves against it, and stabbed Lorathura in the heart.*

*The surprised old man gawked at the stake in his chest,
and gasped "You son of a bitch." Then he died, and the
crystal bauble and other sorcerous treasures and books of
knowledge belonged to Alemar.*

Triss understood now how this human had managed to
gain enough power to challenge Faroc—he had stretched
his years, a thing neither dragon would have suspected.
The poetry of such deceit tantalized her. She reached for
more . . .

*Walking along the marbled columns of the council
chamber of Lealin, capital of Moin, Alemar repeated to
Miranda, "It is not enough."*

*She nodded, essentially agreeing, but she had ques-
tions. "You are already high in the council. In a few years
Moin will be yours."*

*The shadows of his brows hid his eyes, which looked
into the years ahead and what he wanted from them.
"Moin is a small country, beleaguered on three sides. It's
not worth the trouble. I want empire, sister, to rival the
glory of the Calinin realm."*

"Why not start here?" she asked.

*"This is not high ground," he murmured. "And I think I
have found a better place."*

*Miranda betrayed her curiosity with a tiny smile. "To
build an empire, you will need followers in droves. How do
you plan to get them?"*

*"What," he said softly, "could be more spectacular than
killing two dragons?"*

Polk adjusted his footing on the slick rock and accepted
Coller's help in climbing onto the outcroppings at the base
of the crag. Nearby Rand and Miranda brightened to see
the bow that Polk clutched in one hand.

"You found one!" she said, smiling.

Wearily he pulled off the lung, and dropped it into the
tide pool with the others. He was scarred by recent
scrapes, red from the scalding, as were all four of them, the
only survivors of the ship. He looked squarely at Miranda.
She seemed small and exposed in her underclothes—she
had removed Alemar's cloak when she leaped overboard,
because it interfered with swimming. She was the image of
the woman in need, and Polk knew self-consciously it was
why he had not broken down when they had dragged
themselves onto the rock hours before like half-drowned
sacks. Twelve men dead . . .

He handed the bow to her, "I think it's Alemar's own.
All the others must have burned with the ship."

She frowned as she took it. "Where did you find it?"
She cast an apprehensive glance upward.

"Where the debris had collected against the crag. By the
. . . dragon." Polk knew that he looked sick.

Miranda noticed his expression. "And?"

"And I saw Yonni's body . . ."

She pursed her lips, then gently leaned forward. As she
lightly kissed his cheek, he could no longer hold back his
sobs. He bowed his head, painfully aware of the presence
of the other men, but when he looked, they were not
laughing.

"He . . ." Polk gulped.

"He has found his peace," she said.

Miranda stooped down and picked up the coil of rope at her feet. She already held the arrow that had been tied to it. They had found both in the nearby tide pool. She glanced at Rand, at Coller, and then to Polk.

"Let's go up. We have a debt to pay."

*   *   *   *   *

The ache inside Alemar's head was agony, as he opened his eyes. He was still in Triss's grip. Dawn discolored the horizon. Triss had not moved, but he knew much more time had passed than had seemed to. The mind contact was halted, but he was left with a disturbing sense of twoness. It was difficult to identify which thoughts were his own and which were those of the dragon. He knew she was not done; she was still seeking a place in his mind that would yield forever.

He stared up at this creature who was now his closest intimate, and shivered. Bits of her consciousness were soaking into his mind as well, and he understood that the expression with which she regarded him was no longer one of anger, but something akin to . . . identification. She seemed to have withdrawn from the contact in order to be able to consider him from the objective view.

"You should have been a dragon," she said.

Dawn came and went as they climbed. No sounds had come from the crag top, so that they wondered if the dragon were really there at all. They were the longest hours of Polk's life. The crag was steep and treacherous; without the help of Miranda's ropetaming, it would have taken twice as long, if not been impossible. They rested frequently, sipping miserly from their only flask of fresh water. Polk was the first over the edge.

The dragon loomed on the far side of the rock, utterly still. She held Alemar between her talons. Occasional shudders proved he was alive. Gingerly they climbed onto secure footing, aware of their exposure, unwilling to approach the hulking form. The men exchanged nervous glances, while Miranda stared straight at the dragon, her brow marked by her concentration.

"She is dragon-touching him," she whispered into Polk's ear.

Polk felt the despair in her voice. "What do we do? If we kill her, she could crush him to death."

"Worse," she said. "If we kill her when their minds are one, it . . ." She didn't finish the sentence.

"Then what do we do?"

"Shoot her. If we don't, she will finish her task." She handed the arrow to Polk, who already had the bow. "Make that shaft count."

"But . . ."

"There is no choice."

She pressed him gently on the back, and he went. One step, two. His knees would scarcely hold him up by the time he had taken the third. He hesitated, breath tight, saliva gone. He *could* make the shot from here.

It would be stupid to miss at this point, he thought. Abruptly he took several quick strides forward, until he was only a body length from Triss. Behind him he knew Miranda, if she had dared to make noise, would have shouted him back. But better or worse, he had no second chance. He strung the bow, notched the arrow, and aimed at the dragon's heart.

He loosed his arrow. It flew without resistance to its target, burying itself up to the feathers. Polk leaped back, expecting violent results, and ducked behind the same boulder Alemar had used for cover. He heard the gasps of his companions.

But the only indication that Triss had felt the shaft was a spasmodic flutter of her many-layered eyelids. She remained rigid for several agonizing moments, then stunned all the watchers by lifting Alemar to her lips, kissing him gently, and releasing her grip. Alemar flopped onto the stone like a doll, and as for Triss, she simply closed her eyes and went slack where she was. A final breath flowed noisily from her nostrils.

When he could summon the courage, Polk eased forward. Tiny ripples of tension fluttered across Triss, lingering habits of life, which did nothing except to alarm him. Eventually he was able to drag Alemar's limp figure away from the dragon.

The sorcerer was pale, and looked decades older than he had the day before, hardly the man that had inspired Polk to journey across leagues, against his grandfather's advice, and almost into death. Alemar did not respond to Polk's prodding, but his chest rose and fell regularly. Miranda rushed forward.

"He's alive," Polk announced.

As the sister ministered to her kin, Polk and the others stared at the dragon, still trying to comprehend what they had seen. "What do you make of *that*?" Rand said, wiping the sweat off his face.

Polk didn't know. He spent the better part of the next hour staring dumbly at the open sea, at the shards of the ship lapping against Faroc's body, and at Miranda, who still sat with Alemar's head in her lap, seeming lost in her thoughts.

"Milady . . .?"

"Yes," she said faintly.

"What now? How do we survive?"

Without looking up, she said, "Do you see the island on the horizon? The old maps show it is one of the main isles. There will be food and fresh water there."

All three men looked. To the north, a faint blur nearly hidden by the brightness of the sun proved her right. Behind them, they heard a moan.

She would not leave him. As Alemar struggled to rise, feeling Miranda's familiar hands supporting him, he struggled to cast Her from his mind. But She clung, leaving him with a double perception of the people around him, the crag top, the scent of sea air. Questions were being asked of him, but it was as if he had never heard the language. On the third repetition, he understood: "Alemar! What did she do to you?"

Miranda. Yes, he knew Miranda. Sister, companion. He staggered to his feet, held under both arms, and swayed.

"What did she do to you?" Miranda repeated.

Triss could have taken him with her. He had felt the fellit spread through her body as if it had been his own, and shared her confrontation with the certainty of death. She had chosen to let him live. Somehow, he knew, he would be her tool.

Her pawn, her puppet. It was an irk that he could never outlive.

Alemar stumbled forward, where the great mass of Triss' corpse lay, and plunged his hands into her hide until his nails pierced the flesh. He hung from the body, higher than his head, for long moments, as the others watched him silently. He chuckled, at first slowly, then maniacally. Polk, Coller, and Rand backed away, while Miranda shuddered.

Eventually he stood up and walked to the edge of the crag. He stared north, at the island, their source of succor. "She took me to my past, and she showed me my future. I will start there, and before I am done, there will be an empire greater than Tanagaran has ever seen. I will name it . . . Elandris."

He whirled back toward the dragon. "And my realm and my dynasty will survive long after the names of Faroc and Triss are forgotten," he shouted. He spared one strange, haunted glance toward the east, toward deep ocean. "However many children you may send against me."

Empire building required a man of mettle. Growing dragons would need such a man to test their ability against when the time came.

He stayed beside the dragon until the sun drowned, leaving only the forlorn light of the Sister and other stars. When twilight was full, Alemar left Triss and joined the huddle of his companions. He seemed normal by then, but haggard and holding in his eyes a flicker that hinted of something not quite human held within.

"We'll set out in the morning," he announced.

THE END

MORE SCIENCE FICTION FROM BART

☐ 008-9 BLACK IN TIME by John Jakes $2.95
Canada $3.95

☐ 003-8 MENTION MY NAME IN ATLANTIS by $2.95
John Jakes Canada $3.95

☐ 012-7 THE WORLD JONES MADE by Philip K. Dick $2.95
Canada $3.95

☐ 016-X BART SCIENCE FICTION TRIPLET #1 by $3.50
Isaac Asimov, Gregory Benford, Canada $4.50
Poul Anderson

☐ 032-1 BRING THE JUBILEE by Ward Moore $3.50
Canada $3.95

☐ 037-2 DRAGONS OF LIGHT edited by Orson $3.95
Scott Card Canada $4.95

☐ 033-X DRAGONS OF DARKNESS edited by Orson $3.95
Scott Card Canada $4.95

☐ 046-1 THE DEVIL IS DEAD by R.A. Lafferty $3.50
Canada $4.50

☐ 048-8 FOURTH MANSIONS by R.A. Lafferty $3.50
Canada $4.50

☐ 057-7 MISSING MAN by Katherine MacLean $3.50
Canada $4.50

Buy them at your local bookstore or use this handy coupon:
Clip and mail this page with your order

BART BOOKS
Dept. MO
155 E. 34th Street, 12E
New York, NY 10016

Please send me the book(s) I have checked above. I am enclosing
$_____ (please add $1.00 for the first book and 50¢ for each
additional book to cover postage and handling). Send check or money
order only—no cash or C.O.D.'s.

Mr./Mrs./Ms _____

Address _____

City _____ State/Zip _____

Please allow six weeks for delivery. Prices subject to change without
notice.